SGT. PEPPER AND THE BEATLES

Sgt. Pepper and the Beatles
It Was Forty Years Ago Today

Edited by

OLIVIER JULIEN
*Universities of Paris-Sorbonne (Paris IV)
and Paris-Sorbonne Nouvelle (Paris III), France*

ASHGATE

Published by
Ashgate Publishing Limited
Gower House
Croft Road
Aldershot
Hampshire GU11 3HR
England

Ashgate Publishing Company
Suite 420
101 Cherry Street
Burlington, VT 05401-4405
USA

Ashgate website: http://www.ashgate.com

British Library Cataloguing in Publication Data
Sgt. Pepper and the Beatles : it was forty years ago today. –
   (Ashgate popular and folk music series)
   1. Beatles. Sgt. Pepper's Lonely Hearts Club Band
   2. Rock music – England – History and criticism
   I. Julien, Olivier
   782.4'2166'0922

Library of Congress Cataloging-in-Publication Data
Sgt. Pepper and the Beatles: it was forty years ago today / edited by Olivier Julien.
      p. cm. – (Ashgate popular and folk music series)
   Includes bibliographical references (p. 171) and index.
   ISBN-13: 978-0-7546-6249-5 (alk. paper)
1. Beatles. Sgt. Pepper's Lonely Hearts Club Band. I. Julien, Olivier, 1969–

   ML421.B4S47 2007
   782.42166092'2–dc22

                                                              2007035687

ISBN 978-0-7546-6249-5 HBK
ISBN 978-0-7546-6708-7 PBK

Printed and bound in Great Britain by MPG Books Ltd, Bodmin, Cornwall.

Bach musicological font developed by © Yo Tomita.

Contents

List of figures and tables

Figures

Tables

List of music examples

Notes on contributors

Michael Hannan is Professor of Contemporary Music at Southern Cross University, Australia, where in the mid-1980s he established one of the first university degree programmes to train professional musicians for the popular music industry. Professor Hannan is a composer, rock musician and music researcher. His current research interests are focused on film music and sound theory and on ear training for audio engineers. He also was the Chair of the International Society for Music Education's Commission for the Education of the Professional Musician from 2004 to 2006.

Ian Inglis is Reader in Popular Music Studies at the University of Northumbria, Newcastle upon Tyne, United Kingdom. His doctoral research considered the significance of sociological, social psychological and cultural theory in explanations of the career of the Beatles. His books include *The Beatles, Popular Music and Society: A Thousand Voices* (2000), *Popular Music and Film* (2003), *Performance and Popular Music: History, Place and Time* (2006) and *Perspectives on Popular Music* (forthcoming).

Olivier Julien teaches the history and musicology of popular music at the Universities of Paris-Sorbonne (Paris IV) and Paris-Sorbonne Nouvelle (Paris III). During the 1990s, he worked as a songwriter and music journalist while completing studies in Music and Musicology. He graduated in 1999 with a PhD dissertation on the Beatles' sound and has contributed since then to several publications in France and abroad (*L'Education Musicale, Musurgia, Les Cahiers de l'OMF, Analyse Musicale, Canadian University Music Review, British Journal of Music Education, Popular Music, The Continuum Encyclopedia of Popular Music of the World*). He is currently an associate member of the JCMP Research Group of the Observatoire Musical Français (Paris IV).

John Kimsey, PhD, serves as Associate Professor in the School for New Learning at DePaul University in Chicago. He teaches and writes about popular music and modern literature and has also worked as a professional musician. His publications include the essays 'How the Beatles Invented the A-Bomb' in *Proteus: A Journal of Ideas* (Spring 2001) and 'Spinning the Historical Record: Lennon, McCartney and Museum Politics' in the anthology *Reading the Beatles: Cultural Studies, Literary Criticism and the Fab Four* (State University of New York Press, 2006). He is also a contributor to the *Cambridge Companion to the Beatles*, forthcoming in 2008.

Jim LeBlanc is Head of Database Management Services at the Cornell University Library. He holds BA and MA degrees from Miami University (Ohio) and a PhD in French Literature from Cornell University. His current research interests include metadata and library processing workflows, James Joyce and (of course) the Beatles. In addition to his work on librarianship, he has written and/or spoken on Louis-Ferdinand Céline, James Joyce, Alberto Moravia, Jean-Paul Sartre, Joni Mitchell and the Beatles.

SGT. PEPPER AND THE BEATLES

Thomas MacFarlane completed his PhD in Music Composition at New York University, where he teaches courses in Music Theory and Composition. He also co-teaches The Performing Arts in Western Civilization with the Chair of the NYU Department of Music and Performing Arts Professions, Dr Lawrence Ferrara. His doctoral dissertation, *The Abbey Road Medley: Extended Forms in Popular Music*, focused on the impact of recording technology on the compositional style of the Beatles. He subsequently transformed his findings into a book that was published by The Scarecrow Press in 2007.

As a composer, he has had works performed at venues in Italy, Hungary, Romania and the United States. His original score for the film *The Sweetest Sound* was premiered in May 2001 at Lincoln Center, and his orchestral composition, *Suite for Mingus*, was performed and recorded at Merkin Hall on 5 November 2003. In 1997, he released a CD of original works entitled *Longtime*, which was structured as an essay on the development of recording technology. The production of this album employed a wide variety of formats, from 78-rpm sources to analogue and digital multitrack in an effort to raise pertinent questions regarding the existence of paradigmatic shifts in the process of music composition.

Allan Moore is Professor of Popular Music and Head of Music Research in the Department of Music and Sound Recording at the University of Surrey. He gained a first in Music from the University of Southampton and a Master's in Composition from the University of Surrey before returning to Southampton to complete a PhD in 1990 on the late chamber music of Roberto Gerhard and the problem of an adequate analytic method. Until 1999 he led research in the London College of Music and Media at Thames Valley University, and has also taught at Royal Holloway (University of London) and City University.

Subsequent to his doctoral research, Professor Moore changed tack and is now best known for his research in the musicology of popular music, work which has so far produced four sole-authored books (the most recent a study of the Jethro Tull album *Aqualung*), two edited collections and a number of book chapters and articles (principally for *Popular Music*, of which he is joint editor, *Popular Musicology* and *Contemporary Music Review*) in addition to reviewing for various journals including *Music and Letters*, the *British Journal of Music Education* and *Music Analysis*, and regularly for BBC Radio 4's *Front Row*. Still composing and performing, he is a founder member of the Critical Musicology Forum and Founding Co-Editor of the new journal, *twentieth-century music*. He still finds time to take the old guitar down to the local folk club (and sometimes even get it out of its case).

Terence O'Grady is Professor of Communication and the Arts/Music at the University of Wisconsin-Green Bay, United States. He began his work on the Beatles with a 1975 dissertation on the music of the Beatles through *Sgt. Pepper's Lonely Hearts Club Band*. The dissertation was subsequently revised and an abbreviated version was published in 1983 by Twayne Publishers. He has published articles on the Beatles' music in *Ethnomusicology* and *College Music Symposium* and has had articles reprinted in *The Beatles Reader* (Pierian Press, 1984) and *The Lennon Companion* (Macmillan, 1987). He has given presentations on the Beatles and other rock music for the American Musicological Society.

Professor O'Grady has also published articles dealing with the aesthetics of contemporary music, Native American music and other topics in *The Musical Quarterly*, *American Music*, *Perspectives of New Music*, *The Journal of Aesthetic Education* and others.

David Reck, Professor Emeritus of Amherst College, United States, is author of *Music of the Whole Earth* and writings on Indian music and East/West interface. An avant-garde composer in New York in the 1960s, a grant from the Rockefeller Arts Foundation and a Guggenheim Fellowship sent him to Madras and exposure to South India's extraordinarily rich cultural heritage. A disciple of the legendary master musician Mrs Ranganayaki Rajagopalan, he has concertized extensively on the veena in India, the United States and Europe.

Russell Reising received his PhD in American Literature from Northwestern University in 1983. Since then he has taught at the University of Oklahoma, Marquette University, Northwestern University and the University of Toledo. He has also been a Fulbright Teaching Fellow at the University of Jyvaskyla in Finland and a Visiting Fellow in Popular Music Studies at the University of Salford, United Kingdom.

Professor Reising has taught, spoken, and published widely on topics in American literature and culture, Japanese literature and culture, popular culture and popular music. Most recently he was selected to deliver the opening address at the Rock and Roll Hall of Fame and Museum for its special show on psychedelic music, 'I Want to Take You Higher', and he has been writing and editing a series of books on popular music. Two volumes have been published to date: *'Every Sound There Is'*: *The Beatles' Revolver and the Transformation of Rock and Roll*, and *'Speak to Me'*: *The Legacy of Pink Floyd's* The Dark Side of the Moon, both published by Ashgate. The book on *Revolver* was the recipient of the Association for Recorded Sound Collections Award for 'Best Research in Rock, Rhythm & Blues, or Soul', 2003. He is currently at work on a volume on the Jimi Hendrix Experience's album *Electric Ladyland*.

Russell Reising has lived, studied and taught in Taiwan, Japan, Finland, England and the United States. He now lives in Sylvania, Ohio, with his wife, children, and many pets. At the University of Toledo, he teaches courses in American literature and culture, specializing in the film, literature, television and music of the Cold War and the 1960s.

Naphtali Wagner is a senior lecturer in the Musicology Department of the Hebrew University of Jerusalem. His major research projects are: analysis of Western tonal music, based primarily on the theory of Heinrich Schenker; Richard Wagner's leading motifs and their communicative power; rock music (characterization of the Beatles' repertoire); music education (developing courseware for teaching harmony, rhythm, ear-training and more); and developing a methodology for analyzing the relations between prosody and music.

Sheila Whiteley is Professor of Popular Music at the University of Salford, Greater Manchester, the first such appointment in the United Kingdom. She was General Secretary of the International Association for the Study of Popular Music (1999–2001) and Publications Officer (2002–2005). Her publications include *The*

Space Between the Notes: Rock and the Counter-Culture (Routledge, 1992), *Sexing the Groove: Popular Music and Gender* (Routledge, 1998), *Women and Popular Music: Sexuality, Identity and Subjectivity (*Routledge, 2000) and *Too Much Too Young: Popular Music, Age and Identity* (Routledge, 2005). She is co-editor of *Music, Space and Place: Popular Music and Cultural Identity* (Ashgate, 2004) and *Queering the Popular Pitch* (Routledge, 2006) and has contributed chapters to a number of books, including *Reading Pop: Approaches to Textual Analysis in Popular Music* (ed. Richard Middleton, Oxford University Press, 2000), *'Every Sound There Is': The Beatles'* Revolver *and the Transformation of Rock and Roll* (ed. Russell Reising, Ashgate, 2002), *Performance and Popular Music: History, Place and Time* (ed. Ian Inglis, Ashgate, 2006) and *Speak to Me: The Legacy of Pink Floyd's* The Dark Side of the Moon (ed. Russell Reising, Ashgate, 2006). She has recently directed a European Science Foundation-funded project on Women and the Cultural Industries and is now co-directing a project on The Impact of Digitisation on Women in Music, Media and Convergent Media. She joined the Board of Manchester's Performing Arts Network Development Association in 2004 and co-directs FreeFlowUK, a website for showcasing popular music.

General editor's preface

The upheaval that occurred in musicology during the last two decades of the twentieth century has created a new urgency for the study of popular music alongside the development of new critical and theoretical models. A relativistic outlook has replaced the universal perspective of modernism (the international ambitions of the 12-note style); the grand narrative of the evolution and dissolution of tonality has been challenged, and emphasis has shifted to cultural context, reception and subject position. Together, these have conspired to eat away at the status of canonical composers and categories of high and low in music. A need has arisen, also, to recognize and address the emergence of crossovers, mixed and new genres, to engage in debates concerning the vexed problem of what constitutes authenticity in music and to offer a critique of musical practice as the product of free, individual expression.

Popular musicology is now a vital and exciting area of scholarship, and the *Ashgate Popular and Folk Music Series* presents some of the best research in the field. Authors are concerned with locating musical practices, values and meanings in cultural context, and may draw upon methodologies and theories developed in cultural studies, semiotics, poststructuralism, psychology and sociology. The series focuses on popular musics of the twentieth and twenty-first centuries. It is designed to embrace the world's popular musics from Acid Jazz to Zydeco, whether high tech or low tech, commercial or non-commercial, contemporary or traditional.

Professor Derek B. Scott
Professor of Critical Musicology
University of Leeds

Preface

In August 2006, the BBC's Radio 2 *Music Club* commemorated the fiftieth anniversary of the United Kingdom Album Chart by inviting the British public to vote for their favourite number one album among the 787 records that headed the chart since 1956. More than 220,000 people participated in the nation-wide survey, whose results came as no surprise: among the number one albums that made it into the top ten list were four albums by the Beatles, and among those four top ten number one albums was *Sgt. Pepper's Lonely Hearts Club Band*, which was voted 'best number one album of all time'. This poll confirms, if need be, the continuing popularity of the Fab Four over 35 years after they split up. Yet it also reveals that 39 years after its release, *Sgt. Pepper's Lonely Hearts Club Band* was, by far, the album by which they were best remembered. To quote the words of Simon Mayo, who presented the full run-down of the Top 100 Albums: 'It is a very impressive list and no surprise at all that *Sgt. Pepper* is at the top. It revolutionized music and what we expect from an album'.

As its title indicates, *Sgt. Pepper and the Beatles: It Was Forty Years Ago Today* is intended to commemorate the fortieth anniversary of this masterpiece of British psychedelia. It is also aimed at examining the album by addressing issues that will contribute to explain its absolutely unique position in the history of recorded popular music. The chapters are signed by scholars who are world-renowned for their work on the Beatles. These scholars have been selected and approached on the basis that their work had already been concerned with at least one of the aspects that make *Sgt. Pepper* a groundbreaking album (formal unity, cover design, lyrics, connections with psychedelia and, more generally, with the sociocultural context of the 1960s, influence of non-European music and art music, critical reception, songwriting, production, sound engineering) and that the way they would examine the latter aspects would help put the record in perspective. For example, Thomas MacFarlane, who wrote his PhD dissertation in Music Composition on *Abbey Road*, focuses on the formal unity of *Sgt. Pepper* so as to demonstrate why it may be viewed as the first step in a two-year process of experimentation that culminates with the extended form of the *Abbey Road Medley*. As for Terence O'Grady, who graduated in 1975 with a PhD dissertation in Musicology on the music of the Beatles through *Sgt. Pepper's Lonely Hearts Club Band*, his chapter analyzes the aesthetic divergence of Lennon and McCartney on *Sgt. Pepper* and presents it as the outcome of a process whose origins trace back to *Rubber Soul* and *Revolver*.

In addition to Thomas MacFarlane and Terence O'Grady, the list of contributors to this book includes Sheila Whiteley, Michael Hannan, Naphtali Wagner, Russell Reising and Jim LeBlanc, Ian Inglis, David Reck, John Kimsey, and Allan Moore. Sheila Whiteley (whose long-term association with the Beatles, from *The Space Between the Notes* to *Reading the Beatles*, does not need to be emphasized) examines *Sgt. Pepper* and its lyrics in the light of the sociocultural context of the 1960s; Michael Hannan, who established one of the first university degree programmes in the world to train professional musicians for the popular music industry, advances the notion of sound design in music production to encompass the timbres and distinctive playing techniques of the instruments used on *Sgt. Pepper*, the effects and signal processing used on these instruments, the use of recorded sound effects, the noise elements resulting from the recording process and the structuring of all these elements over the whole recording; Naphtali Wagner, author of a book and numerous chapters and articles in which he analyzed the Beatles' songs from a Schenkerian perspective, concentrates on 'Lucy in the Sky with Diamonds' and 'She's Leaving Home' in order to show how the two opposite classical and psychedelic aesthetic ideals can coexist, not only in *Sgt. Pepper*, but even in a single song from the album; Jim LeBlanc and Russell Reising (who edited, among other books, the award-winning *'Every Sound There Is': The Beatles'* Revolver *and the Transformation of Rock and Roll*) examine *Sgt. Pepper* in terms of its sonic and conceptual realizations of the psychedelic experience; Ian Inglis, whose doctoral research considered the significance of sociological, social psychological and cultural theory in explanations of the Beatles' career, focuses on the cover of *Sgt. Pepper* and reveals how it revolutionized the traditional forms and functions of an album sleeve; David Reck, who began working on the Beatles in 1985 after he had already achieved a solid reputation as an avant-garde composer and ethnomusicologist, analyzes the influence of Indian music on *Sgt. Pepper* and, more generally, on the Beatles' music from *Help!* through *Abbey Road*; John Kimsey's chapter extends his previous research on the Beatles by examining ways in which rock purists have responded to *Sgt. Pepper*'s embrace of high artifice, while Allan Moore approaches the question of musicological significance by revisiting the book he published ten years ago on *Sgt. Pepper* in the Cambridge Handbooks Music series; finally, my own chapter puts *Sgt. Pepper* in perspective with regard to the rise of what I called, in my PhD dissertation on the Beatles' sound, a 'phonographic tradition' in twentieth-century popular music.

I would like, of course, to express my most sincere gratitude to all the authors mentioned above. Despite their being leading scholars with heavy writing schedules, their commitment and generosity were beyond compare. In their name and my own, I would also like to thank Heidi May, Derek Scott and everyone at Ashgate for their early enthusiasm and dedication throughout the process of bringing this book into being. On a more personal level, my thanks are due to the Observatoire Musical Français and JCMP Research Group (Paris IV), where this project originated in early 2006. I must particularly acknowledge the encouragement and support of Prof. Danièle Pistone, Prof. Laurent Cugny, Cécile Prévost-Thomas, Hyacinthe Ravet and Catherine Rudent. Last but not least, this list of names would not be complete without those of Daniel Anderson, Andrew Leigh Christie, Marc Naimark and Alicia Sabuncuoglu, who were always there when I needed my English checked by a native speaker.

Olivier Julien
June 2007

'Their production will be second to none': an introduction to *Sgt. Pepper*

Olivier Julien

San Francisco, Candlestick Park, 29 August 1966: the 25,000 people in the audience do not know it yet, but they are attending the last public concert the Beatles will ever give. During the tour that is ending tonight, the Fab Four did not perform any songs from their latest album, *Revolver*, considering that their usual line-up of two guitars, bass and drums could not possibly reproduce songs like 'Tomorrow Never Knows' on stage. Their career has just reached a turning point. Four years of intensive touring and three years of Beatlemania have left them dissatisfied and exhausted. Back in August 1964, they had already expressed their dislike of spending their lives in anonymous hotel rooms and television and radio studios. But this time, it is more than mere dislike: this time, in Cincinnati, they have been frightened to the point of being sick when they found themselves in the middle of 35,000 screaming fans who had just been told that the concert had to be postponed for rain; this time, in the Bible Belt, they also faced hostile demonstrations and received death threats following John Lennon's statement that the Beatles were 'more popular than Jesus'.[1] As Philip Norman observes in his classic biography: 'It did not start out as the Beatles' last tour. It started as their next tour and finished as the one none of them ever wanted to repeat' (Norman 1981, p. 254). On the plane home to London after the concert, George Harrison will be the first to answer the question that was on everybody's mind over the past two months by announcing: 'Well that's it, I'm not a Beatle anymore' (quoted in Martin with Pearson 1994, p. 11).

Back in England, the Beatles will do nothing to confirm or deny their intention to give up touring, which will eventually lead to rumours of the band splitting. However, it is obvious that their decision has already been made. In private, Ringo Starr confesses to Hunter Davies:

> We got in a rut, going round the world. It was a different audience each day, but we were doing the same things. There was no satisfaction in it. Nobody could hear … It was wrecking our playing … The noise of the people just drowned anything. Eventually I just used to play the off beat, instead of a constant beat. I couldn't hear myself half the time, even on the amps, with all the noise. (Quoted in Davies 1992, p. 292)

---

1   Lennon made this now-famous statement during an interview with Maureen Cleave that was published in the London *Evening Standard* on 4 March 1966. The scandal began after the latter interview was reprinted in an American teenage magazine, *Datebook*, in July 1966. The exact text was: 'Christianity will go … It will vanish and shrink. I needn't argue about that; I'm right and I will be proved right. We're more popular than Jesus now; I don't know which will go first – rock 'n' roll or Christianity' (reprinted in Thomson and Gutman 1988, p. 72).

As for John Lennon, his view on the matter is even clearer: 'We've had enough of performing forever. I can't imagine any reason which would make us do any sort of tour again' (Ibid.). Even Paul McCartney – who will appear, in years to come, as the most anxious Beatle for the band to take to the road again – is beginning to admit his weariness when reminded of the Cincinnati incident:

> … we had just a little tarpaulin over the thing and it was really unpleasant to play … I remember we all used to run into the back of these big vans they'd hired, and this one was like a silver-lined van, chromium, nothing in it, like a furniture van with nothing in it, just chrome; we were all piled into this after this really miserable gig, and I said, 'Right, that's it, I agree with you now … between the four of us let's give up the gigging up.' (Quoted in Martin with Pearson 1994, p. 11)

Ever since the beginning, touring has been the *raison d'être* of the Beatles. And even though they all agreed on the decision to 'give up the gigging up', they now find themselves at something of a loss. During the following weeks, they take a break and start considering individual projects. In September, George Harrison, whose recent interest in Indian music has turned into a passion, flies to Bombay for six weeks of sitar lessons with Ravi Shankar. That same month, John Lennon flies to Germany to make his acting debut in Richard Lester's *How I Won the War* and then on to Spain to continue filming in Almeria. He also attends private views at London art galleries such as the Indica, where he will meet a conceptual artist named Yoko Ono in early November. Ringo Starr, the most family minded of the four, takes advantage of his new freedom by spending most of his time home with his wife Maureen and their first child Zak. At the other extreme, Paul McCartney helps a friend who owns a gallery to hang a few paintings by Richard Hamilton, moves into the house he has bought on Cavendish Avenue (close to the EMI Studios), becomes a fixture at underground clubs like the UFO, produces a single for the Escorts, composes the soundtrack for the Boulting brothers' film *The Family Way* and goes off on a long trip to Africa with Mal Evans and girlfriend Jane Asher.[2] It is on the flight back to London from Kenya that he first comes up with an idea that will soon develop into a song and, subsequently, into the concept for the next Beatles' album:

> Sipping the first of several in-flight Scotch and Cokes, [he] asked for a pen and paper, opened the tray table in front of him, took another sip, then wrote 'Big Brother Holding Nitty Gritty Quicksilver Fabs' on the sheet of blue airline stationery, drawing a circle round the last word. Just then lunch was served and Evans leant over to ask what [he] was doing.
> 'We need a freaky name. Like those California bands. Any ideas?'
> 'Pass the pepper', said Mal.
> Once more Paul sipped his drink, then took up the pen again. Underneath 'Fabs' he wrote 'Pepper', drawing another circle round the word, which he attached to the first circle by a line. 'I can use that', he said. (Sandford 2005, p. 128)

---

2   Mal Evans was a friend of the Beatles' since the days of the Cavern Club. He worked for them as their equipment road manager and then as one of their personal assistants after they ceased touring.

A few days later, on 24 November, the Beatles are back in Abbey Road, ready to enter the new phase of their career. They are closing the chapter of Beatlemania and beginning a new chapter: the chapter of the 'studio years'.

The beginning of the 'studio years'

In his autobiography, George Martin remembers the frame of mind in which he and the Beatles met in their usual studio, Studio Two, in late 1966: 'The time had come for experiment. The Beatles knew it, and I knew it. By November 1966, we had had an enormous string of hits, and we had the confidence, even arrogance, to know that we could try anything we wanted' (Martin with Hornsby 1979, p. 199). The tremendous success the Fab Four had achieved in over four years had certainly put them in a position to experiment with new approaches to songwriting and instrumentation (which they had actually begun to do on *Help!* and, more significantly, on *Rubber Soul* and *Revolver*). But it had also led them to the point at which they could enjoy almost complete freedom of the EMI Studios. On their first visit to Abbey Road, in June 1962, they had discovered a very formal place: studio time, for instance, was limited to three three-hour sessions per day (10.00am–1.00pm, 2.30–5.30pm and 7.00–10.00pm); engineers wore white coats, producers wore a collar and tie and a suit and all those people stood very pompously in the control room where artists were not allowed to touch anything. In those days, as Paul McCartney recalls, 'you just went in, sang your stuff and went to the pub. And then *they* mixed it, and *they* rang you up if they thought there was a single, you'd just ring them up "Have we got a hit?" – that's all you wanted to know' (Lewisohn 1988a, p. 10).

Yet it was not long before the Beatles' interest in the recording process of their songs had become apparent. As early as late 1963, in the very early days of Beatlemania, Paul McCartney had declared in the first annual Official Beatles Fan Club Christmas message:

> Lots of people have asked us what we enjoy best, concert, television, or recording. We like doing stage shows, 'cos, you know, it's great to hear an audience enjoying themselves. But the thing we like best is going into the recording studio to make new records ... What we like to hear most is one of our songs taking shape in the recording studio, one of the ones that John and I have written, and then listening to the tapes afterwards to see how it all worked out. (Quoted in Riley 1989, p. 3)

The way those songs had been taking shape in the studio during the first two years of the Beatles' recording career had been basically determined by George Martin's desire to 'give the fans on record what they [could] hear on stage – as quickly as possible' (Martin with Pearson 1994, p. 77). There was just no time for sophisticated arrangements or experiments of any kind:

> My time with the Beatles was issued to me in little driblets, little sealed packages. I could have an afternoon with them there, an evening with them here ... I never really got much time with them. And in order to talk about records, I had to go and chase them, and see them wherever they were. (Martin 2004)

This situation, however, had begun to evolve in 1965–66, as the Beatles, according to Paul McCartney, had 'started to take over things' (quoted in Southall, Vince and Rouse 1997, p. 109). By featuring a string quartet on 'Yesterday', *Help!* had marked their first major departure from their usual live-oriented approach to arrangements; while confirming the latter trend, *Rubber Soul* and *Revolver* had then seen them experimenting with new approaches to the recording studio. Those new approaches were probably the most obvious signs of the freedom that they were beginning to enjoy in Abbey Road. As George Martin puts it, 'We were given very much *carte blanche* with Studio Two' (Ibid., p. 77).

In concrete terms, this '*carte blanche*' meant that the Beatles now had priority access to the EMI Studios; they came and went as they pleased, spent the time they wanted in Studio Two and did not hesitate to demand studios that had already been booked by other artists:

> As the success story of the Beatles unfolded, a new chapter was being written with every new release, so their every whim and fancy was catered for and when it came to recording schedules at Abbey Road there was never any question of them being kept waiting for a studio. People, perhaps unkindly, suggested that the wealthy young men from Liverpool would have bought the studios had they been refused a session or a particular studio. (Ibid., p. 109)

They also enjoyed an almost unlimited studio budget, using extra musicians whenever they needed to, choosing the technicians they wanted to work with and affording themselves the luxury of encouraging those technicians to try and 'abuse the equipment [they] had to achieve a certain sound' (Chris Thomas, quoted in Cunningham 1996, p. 143). The dedication of a house technical engineer named Ken Townsend and the arrival of Geoff Emerick as their regular sound engineer in April 1966 had certainly been among the reasons that led them to explore the latter option throughout the recording of *Revolver*.[3] On several occasions, Townsend and Emerick had even got themselves into trouble with the studios managers for breaking the unwritten studio rules or damaging microphones. But Sir Joseph Lockwood (Chairman of EMI from 1954 to 1974) had never pursued it. As he later admitted:

> I had a pretty close relationship with the Beatles, largely because they were so successful. I knew them better than I did most of the pop artists, and the situation developed that where they were refused something by EMI's management, which was quite often – some disagreement about a minor thing maybe – Lennon and McCartney would come to me. (Quoted in Taylor 1987, p. 36)

Virtually unlimited studio time, a nearly unlimited studio budget: such were the conditions the Beatles faced on the eve of recording their eighth album. Once again,

---

3   Ken Townsend is known for having invented Automatic Double-Tracking (ADT) and the 'frequency changer', which the Beatles used extensively throughout the *Rubber Soul*, *Revolver* and *Sgt. Pepper's Lonely Hearts Club Band* recording sessions. Even though Geoff Emerick only worked as their regular sound engineer from April 1966 through July 1968, the contribution of his close-miking techniques to the Beatles' sound was as important as that of Townsend's inventions during that period (see Julien 1999; McDonald and Hudson Kaufman 2002).

they had already begun enjoying such conditions before they stopped performing live; but now that they had actually retired from touring, they found themselves in a situation where they could, at last, make the most of them. And this was exactly what they were about to do: make the most of their unlimited studio time and studio budget. As an example, their first album, *Please Please Me*, had been recorded in less than 20 hours from start to finish and cost about £400; by comparison, *Sgt. Pepper's Lonely Hearts Club Band* would take no fewer than 700 hours to record and would cost over £25,000 – according to George Martin, 'a fortune in 1967' (Martin with Pearson 1994, p. 168).

From 'Strawberry Fields' to 'All You Need Is Love'

The song that inaugurated the *Sgt. Pepper* recording sessions was a song John Lennon had written during his stay in Spain about a Liverpool Salvation Army house named Strawberry Fields. And even though this song would ultimately be released separately, George Martin gives it a special place in his account of the making of the album:

> It is impossible for me to talk about *Sgt. Pepper* without mentioning two crucial songs that neatly bracket it: 'Strawberry Fields Forever' and 'All You Need Is Love'. If 'All You Need Is Love' says everything about where the Beatles were in terms of popularity and success, 'Strawberry Fields Forever' shows us where they were musically. Destined originally to be on *Pepper*, it set the agenda for the whole album. (Martin with Pearson 1994, p. 13)

If 'Strawberry Fields Forever' must be regarded as a groundbreaking track in the Beatles' recording career, it is firstly because it represents an unprecedented 55 hours of studio time spread out over five weeks. Furthermore, the band spent most of those 55 hours experimenting with different instruments and different sound treatment techniques, literally building the structure and the sound of the song as they advanced. On 24 November, the recording began with an arrangement featuring a rhythm track and a Mellotron; it then underwent additional changes and overdubs on 28 and 29 November, but the latter session was only nine days before Lennon decided to record a remake with extra musicians. This new series of recording sessions led to a second version with a much heavier drum sound and a four-trumpet and three-cello arrangement that was completed with new overdubs on 21 December. And yet, on 22 December, Lennon was still uncertain about which of the two versions he liked best. So he asked Martin to try and combine them by splicing the beginning of the first one and the end of the second one together. It so happened that both versions were in different keys and different tempos; but as chance had it, the faster version also happened to be the one whose key was about a semitone higher.[4] With the help of Ken Townsend's 'frequency changer', Martin took advantage of those slight

---

4   In *Summer of Love*, George Martin recalls the two versions being a whole tone apart (Martin with Pearson 1994, p. 22), but he mentions a semitone in *All you Need Is Ears* (Martin with Hornsby 1979, p. 201). Geoff Emerick confirms the latter interval in *Here, There and Everywhere* (Emerick and Massey 2006, p. 139).

differences to achieve, on a memorable four-and-a-half-hour session, what he calls 'the edit of the century' (Ibid., p. 22).

Beyond technical prowess, the determination of the overall sound and structure of 'Strawberry Fields Forever' by this manipulation of the phonographic medium clearly shows that by the time they had completed that song, the Beatles were no longer concerned with the performability of their music. To quote the words of George Martin again, '… that was going to be what became *Pepper*. It wasn't *Pepper* – no one heard of *Sgt. Pepper* [yet] –, but it was gonna be a record that was gonna be made in the studio … [with] songs which they had written which couldn't be performed live: they were designed to be studio productions. And that was the difference' (Beatles 2003b). Paul McCartney says nothing else when he remembers the Beatles starting to get 'full-time into the studio and saying, at the time: "Now our performance *is* that record"' (Ibid.).

Nevertheless, with the completion of 'Strawberry Fields Forever' came Christmas time and then the 1966 Christmas market, for which EMI and the Beatles' manager, Brian Epstein, needed a brand-new single. Having finally resigned himself to formally announcing that the Fab Four were through with touring a few weeks earlier, Epstein was all the more desperate for a hit that would help to bolster their declining popularity. In addition to 'Strawberry Fields Forever', they had almost completed two tracks so far: 'Penny Lane' and 'When I'm Sixty-Four'. In many ways, the first song appeared as McCartney's answer to Lennon's 'Strawberry Fields Forever': both titles referred to areas of Liverpool close to where the Beatles had been brought up and both recordings had seen them experimenting with abandon for over 50 hours.[5] Determined to provide Epstein with a strong combination, Martin decided to let him have a double-A-sided single.

'Strawberry Fields Forever'/'Penny Lane' came out on 17 February 1967 in the United States and four days later in the United Kingdom. It was the Beatles' third double-A side in a four consecutive British releases;[6] and quite ironically, considering it was to become 'what many still regard as the greatest coupling ever' (Cunningham 1996, p. 130), it was also the Beatles' first single to fail to reach number one in the United Kingdom since 'Please Please Me' had topped the charts in January 1963 – 'Strawberry Fields Forever'/'Penny Lane' actually stalled at number two, being outstripped by Engelbert Humperdinck's 'Release Me'. Naturally, the press began suggesting that the band was finished: '… to *Melody Maker*, for one, it seemed as if the dream would be over before you could say "Bee Gees"' (Sandford 2005, p. 130). But the Beatles did not seem to worry so much; during an interview on the British radio, Paul McCartney was even heard commenting: 'It's fine if you're kept sort of from being number one

---

5   As an example, the distinctive keyboard sound of 'Penny Lane' resulted of the combination of six piano tracks that were superimposed onto each other between 29 December 1966 and 6 January 1967 – one of those tracks consisted of a piano played through a Vox guitar amplifier with added reverberation and another one of a piano recorded at half speed and then sped up on replay.

6   'We Can Work It Out'/'Day Tripper' (issued on 3 December 1965 in the United Kingdom and 6 December 1965 in the United States) was the Beatles' first single officially released as a double-A side. Eight months later, 'Eleanor Rigby'/'Yellow Submarine' (issued on 5 August in the United Kingdom and 8 August in the United States) was the second.

by ... a record like "Release Me", 'cos you're not trying to do the same kind of thing as "Release Me"'s trying to do ... So that's a completely different scene altogether ... it doesn't really matter, anyway' (Beatles 2003b). Such a diplomatic statement was obviously the least one might have expected from 'the most cautious and image-conscious Beatle' (Norman 1981, p. 289). Still, there was more than diplomacy behind those words; beyond caution and possible calculation, they revealed first and foremost an incredible self-confidence as the Beatles had just embarked upon a project that was going to revolutionize the concept of an album: '... a month or two earlier the press and the music papers had been saying, "What are the Beatles up to? Drying up, I suppose." So it was nice, making an album like *Pepper* and thinking, "Yeah, drying up, I suppose. That's right"' (Beatles 2000, p. 252).

By 1 February 1967, the idea of a fictitious band whose name would be inspired by the Californian psychedelic scene had finally developed into a song: 'Sgt. Pepper's Lonely Hearts Club Band'. And just around the time the Beatles had started recording that song, it had begun evolving into a more ambitious scheme that consisted of extending the concept of a fictitious band to the Beatles themselves and to the whole album that they were working on. As Mark Lewisohn points out:

> It wasn't going to be *Sgt. Pepper's Lonely Hearts Club Band* until 'Sgt. Pepper's Lonely Heart Club Band' had come along. That is, the album was not 'The Sgt. Pepper Project' until the recording of this Paul McCartney's song and Paul's realization soon afterwards that the Beatles could actually pretend they were Sgt. Pepper's band, the remaining songs on the LP forming a part of a show given by the fictitious band. (Lewisohn 1988b, p. 95)

It would take a little less than three additional months for the Beatles to see the 'Sgt. Pepper Project' through. The recording, properly speaking, was completed on 21 April 1967, with the taping of nonsense gibberish that they had decided to cut into pieces, stick together at random and play backwards before putting it in the concentric run-out groove of side two of their new album. At John Lennon's request, a high-pitch whistle of 15 kHz especially intended for dogs was also inserted across the spiral of the run-out groove – that is, between the final chord of 'A Day in the Life' and the concentric nonsense. As the recording had been progressing, this type of experimentation for art's sake had become one of the most characteristic features of what was now known as *Sgt. Pepper's Lonely Hearts Club Band*; on certain sessions, it had gone to such extremes that George Martin had even been led to wonder whether he and the Beatles were going too far:

> Five per cent of me was thinking, 'This is never going to work, we've been too pretentious, it's all too complicated and uncommercial, far too different from what the Beatles have done before.' The other ninety-five per cent of me were thinking, 'This is brilliant! They're going to love it!' (Martin with Pearson 1994, p. 151)

A few weeks later, as the release date was coming closer, he simply found himself in a true state of uncertainty: 'With the "failure" of "Strawberry Fields Forever" and "Penny Lane" ... fresh in our minds, we all held our breath to see what the reaction to it would be. Would it sell? Would the critics savage it?' (Ibid.). Needless to say, he worried for no reason.

The toppermost of the poppermost

If 'Strawberry Fields Forever' set the agenda for the *Sgt. Pepper's Lonely Hearts Club Band* recording sessions, 'All You Need Is Love' does say everything about where the Beatles were in terms of popularity as the 'Summer of Love' was blossoming. They had begun recording this new song on 14 June 1967, as a commission for the BBC who had invited them to appear on a live television programme to be broadcast worldwide during the evening of 25 June. This programme, *Our World*, was the first global television satellite link-up; it was to be seen by a potential audience of 400 million people across five continents and the British contribution to this world premiere was a performance by the Beatles from Abbey Road's Studio One.

In *Shout!*, Philip Norman concludes the short paragraph he spares for the event with the following remark: 'So, on 25 June 1967, was registered the ultimate statistic of [the Beatles'] career' (Norman 1981, p. 290). In *Summer of Love*, George Martin's analysis of the broadcast is quite a similar one:

> The huge success of the Beatles' live performance of 'All You Need Is Love' on that show is important. It shows that they had become, in the words of a little rhyme John [Lennon] had long ago composed to keep up group morale on those endless drives to dreary dance halls, 'the toppermost of the poppermost'.
> JOHN: 'Where are we going, fellas?'
> CHORUS: 'To the top, Johnny, to the TOP!'
> JOHN: 'And where is the top, fellas?'
> CHORUS: 'To the toppermost of the poppermost!'
> Important, too, is the fact that the Beatles were the automatic choice to represent Britain worldwide. (Martin with Pearson 1994, p. 160)

Indeed, the Beatles' participation in *Our World* says everything about the position they had achieved in popular music and British culture a few weeks after *Sgt. Pepper's Lonely Hearts Club Band* had come out. In the United Kingdom, the album had been an immediate popular sensation: it had been released on 1 June 1967 and had sold 250,000 copies in the first week; within one month, sales would exceed half a million copies (they would eventually mount to one million by April 1973). In the United States, it had been issued a day later: advance sales had been one million and, within the first three months, it would sell two and a half million copies while occupying the top slot on the *Billboard* album chart for 15 weeks – a position it would hold in the United Kingdom Album Chart for 27 weeks as well. In other words, on 25 June 1967, *Sgt. Pepper* was already on its way to becoming the most successful British album of all times.

On the critical front, the record had also received significant acclaim. In the *New Musical Express*, Allen Evans ended his review by noting: 'No one can deny that the Beatles have provided us with more musical entertainment which will both please the ear and get the brain working a bit too!' (quoted in Taylor 1987, p. 42). In *Melody Maker*, Chris Welch had written: 'The lads have brought forth yet another saga of entertainment and achievement that will keep the British pop industry ticking over securely for another six months at least' (Ibid., pp. 41–2). By 1967, the Beatles were certainly used to (or at least prepared for) such reviews. But this time, the difference was that the most spectacular comments had come from the most unexpected critics. For example, in the 29 May issue of *The Times*, William Mann had called *Sgt. Pepper* a 'pop music master-class' (reprinted in Thomson and Gutman 1988, p. 93); in *Newsweek*, Jack Kroll had compared its lyrics with T.S. Eliot, while the *Times Literary Supplement* had called them 'a barometer of our times' (quoted in Norman 1981, p. 287); the *New York Times Review of Books* had announced that *Sgt. Pepper* heralded 'a new and golden Renaissance of Song' (Ibid.) and the *New Statesman*'s Wilfrid Mellers had summed it all up by stating: '... though it starts from the conventions of pop it becomes "art" – and art of an increasingly subtle kind' (quoted in Martin with Pearson 1994, p. 153).

Referring to William Mann's review in *The Times*, Philip Norman observes:

> Tunes that made little boys jig up and down were, at the same moment, receiving praise ... for their 'sweeping bass figures and hurricane glissandos'. Elsewhere, the practice begun by that paper's music critic, of burying something direct and enjoyable under tormented technical gibberish, was greatly assisted by the provision of the lyrics in full. (Norman 1981, p. 287)

As a matter of fact, Mann did not mention 'sweeping bass figures' but the 'shapely bass line of "With a Little Help from My Friends"' (reprinted in Thomson and Gutman 1988, pp. 92–3) and, more generally, bass lines that were more 'vivid' (Ibid., p. 92) than they used to be in beat music. What is more, those lines were not even the ones that contained the most technical jargon: among such examples, the critic also evoked 'the Alberti string figuration in ... "Eleanor Rigby"' (Ibid., p. 91), a music that needed no more 'to be harmonized entirely diatonically in root positions' (Ibid., p. 92) and the 'recognisably mixolydian' (Ibid.) tune of George Harrison's 'Within You Without You'. This quite unusual way of approaching a popular work reveals another important feature of *Sgt. Pepper*: it was, finally, the album that achieved the 'cultural legitimization of popular music' (Moore 1997, p. 62). To put it differently, those reviews, whatever the true motivations of their authors, represented the final steps in a process that was pointing towards the emergence of popular music as a worthy field of research for scholars in disciplines like musicology, sociology, literature, history or cultural theory (to name but a few).[7] As for illustrating the appropriateness of such disciplines to explain the position *Sgt. Pepper* has held over the past 40 years in the Beatles' discography, in the history of songwriting, in the history of record production, in the history of popular music and, why not say it, in the history of Western music, it is, precisely, the aim of the chapters that follow.

---

7   The very origins of this process may be traced back to the publication of an article entitled 'What songs the Beatles sang...' in the 27 December 1963 issue of *The Times* (reprinted in Thomson and Gutman 1988, pp. 27–9). Although the latter article was printed unsigned, it has since been attributed to William Mann.

Chapter 1

'Tangerine trees and marmalade skies': cultural agendas or optimistic escapism?

Sheila Whiteley

It may have been superseded by *Revolver* as 'the best Beatles' album ever', but for those of us who were around at the time, there is no doubt that *Sgt. Pepper* summed up our mood. Released slap bang in the middle of the so-called 'Summer of Love', it was, as Allen Ginsberg recalls, 'an exclamation of joy, a discovery of joy and what it was to be alive' (Sheppard 1987). Despite the murder of Che Guevara, the race riots in Detroit and the gathering discontent at universities both in the United States and the United Kingdom, it was actually 'a cheerful look around the world: the first time, I would say, on a mass scale' (Ibid.). *Sgt. Pepper* seemed, at the time, to exemplify a mood of 'getting better'. 'Holes' were being 'fixed', love would still be there at 64, and the band promised to 'turn you on'.

Of course, I am considerably older than I was in August 1967. I am also older than when I published my first piece on *Sgt. Pepper* in 1992, and I recognize that with age comes an increasing nostalgia. But as George Harrison said:

> The summer of 1967 was the Summer of Love for us ... A lot of it was bullshit; it was just what the press was saying. But there was definitely a vibe: we could feel what was going on with our friends – and people who had similar goals in America – even though we were miles away. You could just pick up the vibes, man. (Beatles 2000, p. 254)

In *The Space Between the Notes* (Whiteley 1992, pp. 39–60), I attributed those vibes to the underlying hallucinogenic mood of the album and, in many ways, this chapter is a revisiting of my original analysis. I have no sudden new insight, despite the ever-increasing number of texts that have appeared over the last decade, but I have listened again to the album, albeit with a none-too-innocent ear, to evaluate whether the tracks constitute optimistic escapism or whether the Beatles gave voice to a more generalized feeling that the old ways were out, so setting the agenda for cultural and political change.

Even at the time, it was apparent that the Beatles held a privileged position within the pop world, that they were able to voice opinions on current situations and be heard by their thousands of fans worldwide. They had become, in effect, the socio-political zeitgeist for their generation, and this is reflected in Peter Blake's pop-art design for the album sleeve, which shows the Beatles, as the Sgt. Pepper Band, surrounded by life-size cut-outs of famous figures past and present – philosophers, artists, painters, writers, film stars, comedians and, at Harrison's request, a number of Indian gurus. Waxwork figures of the Beatles (borrowed from Madame Tussaud's) confirm their celebrity status and hint at their historical significance; they had 'not only changed pop music, but transformed how we perceived that music and, in a very literal sense, how we perceived ourselves' (Dowlding 1989, p. 152). Within three months of its release, *Sgt. Pepper* had sold two and a half million copies in the United States, tapping into the mood of the summer, its evocation of 'Edwardian military music' (Mellers 1973, p. 87) drawing on the current craze for military uniforms, quickly echoed in Biba's Carnaby Street fashions and copied by fans worldwide. Even the pseudo-military figure of Sgt. Pepper himself seemed little more than a lampoon on the infamous Kitchener recruitment poster of the 1914–18 war. What we remember, with increasing nostalgia, are the good times, the feeling of optimistic escapism promised by the sound of a band tuning up, the beautiful Lucy, still up there, in the sky, with diamonds, the camaraderie of friends long past, and the final 'hup, hup, hup' of Sgt. Pepper himself, as he leads his band into the final reprise. Why, then, that earth-shattering coda to 'A Day in the Life'? Why that final apocalyptic vision of chaos and anarchy? Does it provide a particular insight into the underlying philosophy of the album, or is it, as Richard Goldstein commented, part of the 'slicks and tricks' of production that situate the album as 'the Beatles baroque' (reprinted in Heylin 1992, p. 542)?

While Goldstein's observation can be countered by reviews that situate the Beatles as 'standard bearers for the long march into the new dimensions which pop took during the sixties' (Connolly 1983, p. 24), his identification of 'the surrogate magic of production' (reprinted in Heylin 1992, p. 543) provides one specific insight into the distinction between their first album, *Please Please Me* (1963), which had taken less than 20 hours to record, and *Sgt. Pepper*, which literally took hundreds of hours to complete. It is also apparent that his identification of the album's dangerously dominant sense of what is chic spotlights the summer of 1967 itself, when so many of the radical issues of the counterculture had become subsumed by the boutique culture of 'swinging London', and when such iconic underground bands as Cream, Pink Floyd and the Jimi Hendrix Experience could feature on *Top of the Pops*. Clearly, the Beatles were not the naïve band who, some four years earlier, had hit the headlines with their launch single, 'Love Me Do', who had wooed six million viewers with 'Please Please Me' on their subsequent appearance on British television's *Thank Your Lucky Stars* (13 February 1963), and a year later stormed America in February 1964 on the *Ed Sullivan Show*. There is, in particular, an underlying 'knowingness' that extends both into their experimentation with mind-expanding drugs and a world-weary cynicism, which had earlier emerged in such songs as 'Nowhere Man' and 'Taxman', and which also surfaces in *Sgt. Pepper*, despite its air of apparent cheerfulness. Even so, there are certain continuities, not least, their lack of reverence for all things Establishment.

John Lennon's pungent wit is, of course, well documented. Invited to perform at the televised Royal Command Performance in November 1963, he prefaced 'Twist and Shout' with: 'The people in the cheaper seats clap your hands, and the rest of you if you'd just rattle your jewellery' (Beatles 2000, p. 105). His attitude towards the Prime Minister was equally challenging: at the 1964 Royal Variety Show, the Beatles were presented with the Variety Club Silver Heart Award and Lennon's 'Thanks for the purple hearts, Harold' (Ibid., p. 145) was another indication that the age of blind deference was coming to an end. Nevertheless, the award of Member of the Order of the British Empire in 1965 was considered by many inappropriate, with some existing MBEs returning their medals. Lennon's response, that the award was 'for exports', can be interpreted both as an astute recognition of the Beatles real value to the country and a refusal to acquiesce in the 'somewhat patronizing endorsement' of their artistic merit. Either way, it was the first step into today's world where celebrities are rewarded for their services to Queen and country, and an indication that the separation between high culture and popular culture was on the wane, as evidenced in the musical sophistication of the Beatles' highly acclaimed album, *Revolver*.

By 1967 the Beatles were fully aware of their own significance as musical leaders and trendsetters. Their lyrics overall showed a new seriousness of tone, which was complemented by George Martin's distinctive and innovative arrangements (including overdubbing and mixing), unconventional instrumentation (including French horn, string quartet, sitar and sophisticated collages of electronic sounds and *musique concrète* effects) and an occasional classic restraint that was far removed from conventional rock/pop. 'They're untouchable', said Cass Elliott of the Mamas and the Papas. 'No matter how hard anyone tries, no matter how good they are, almost everything we do is a cop on the Beatles' (quoted in Shaw 1969, p. 81). Even so, the fact that the growing complexity of their studio-engineered music was impossible to recreate on stage meant that their live concerts consisted largely of songs from 1963–64, albeit largely unheard due to the mass hysteria of the fans. Their final tour of Germany, Japan, the Philippines and the United States (June–August 1966) was offset with personal tensions and controversy[1] and the realization that 'Beatles concerts are nothing to do with music anymore. They're just bloody tribal rites' (Beatles 2000, p. 229). Lennon's cynical 'more popular than Jesus now'[2] thus evidences an astute insight into the hysteria accompanying so-termed Beatlemania and an awareness of where such adoration could lead.

> One night on a show in the South somewhere (Memphis) somebody let off a firecracker while we were on stage. There had been a lot of threats to shoot us, the Klan were burning Beatle records outside and a lot of the crew-cut kids were joining in with them. Somebody let off a firecracker and everyone of us … looked at each other, because each thought it was the other that had been shot. It was that bad. (Ibid., p. 227)

Sgt. Pepper thus finds the Beatles retreating to the safety of EMI Studios, their past represented by the mop-top wax effigies on the album sleeve, their present by the colourful uniforms of the 'Lonely Hearts Club Band'. But even here, in their imaginary world, there is an awareness of the vicissitudes of fame: Jesus Christ, Mahatma Gandhi and Hitler were removed from Blake's cover design. Given the earlier death threats and bomb scares, their images would have been far too controversial. Even so, it is considered that Lennon's attitude towards the Establishment, not least the

---

1   The Beatles were accused of snubbing the wife of the Filipino president while on tour. In the United States the cover art of the Beatles' first album of 1966, *Yesterday... and Today*, attracted controversy owing to its photo of the Beatles posed amidst 'slabs of raw, red meat and a decapitated baby' (O'Grady 1983, p. 89).

2   Lennon's 1966 oft-quoted comments on Jesus Christ to rock journalist and friend Maureen Cleave caused outrage across the southern United States.

US government, his well-documented anti-war philosophy and his characteristic humour would surface in *Sgt. Pepper*, albeit in a more covert frame of reference. Whether characterized as 'sarcasm masquerading as cool', as continuing cynicism and wit or as an acute awareness of social and political inequalities was, as discussed earlier, dependent upon individual interpretation.

First, however, the question arises as to why Sgt. Pepper? What was the significance of this Edwardian figure and his Lonely Hearts Club Band? The concept for the album was McCartney's, and his use of an alter ego is characteristic of his love of creating colourful figures and constructing stories. Here, however, he moves from the third person, submerging himself in the persona of a bandmaster playing to the lonely, the alienated, in that imaginary (and most English of settings) music hall Palace of Varieties.[3] The use of sound collage – crowd noises, an orchestra tuning up – functions both as a narrative source and as a psychological trigger, creating for the listening audience (both imagined and real) a mood of shared festivity as they are invited to 'enjoy … sit back and let the evening go'. For the more perceptive, the colourful uniforms and vaudeville-style banter also evoked the cultural politics of the drop-out hippies and student and graduate activists: 'Eradicate the Victorian ethic of virtuous sacrifice and remind the world that love must be a constantly original and divine word' (Gillett 1970, p. 352). The intense high-volume guitar and active syncopated bass (reminiscent of 'Taxman') add their own connotations as they invade the superficial mood of old-time camaraderie; by wearing the uniforms of the past within the context of a psychedelically charged rock album, *Sgt. Pepper* undercuts traditional values and its 'military' aspect, as producer George Martin confirms, is shown to be 'a send-up of the US in Vietnam' (quoted in Moore 1997, p. 21).

By 1967 the War in Vietnam was in its sixth year and television coverage had brought the atrocities into the family living room. Protests escalated, with student demonstrations, teach-ins and silent Vietnam vigils across American campuses, horrifying self-immolations,[4] and uprisings in Paris, Rome, Berlin and the United Kingdom, where British students were acquiring a reputation for extremism, with many supporting the North Vietnamese in their war with the United States. This was later evidenced in July 1968 when 3,000 VSC (Vietnam Solidarity Campaign) militants charged the US Embassy in London's Grosvenor Square, the demonstration turning into a riot after an 18-year-old girl became trapped underneath a police horse.

It would be misleading to suggest that the Beatles were directly involved in political protest against the War in Vietnam. Unlike Mick Jagger, who was at the Grosvenor Square demonstration and whose song 'Street Fighting Man' resonated with his personal experiences on the day, the Beatles were more aligned with the

---

3   While there is no evidence to support my 'imaginary' venue, the format of the album and the introduction of Billy Shears with the ♭VI–♭VII–I harmonic music hall cliché (which establishes McCartney as Master of Ceremonies) do suggest the Palace of Varieties (as many music halls are called) to be an appropriate setting.

4   These included Alice Herz, an 82-year-old survivor of Nazi terror, who set herself on fire in Detroit shortly after President Johnson announced major troop increases and the bombing of North Vietnam (15 March 1965); Quaker Norman Morrison, setting himself on fire and dying outside Secretary of Defence Robert McNamara's Pentagon office (2 November 1965); Catholic Worker Roger Laporte, self-immolating opposite the United Nations Building.

philosophy of love that characterized hippy philosophy. However, as Steven Fielding observes, despite the visibility of Tariq Ali and the VSC, the motives of most student protesters and drop-out hippies were closer to the Beatles' sentiments than those of Mick Jagger.[5] Their 1968 song, 'Revolution', spelt it out: 'we all want to change the world. But when you talk about destruction, don't you know that you can count me out'. Their solution, 'change your head ... free your mind' and the importance of love as empowering change ('All You Need Is Love', 1967) is, I would suggest, the philosophy underpinning *Sgt. Pepper*, relating to drug culture,[6] the metaphysical[7] and 'flower power', a slogan used by hippies in the late 1960s and early 1970s as a symbol of their non-violence ideology, rooted in their opposition to the Vietnam War.[8]

As such, the 'twenty years ago today' reverberates uneasily with the surface optimism of Sgt. Pepper's promised evening of fun and frolics, taking the listener back to the 1940s, where it seemed the promised peace was, at best, fragile. 1945 had seen the end of World War II, the surrender of the German forces, Hitler's suicide, Mussolini's arrest and execution, the liberation of the Buchenwald and Dachau concentration camps and the dropping of the nuclear bomb on Hiroshima and Nagasaki, which ended US conflict with Japan. 1945 also saw the onset of the Cold War between the United States and Soviet Russia, with the former refusing to share nuclear secrets and the latter fearing American attack. Then, on 25 June 1950, the Cold War suddenly escalated. North Korea's invasion of South Korea had brought about a United Nations' 'police action' against the aggressors which involved heavy military and naval involvement by the United States. While there were no illusions that the task would be easy, it was not anticipated that the violent conflict would continue for more than three years. By the 1950s the Americans were also engaged in the conflict in Vietnam, although President John F. Kennedy's 1961 despatch of 400 Special Operations Forces-trained (Green Beret) soldiers to teach the South Vietnamese how to fight what was called a 'counterinsurgency war against Communist guerrillas in South Vietnam' provides one starting date for the actual war itself. When Kennedy was assassinated in November 1963, there were more than 16,000 US military in South Vietnam, and more than 100 Americans had been killed. By 1968 the figure had risen to 550,000 combatants, with more than 1,000

---

5   Discussion with Steven Fielding, Professor of Contemporary Political History, University of Salford (see Fielding 2002).

6   Their 1966 album, *Revolver*, is now interpreted as transforming the vocabulary of popular music with 'Tomorrow Never Knows' topping the list of British psychedelia (Savage 1997, p. 61), attempting to 'recreate what tripping actually *sounds* like' (Reising 2002, p. 238).

7   In 1966, the Beatles retreated into Hinduism, Transcendental Meditation and the adoption of the Maharishi Mahesh Yogi as spiritual guide, and admitted that they had all taken drugs – including LSD.

8   America's continuing commitment to winning the war in Vietnam through massive B52 bombing campaigns also involved a determination, on the part of Robert McNamara and Lyndon B. Johnson, to involve the United Kingdom by sending British troops to Vietnam. Prime Minister Harold Wilson's refusal resulted in the United States withdrawing support for sterling and Britain's economic situation worsened. Wages were frozen and the Labour Government began to fall apart.

American soldiers killed each month. Meanwhile, in April 1961, the CIA encouraged, funded and transported an attempt by anti-Castro Cuban exiles to invade Cuba. It failed miserably, greatly embarrassing Kennedy. In September 1961, Castro asked for – and Russia publicly promised – weapons to defend Cuba against America. With war continuing in Vietnam and the spectre of the atomic bomb constantly in the media (see Nuttall 1970), the stand-off between Soviet Russia and the United States, communism vs capitalism, made the threat of global warfare ominously real. It would seem, then, that Sgt. Pepper had a more serious agenda for his audience of lonely hearts; they may be there to be entertained, but there is a sting in the tail. First, however, lulled into a false sense of security by the vaudeville introduction to 'Billy Shears', they can sit back and 'enjoy the show'.[9]

In many ways, the characters presented across the album provide a particular insight into the swinging sixties and, more specifically, the so-called 'Summer of Love'. There are the insecure Billy Shears and the anonymous girl of 'She's Leaving Home', looking for love and reassurance at a time when, it seemed, love-ins, the pill (no more unwanted pregnancies) and the Kinsey Report[10] (a discussion of previously taboo subjects, including masturbation and the female orgasm) heralded unlimited sexual pleasure. Parliament confronted outmoded laws concerning sexuality with the Homosexual Reform Act (1967) and the Abortion Act (1967),[11] and the attraction of 1960s London as the epicentre of the 'swinging scene' was, for many, an alluring prospect that far outweighed the security of the parental home. As the focus for European fashion, art, design, music and theatre, it was 'the place to be seen', with Allen Ginsberg, Julie Christie, Mick Jagger, Michael Caine and David Bailey, to name but a few, frequenting the most glamorous restaurants and nightclubs. Captured by Peter Whitehead in his documentary *Tonite Let's All Make Love in London* (1967) and in the American weekly magazine *Time* which, in 1966, dedicated an entire issue to 'the Swinging City', London was eulogized as the epitome of modern urban culture. Small wonder, then, that Mike Leander's lush string arrangement, which underpins the traditional waltz of 'She's Leaving Home', comes across as curiously

---

9   The format would have been well known to the Beatles and, indeed, George Martin, not least because of the media attention paid to the closing of so many venues that belonged to the Moss Empire music hall chain and its continuing popularity in the north of England. In Manchester, early Beatles performances were prefaced by a warm-up spot by the resident comedian, a common practice at the time. The BBC also featured a regular vaudeville programme, *A Night at the Music Hall*, and the Beatles had also experienced the famous London Palladium, first hand, in 1963 and 1964.

10   The Kinsey Reports are two books on human sexual behaviour, *Sexual Behavior in the Human Male* (1948) and *Sexual Behavior in the Human Female* (1953), by Dr Alfred C. Kinsey, Wardell Pomeroy and others. Kinsey was a zoologist at Indiana University and the founder of the Institute for Sex Research. The findings challenged conventional beliefs about sexuality and discussed subjects that had previously been taboo, including masturbation, the female orgasm, homosexuality and sadomasochism.

11   The Abortion Act (1967) regulates abortion by registered practitioners and provides free medical aid through the National Health Service. It was introduced by David Steel as a Private Member's Bill but was backed by the Government and after a heated debate and a free vote passed on 27 October 1967. It came into effect on 27 April 1968.

old fashioned when compared with the dream-like scoring of 'Lucy', the girl with the fashionable kaleidoscope eyes, favoured by such trendy models as Twiggy. But then, growing up in the 1960s for most people was more conservative than they would like to make out, and McCartney's perceptive insight into everyday life in suburbia highlights both the loneliness of the individual and the tabloid take on the period as one of 'loose living'.

In the early 1960s, for example, the consequences of sex before marriage were considered a serious matter. There were still shotgun weddings; John Lennon married Cynthia Powell, whom he had been dating since 1958, because she was pregnant.[12] His possessiveness and jealousy are well documented, and it seems that 'Getting Better' provides a particular insight into the fate of many women at the time: 'I used to be cruel to my woman I beat her and kept her apart from the things that she loved'. Brutality in the home was, however, no grounds for divorce and the institution of marriage, as sanctified by the Church and authorized by the State, was dissolvable only by proven adultery. With marriage considered by many both oppressive and out of touch with social reality – a social institution that had little to do with love and (historically) everything to do with private property –, Roy Jenkins's (Labour Home Secretary from 1965 to 1967) 'no blame' divorce legislation was welcomed as providing a legal framework which would allow for greater self-determination in social life and relationships.[13] Even so, Cynthia Lennon filed for divorce in 1968 on the grounds of John's adultery with Yoko Ono; in turn, Lennon blamed Cynthia for the breakdown of the marriage, claiming his public image would suffer if he were 'the guilty party'. As such, the seemingly flippant 'it can't get any worse' and the bantering response 'I can't complain' suggest an underlying irony, which is musically reinforced by the stepped falsetto barber-shop effect on 'better, better, better'. Nevertheless, with Yoko now on the scene,[14] life was, it seems, improving, 'getting better since you've been mine'.

In keeping with the theme of lonely hearts, there are, however, insecurities still to be confronted, not least those of growing old together. As such, 'When I'm Sixty-Four''s rhyming incantation – 'will you still need me, will you still feed me' and the 'give me your answer, fill in a form' – reads like a parody of the lonely hearts' bureau, tying the song to Lennon's angry young man, to the anonymous girl of 'She's Leaving Home' and the insecure Billy Shears. The links with music hall are also there in the shuffling syncopation of the introductory clarinet duet, the simple vocal melody, the neatness of fit between lyrics and accompaniment. It is both nostalgic and child-like, with a 'touching contrast between the first phrase, naïvely pentatonic despite the chromatic passing note, and the piquant rising and falling chromatics of the second phrase: while the middle section – minor thirds for the cottage in the Isle of Wight, sustained minims arching up to a high G for the recognition that "you'll

---

12 John Lennon married Cynthia Powell on 23 August 1962. He later said he married Cynthia because she was pregnant with his child (Julian) and he felt it was the right thing to do.

13 Roy Jenkins was also responsible for the abolition of theatre censorship. As Home Secretary he had given government support to David Steel's Private Member's Bill for the legalization of abortion and Leo Abse's Bill for the decriminalization of homosexuality.

14 John had met Yoko Ono in 1966.

be older too" – reveals a pathos that is disturbing as well as wistful' (Mellers 1973, pp. 95–6). Written by Paul as a tribute to his aging father, James, its sense of nostalgia is nevertheless offset by a tongue-in-cheek recognition that times have changed. To ask for a written guarantee, whether a postcard or a form, promising 'mine for evermore' is shown to be unrealistic. The 1960s are a time of generational change, and the bantering style, the 'ho's', 'hums', 'ooos' and clarinet countermelody gently poke fun at the singer's need for certainty, a possible reference to his affair with Linda Eastman, whom he had met at the Bag O' Nails club in May 1967 when she arrived to photograph the Beatles for the book *Rock and Other Four Letter Words*.[15]

The sense of biographical detail is also there in 'Fixing a Hole' where the 'Hey, hey, hey' which precedes the guitar solo suggests another instance of Lennon's sarcastic digs. Paul McCartney was the last Beatles to take LSD, 'his cautious reluctance finally broken down as the group began recording its acid-inspired masterpiece, *Sgt. Pepper* early in 1967 … Lennon rarely misses an opportunity to put down McCartney … because [he] was slower than he to capitulate to the hallucinogenic powers of the drug. One thing is certain. After his initial experiences with LSD, Paul McCartney became convinced that *Sgt. Pepper*, with its many drug connotations, was a work of great artistic and social significance' (McCabe and Schonfield 1972, p. 80).

Comparable with 'Lucy in the Sky with Diamonds' in exploring the potential of LSD for changing perceptions, 'Fixing a Hole' floats above a secure diatonic base, the mind freed to wander 'where it will go'. Both songs identify changing visual perceptions: 'with the eyes closed, kaleidoscopic colors and a wide array of geometric shapes … are often seen' (Fort 1969, p. 182). For the initiated, the connotations of the lyrics are less than subtle. 'Holes' have been filled, 'cracks fixed' and barriers erected between the initiates and the Establishment who 'wonder why they don't get in my door'. Like Lucy's experience, where 'rocking horse people' float against 'tangerine trees and marmalade skies', those in the know are free to explore their minds, enjoy the heightened sensations experienced on a trip, 'get high with a little help from my friends' as Ringo had earlier sung.

> For acid wasn't just a private pleasure, it was a revolutionary tool for inspiring within common clay a cornucopia of poems, moods, paintings and music … it could unite the world and achieve Nirvana. Acid was a crash course in the solution of the old occidental problem of alienation. LSD said 'We are one'. (Nuttall 1970, p. 211)

Hallucinogenic connotations inform much of the album, as my analysis in *The Space Between the Notes* suggests (Whiteley 1992, pp. 39–60). Electronically manipulated timbres including the voice, blurred, bright, overlapping timbres, upward movement (and its comparison with psychedelic flight), lurching, oscillating harmonies and curious collages create musical metaphors for hallucinogenic experience. Even where there is an explicit reference to reality (as in the nineteenth-century circus poster, 'For the benefit of Mr. Kite', purchased by Lennon in an antique shop while filming the promotional video for 'Strawberry Fields Forever'), the connotations emerge in the increasingly lurching rhythms, the electronic manipulation of fairground sounds – the

---

15 Paul McCartney and Linda Eastman married on 12 March 1969, eight days before John Lennon married Yoko Ono.

chromatic runs of the hurdy-gurdy with its simple vamped accompaniment – which take over in the song's outro.[16] Thus, while there is a comparability with Sgt. Pepper's opening track in the evocation of past and public showbiz, the carousels, trapezes, men and horses, hoops and garters of Mr. Kite's benefit by Pablo Fanque's Circus Royal, the track also provides a more contemporary analogy with the Spontaneous Underground, held at the Marquee Club in Wardour Street, Soho. Here, the mixture of bands, poets, jugglers, fire-eaters and the ready availability of marijuana and LSD 'turned men into stoned Houdinis, who can escape the straitjacket of Aristotelian logic'. As Richard Neville wisely points out, 'Lateral thinkers, mystical drifters rarely maim other people' (Neville 1970, p. 142).

This observation also informs George Harrison's metaphysical track, 'Within You Without You', which provides an alternative and complementary approach to changing consciousness: 'When you've seen beyond yourself … the time will come when you see we're all one, and life flows on within you and without you'. The individual Beatles are, it seems, providing their own solutions to world problems and by the time the album went into production, George was 'convinced that acid wasn't the answer' (Poirier 1969, p. 174). Rather, he turned to the teachings of Krishna and the Maharishi Mahesh Yogi,[17] furthering his exploration of Indian spirituality through a study of Indian classical music under the guidance of his friend, sitar virtuoso, Ravi Shankar. The merging of the Beatles' familiar pentatonic/modal melodicism with the Asian sound of the sitar can thus be interpreted as Harrison's solution to the problems of alienation and loneliness which underpin much of the album, 'the space between us all … the people who gain the world and lose their soul'. The mood of orientalism 'is recreated in terms of the Beatles' newborn innocence … the freeing of the mind literally breaks the time-barrier, so that the metres shift, over the endless drone, between fours, fives and threes' (Mellers 1973, p. 94), but while the raga motifs and instrumentation – tamburas, dilruba, tabla and sitar – heighten the mood of contemplation, the leery laugh, with which the song ends, evidences once again an underlying cynicism.[18] '… if religion is the opium of the people, the Hindus have the inside dope' (Alan Watts, quoted in Neville 1970, p. 215). Regarded as 'the heavenly guide', 'the soother of grief' (Fort 1969, pp. 15–16), cannabis took its place alongside LSD as the favoured drug of the period.

---

16 The track was banned from playing by the BBC, supposedly because of its reference to 'Henry the Horse', two common terms for heroin.

17 Harrison visited India with his wife Patti in 1966 after the completion of the Beatles' final tour. On their return to the United Kingdom, she introduced him to the Maharishi Mahesh Yogi, who further developed his interest in Indian mysticism, including Transcendental Meditation. Harrison's interest in Indian culture may have originated in 1965, when his friend David Crosby of the Byrds introduced him to Indian classical music and the work of sitar maestro Ravi Shankar, with whom he subsequently studied. Harrison converted to Hinduism, retaining his faith throughout his life.

18 While some writers consider the laugh to represent the outlet of tension on the part of the audience who were, perhaps, somewhat thrown by the trance-like mood of the track, songs with Eastern or Indian themes were no stranger to music hall, as evidenced by, for example, Wilson, Keppel and Betty's famous 1930s sand dance.

> ... it aids concentration and helps you do almost anything a little bit better ... A pot nation is a powerful nation. You think Zambia's moon project is a joke? Watch them reach Mars first. *Possible side effects*: A feeling of dreamy nonchalance, heightened sense of awareness, bursts of introspection, a mellowing attitude towards one's fellow man (especially if he's stoned beside you) and a formidable sense of contemporaneity. (Neville 1970, pp. 127–8)

While the laugh may well reflect Lennon's cynicism with regard to the whole Maharishi experience as another version of what they already knew – 'You know like some are EMI and some Decca, but it's still really records' (Poirier 1969, p. 176) – the association of mysticism with flower power and drugs was picked up by the tabloid press,

> ... with that menopausal tone of total scandal that is guaranteed to bring the English clustering like flies to the subject as participants or sightseers. Nine months after the first gathering in Haight Asbury mill-girls and office workers were wandering down Brighton and Blackpool seafronts, jangling their souvenir prayer-belts, trailing their paisley bedspreads, brandishing daffodils and trying to look tripped out. The Beatles had gone 'flower power' and it was up to the kids to do their best to follow. (Fort 1969, p. 130)

As such the strident 'good morning, good morning' is like a wake-up call to the remaining 'lonely hearts'. Time to 'tune in and turn off' from the boring repetitiveness of nine-to-five everyday life, 'nothing to do ... nothing to say', 'nothing has changed, it's still the same'. Momentary diversions 'watching the skirts', 'go to a show' are equally part of the routine, a night-time escape from 'going to work, don't want to go, feeling low down'. This is also Rita's world, her total personality summed up in her meter-maid uniform, 'the bag across her shoulder' which 'made her look a little like a military man', supported musically by the bugle-like shape of the melody. Uncomplicated and predictable, the song bounces and with it Rita, 'sitting on the sofa with a sister or two'. To an extent, both songs presage the conformity of the 'crowd' in 'A Day in the Life', the amorphous mass who 'stood and stared' or 'turned away'. Life, as the Beatles had discovered, could be more colourful and the outro of 'Good Morning' takes off in an unexpected direction as dogs, cats, roosters, birds invade the music and, metaphorically, the boring routines of daily life. It is a flight from reality into a new non-reality, the mundane of everyday existence transformed into the sensational of hallucinatory experience.[19]

At this point 'Good Morning' pre-empts the psychedelic coding of 'A Day in the Life' in its contrast of everyday life with the heightened colours and the changed perceptions associated with tripping. As Richard Neville astutely observed, 'If Pavlov's dogs had taken LSD they would have danced to the sound of the bell, not salivated' (Neville 1970, p. 144). The outro thus prefaces and highlights the need for a new form of consciousness: the cockerel stands for life, the rebirth of each day and within the context of acid rock, the outro also reveals that after hallucinogenic experience, 'you will almost certainly come down safely ... but not necessarily in the same spot you took off from' (Ibid., pp. 143–4). The 'Sgt. Pepper' reprise is thus

---

19 As Richard Neville confirms, the sensational effects of LSD apply to 'sounds, smells, colours, tastes, touch, everyday experiences' (Neville 1970, p. 144).

subtly changed, the 'hup, two, three, four' setting a faster pace as the band prepares the audience for the final, traditional encore: 'it's getting very near the end'. But instead of a more traditional upbeat finale to the show, the opening acoustic guitar chords of 'A Day in the Life' are reflective, with the verse describing a suicide with a conciseness comparable to that displayed in 'Eleanor Rigby': 'I read the news today, oh boy'.

Built on a series of tense, reflective passages, followed by soaring releases, the dispassionate account of events, 'he blew his mind out in a car', is reinforced by the simplicity of narration, both verbally and through the music. There is no extraneous detail, and the pentatonic melody follows the natural inflection of the words. The lack of modulation also works to make the imagery more powerful as it evokes the monotonous repetition of newscasting and the reading of horrendous events which are passively consumed and then forgotten. Materialism is confronted by the headlines 'about a lucky man who made the grade', the response, 'Well I just had to laugh', linking the song to George Harrison's metaphysical 'Within You Without You', 'the people who gain the world and lose their soul'.[20] The out-there is then rejected, with the refrain 'I'd love to turn you on' precipitating an electronic crescendo, a musical metaphor for a drug-induced 'rush', as the audience is moved on to a differently coded, though thematically connected idea. The music has a nervous dissonance as the percussive drumbeat melts into a panting chug, but again there is a move towards a drug-enhanced release, 'Found my way upstairs and had a smoke, somebody spoke and I went into a dream'. The dream, however, is more an evocation of a nightmare and the final 'I'd love to turn you on' leads directly into a cacophony of noise, suggesting both anarchy and chaos.

As the final song on the album, 'A Day in the Life' takes on board 'the lonely people' and with wit, tenderness, and a cutting-edge musical arrangement by George Martin, calls into question the meaning of contemporary society. To ignore the vision is to invoke the consequence, and the final instrumental crescendo paints a scenario of devastation that is balanced only by Lennon's invitation to psychedelic experience, 'I'd love to turn you on'.

And so to my initial question: did the *Sgt. Pepper* album simply constitute optimistic escapism or did it set an agenda for cultural change? As Eric Hobsbawm suggests, the 1960s fell within 'a sort of Golden Age', which began with Western Europe's recovery from World War II in the early 1950s and ended with the onset of global recession two decades later (Hobsbawm 1994, p. 6). It was a period which 'changed human society more profoundly than any other period of comparable brevity' (Ibid.). The fact that the Beatles had embarked upon their musical career at the beginning of the decade, ending it in 1970, made them, for many, the spokesmen for their generation. Even UKTV History dubbed the 1960s 'the Beatles generation'. But were they the instigators of cultural change or did they simply have well-developed antennae for the ideological shifts taking place and an ability to situate these within 'a sequence of intricately related numbers' (Mellers 1973, p. 86)?

---

20 By 1967, after 300 concerts worldwide, the Beatles withdrew from public performances and engaged totally with studio production. They also embraced Transcendental Meditation under the guidance of their Hindu guru, the Maharishi Mahesh Yogi. George Harrison remained a Hindu throughout his life, donating a manor house in Watford, UK, to the Krishna movement.

In many ways, the album provides a historical snapshot of England during the run-up to the so-called 'Summer of Love', recording the outside world's images with an astute and often cynical perception, and arranging the characterizations of the lonely and alienated into dramatic monologues. Jobs, money and status are shown to be blind and destructive, the audience of lonely hearts, like the outside world, full of people who hide behind a wall of illusion.[21] The digs at convention are, however, typical of the Beatles' compositional techniques with Lennon writing first-person, often cynical testimonies, McCartney constructing stories and characters and Harrison making his first full-blown attempt at raga rock in 'Within You Without You', albeit that his presence is also felt in the strains of 'Taxman' which intrude into the first track of the album. Even so, as alluded to earlier, why that chaotic ending to 'A Day in the Life'?

Of all the problems associated with the 1960s, the threat of war seemed the most terrifying. With the devastation of World War II still evident in the bombed buildings and the United Kingdom's continuing financial indebtedness to the United States, the threatening backdrop of potential nuclear cataclysm underpinned much of the countercultural politics of the time. Anti-war protests, student rebellion and artistic and social experimentation were part of the same agenda, and Jeff Nuttall's perceptive book *Bomb Culture* (1968), with its cover images of Fidel Castro, Elvis Presley, Marilyn Monroe, Marlon Brando, a student protester and a self-immolated monk, highlights the links between culture and protest. As such, the Beatles, in their position of spokesmen for their generation were, in a way, unable to escape their responsibilities,[22] and Harrison subsequently defended the Beatles against charges that they were skirting reality (Northcutt 2006, p. 140). Thus, while much of the album can be read as exploring and celebrating alternative consciousness (whether metaphysical or through LSD and marijuana), there is nevertheless a seriousness about the threat of war which resonates with the final song and its cacophonous outro. It 'depicts the "real" world as an unenlightened construct that reduces, depresses, and ultimately destroys' (MacDonald 1994, p. 181) and aligns the Beatles with the philosophy of the drop-out hippies in their emphasis on 'make love not war'.[23] The connections between hallucinogenics and visionary religion thus fall into place: they are complementary pathways in the search for an alternative reality to the atrocities of war, as hinted at in the opening track. As Timothy Leary observed at the time, the album 'gave voice to a feeling that the old ways were over ... it came along at the right time in that summer' (quoted in Gillett 1970, p. 353), highlighting the need for cultural change and setting an agenda based on love.

---

21 As MacDonald observes, 'The Beatles offered an inclusive vision which, among other things, served to defuse the tensions of the generation gap' (MacDonald 1994, p. 185).

22 As Mick Jagger observed at the time, 'The Stones might speak to one's personal condition in a way that the Beatles did not, but the Beatles were universal' (Schofield 1983, p. 130).

23 Their refusal to engage in 'Revolution' and their awareness of the horrors of war had certain parallels with Prime Minister Harold Wilson's courageous refusal to send British troops to Vietnam despite being asked by Robert McNamara (US Secretary of Defence, commonly dubbed Mac the Knife) to support the United States, and threatened that non-compliance would result in the United States withdrawing their support for sterling.

Chapter 2

Sgt. Pepper and the diverging aesthetics of Lennon and McCartney

Terence O'Grady

Early 1967 represented a turning point in the evolution of the Beatles' music. It was neither the first nor the last for the quartet, whose coming-of-age conquests had already included the production of the *Rubber Soul* album in 1965 and the *Revolver* album in 1966. Both had been monumental achievements, the first every bit as original as the second, if less spectacularly so. But as remarkable as the music from these two innovative records had been, the degree to which Lennon and McCartney, the two prime movers behind the creative juggernaut, had shown compatibility was even more remarkable. While it is easy now, 40 years later, to bemoan the fact that the songwriting 'team' (such as it was) of John and Paul faltered all too soon, the fact is that their artistic relationship was exceptionally resilient for a long time under terrible pressures. While it is all well and good to suggest that productive relationships can be expected to flourish in prosperous times, the histories of other late-1960s groups make it clear that substantial commercial success doesn't necessarily make for smooth sailing in creative terms.

And yet, the Beatles had remained not only overwhelmingly successful, both in commercial and critical terms, into 1967, but also surprisingly compatible in their artistic perspectives. Interviews given by the ex-Beatles in the 1970s and 1980s called this into question from time to time, for example, George Harrison's resentment about having his songs accorded little respect within the group's repertoire, but it is likely that this sort of discontent was sharper and more focused in retrospect than it was at the time. While petty quarrels certainly surfaced from time to time in the early and mid-1960s, the Beatles' history up to the time of *Sgt. Pepper* was remarkably free of sharp artistic differences.

There were certainly challenges along the way that might easily be seen as requiring a leap of faith by George and Ringo, as well as by John and Paul. While conventional wisdom has long held that the Beatles' *Rubber Soul* album (released in December 1965) represented no risk of any sort to the group's enormous popularity, it was not so clear at the time that releasing a 'theme' album (if not a concept album per se) almost completely devoid of music respecting the dance-oriented conventions of mid-1960s rock would not at the very least slow down the Beatles' remarkable momentum. Whereas Lennon and McCartney had always been capable of going their own ways stylistically, there was also clear evidence of a songwriting empathy between them that was so strong that each could effortlessly step into the other's shoes and echo the stylistic tendencies of their partner. By the time of *Rubber Soul*, the songwriting differences between Lennon and McCartney were beginning to be magnified to a certain degree; it was no longer merely a question of contrasting melodic or harmonic tendencies on the part of each, but an increasing inclination to tilt towards separate genres. Yet in *Rubber Soul* there was still to a great degree a unity of spirit, a compatibility of genre and style, and a mutual desire to make an album that was remarkably cohesive in its aesthetic and yet markedly different from any previous Beatles album.

This new direction can be seen immediately in the song that opens the American version of the album, McCartney's jaunty, bluegrass-inflected 'I've Just Seen a Face', which had little resemblance to anything that the Beatles had recorded up to that time. But 'I've Just Seen a Face' was written several months earlier than the other *Rubber Soul* songs and had already been included on the British version of *Help!*, so its credentials as the 'signature song' for the album are, regardless of its quirky charm, suspect at best. The lyrics of McCartney's 'Drive My Car' (put together with some significant assistance from Lennon) encapsulate the ironic intent of the album perfectly, but the music – despite its clever vocal dissonances and catchy ostinato – represents no new direction for the Beatles. Among Paul's other offerings, 'Michelle' was seen as the most unique at the time, a witty and poignant evocation of a French *chanson* or cabaret song. The song's bridge, clearly a Lennon contribution, is based initially on the wailing repetition of the familiar $1-\flat7-5$ blues pattern followed by a more sentimental and affective use of non-harmonic tones as Lennon's tune works its way neatly back to the verse, making an effective contrast to the suavely chromatic motion under McCartney's melody while still preparing the way for it.

Paul's 'I'm Looking Through You' brings back the folksy acoustic guitar strum of 'I've Just Seen a Face', and there are hints of the same bluegrass style in the bridge, but the overall quality is more expansive, and the lyrics at times more penetrating than was typical for a 'personal' McCartney song at that point. The lyrics of Paul's halting 'You Won't See Me' vary a similar theme, while the 'ooh-la-la' background vocals once again suggest that 'period'-flavoured coyness was – at least for Paul – one of the components in the album's emphasis on irony.

Lennon's contributions to the album, while distinctive and individualistic, appear to be stylistically compatible with McCartney's, if not directly commensurate. Even though John's contribution to 'Michelle' had managed to strike a distinctively Lennonesque tone, it was perfectly in sync with (and provided a smooth segue into) McCartney's smoother style in the verse. The same is true for the majority of Lennon's songs on the album. Whereas McCartney tilted towards bluegrass in his contributions to *Rubber Soul*, Lennon manoeuvred closer to a traditional folk style, equally 'undanceable' by the standards of the day and perfectly compatible with Paul's offerings.

And, of course, irony abounds in the songs of both. Lennon's 'Norwegian Wood (This Bird Has Flown)' is a striking song that makes its effect through a combination of unusual sonorities (the famous debut of Harrison's sitar combined with folk-like guitar strums accentuating the song's triple metre); lyrics that combine the sense of a traditional narrative ballad with the sort of surprising twists more typical of Lennon's literary attempts (for example, *In His Own Write* and *A Spaniard in the Works*) than most of his earlier lyrics; and a haunting melody, unusually jagged in its contour for a Lennon tune, paired with archaic modal harmonies and a plaintive bridge sung in the parallel minor. The song is very much a package: words, music and instrumental timbre all contribute to its unique and introspective, yet self-consciously hip quality. No song on the album makes it clearer that the Beatles have entered a new world with *Rubber Soul*.

Lennon's other contributions to the album are almost as strong. 'Girl' projects the quality of a folk-song narrative while expressing some of Lennon's old themes of betrayal (echoed also in 'Run for Your Life', a conventional and somewhat dated rock song co-authored with McCartney). 'In My Life' is somewhat less remarkable than 'Norwegian Wood' in terms of its sonic quality (George Martin's clever 'Baroque' interlude notwithstanding) but equally successful in terms of projecting the global essence of the album. While the lyrics – unusually sensitive and more affirmative than usual for Lennon – have received the most attention over the years, the melody combines typically Lennonesque pentatonic gestures with an expansive use of a major sixth in a way that is less characteristic of his style but extremely effective nevertheless. But it is the relative delicacy of the lyric's sentiments, combined with the low-key, folk-like instrumental accompaniment, which marks the song as a full partner in the distinctive identity of the album.

Lennon's 'Nowhere Man', not included on the original American version of the album, also assumes a serious posture, albeit in a manner that is more preachy than plaintive, and its simple pop-oriented melody is one of the most conventional on the album. This was the only single taken from the British album and, while its lyrics suggest a search for 'meaning' compatible with the album's overall identity, the song seems out of place stylistically, once again suggesting that the American version of the *Rubber Soul* album may represent the 'purer' manifestation of the concept of the album.

Taken as a whole, Lennon's songs are fully compatible with McCartney's and contribute even more strongly to the unique identity of *Rubber Soul*. At this point in their careers, Lennon and McCartney seemed largely in sync in terms of their artistic goals, at least so far as they concerned the distinctive identity of a particular album.

Revolver, the next Beatles album to have a marked conceptual focus, was released in August 1966. Once again the British and American versions of the album differed, with the shorter American version (omitting three Lennon songs that had been released earlier on the American *Yesterday... and Today* album) the more satisfying in terms of conceptual unity. It has always been assumed that the burgeoning interest in psychedelia displayed by the album was kicked off by George Harrison's west-coast pilgrimage, combined with his increasing interest in the sitar and the classical music of India. Harrison's aggressive and gritty 'Taxman' (with its San Francisco-inspired distortion and Indian-inspired guitar solo by McCartney) certainly sets the table nicely for what is to come, but Lennon's contributions are anything but timid. 'Tomorrow Never Knows' is a dark, drone-dominated exercise in psychedelic hallucination and tape effects that defines the album as effectively as any single song. (By comparison, Lennon's earlier B-side 'Rain' seems gratuitous in its use of tape-reversed effects.) Its companion piece on *Revolver*, 'She Said She Said', also heavily steeped in psychedelic imagery, is even more successful musically, especially in its elastic bridge section which moves from duple to triple metre, eventually floating off into a dream-like reverie before returning to the more predictable verse. 'I'm Only Sleeping' again celebrates the dream-like state between waking and sleeping, but is less remarkable musically than either 'Tomorrow Never Knows' or 'She Said She Said'.

The two additional Lennon songs included on the British version of *Revolver* do little to enhance the unique personality of the album. The lyrics for 'Doctor Robert' may in fact concern a drug-dealing New York physician, but there is little distinctive about the song's musical personality, and 'And Your Bird Can Sing' sounds almost archaic by the standards of 1966, despite an innovative double lead guitar part in the bridge.

McCartney's contributions to the album are in many cases quite striking, but rather different in tone than Lennon's and less in keeping with the psychedelic ambiance that Lennon and Harrison's songs so effectively establish (at least in the American version of the album). 'Eleanor Rigby' is surprisingly dark and cynical for a McCartney song as well as being more self-consciously literary in its tone than was usual for the composer – Lennon later claimed that he provided substantial assistance with the lyrics, a claim disputed by McCartney (Dowlding 1989, pp. 134–5).

Its string arrangement provides a framing device that distances the song from any other on the album, but the song's power to bring life to a series of powerful images in the lyrics is undeniable. Nevertheless, the song stands alone on the album, McCartney's other offerings all being decidedly different in mood. 'Good Day Sunshine' is a barrelhouse-piano flavoured 'period' piece (its compelling cross-accents notwithstanding) of the sort that McCartney always had a weakness for and of which he would become increasingly fond in the next couple of years. The good-natured, old-time quality of the verse would be echoed in his much simpler 'Yellow Submarine', these being the only two McCartney songs to resemble each other closely in terms of mood.

McCartney provided two ballads for the album, each distinctive in tone. 'For No One' traces a bleak and cynical landscape not unlike that heard in 'Eleanor Rigby', although the two songs feature few meaningful musical similarities. 'Here, There and Everywhere' occupies a different musical universe than both, its smooth and predictable chord progressions in the verse being forced into more remote (and decidedly more expressive) territory by a bridge melody that refuses to stay earthbound and provides a sense of romantic epiphany to the song that is lacking elsewhere in the album.

While 'Here, There and Everywhere' contrasts strongly with 'For No One', McCartney's 'Got to Get You into My Life' is absolutely unique on the album, the blues-inflected refrain melody joining with a punchy Stax-Volt horn line to summon up the modern soul sound in a way the Beatles had never attempted before.

What is lacking from McCartney's contributions, of course, is the sort of overt psychedelic influence so clearly heard in the songs of both Lennon and Harrison (although the latter's Indian-influenced rock songs will always remain a special case). McCartney refuses to dabble in either mysticism or exotic, hallucinatory imagery, at least for now. Instead, he insists on his own, ever-changing type of novelties. Certainly, 'Eleanor Rigby', in its social consciousness, lamenting lyricism and distancing string arrangement, is unique among the Beatles' songs to that point. But then so is 'Good Day Sunshine', with its good-natured period travelling given a modern rhythmic twist. McCartney's ballads, on the other hand, are less exceptional as types, even the highly successful 'Here, There and Everywhere' with its brilliantly crafted modulations. But on the whole, McCartney's songs remain as masterfully inventive as Lennon's, even if they do not seem so attuned to the psychedelic spirit of the album.

But what of *Sgt. Pepper's Lonely Hearts Club Band* itself? The album's status as a cultural landmark was asserted almost immediately (at least in part due to the striking cover art which seemed to suggest subtle relationships between the popular culture icons that populated it) and the conceptual basis for the album – the notion of the Beatles' alter ego period brass band performing in a traditional, pre-World War II British music hall entertainment adorned with aspects of the circus and a colourful magic act – was widely discussed and celebrated. From the beginning, McCartney encouraged this sort of interpretation and seemed to be most proud of the uniqueness of the Beatles' achievement. In later years, Lennon expressed strong reservations about the 'conceptual' basis of this much-celebrated 'first' concept album as well as the quality of his own contributions to the record (Sheff 2000, p. 197). But there is no question that – at least in McCartney's mind – the songs for this album were to demonstrate a unity of purpose that was different from – if not necessarily better than – the sort of unity exhibited by the songs of *Rubber Soul* and *Revolver*.

McCartney guaranteed that the songs of *Sgt. Pepper* would be framed for a unifying concept by the masterful stroke of the introductory song, 'Sgt. Pepper's Lonely Hearts Club Band', which alternately evokes San Francisco psychedelia, with its high-volume, distorted guitar sound, hand tremolo effects, and rhythmically reiterated pitches alternating with wide melodic leaps, with the quaint posturing of a pre-war village band. It is of course the timbre of the instrumental introduction that establishes the psychedelic identity of the song. Sung over a standard Beatles pop-rock progression of I–II⁷–IV–I (heard in 'Eight Days a Week' and 'You Won't See Me' among others), the melody of the verse, consisting of short phrases with many repeated notes, could be interpreted either as an emotionally heightened 'reciting tone' style used by an announcer to build tension and excitement in anticipation of the appearance of the Master of Ceremonies ('Let me introduce to you … the one and only Billy Shears …'), or more conventionally as the sort of repeated-note incantation found frequently in the 1950s and early 1960s songs of rhythm and blues rockers like Chuck Berry and Little Richard (as well as McCartney's earlier homage, 'I'm Down'). But it is the 'side show', carnival-barker implications that seem to be the most important here, as Sgt. Pepper's band is introduced and allotted a five-measure solo section of four horns playing patently old-fashioned military band music (courtesy of George Martin) to bemused applause from an audience who is quite anxious to be pleased.

Following this brief but evocative interlude, Sgt. Pepper's band itself takes the stage, intoning a somewhat more tuneful melody over a chord progression (I– this brief but evocative ♭III–IV–I) that is unambiguously blues saturated and rock styled ('We're Sgt. Pepper's Lonely Hearts Club Band') as the 'heavy' guitar accompaniment in open fifths completes the sonic image. But the style shifts again just seconds later, as the next phrase reminds us that Sgt. Pepper's band is, after all, the house band for a larger show to be presented for the listener's entertainment ('Sit back and let the evening go'). Here the progression shifts from the psychedelic or 'heavy blues' progression to include a milder, more 'dated' secondary dominant

(V^7/V), coinciding with another brief brass band segment. The five-measure bridge ('It's wonderful to be here, it's certainly a thrill, you're such a lovely audience, we'd like to take you home with us, we'd love to take you home') continues in its expression of old-fashioned sentiments with the repeated-note melody delivered in a more 'sedate' tone, the 'period' chords and the sustained brass band chords underneath following suit.

At this point, the original verse section returns in full psychedelic regalia and is greeted enthusiastically by the crowd, which seems equally enchanted with both the San Francisco and period brass band styles. But just as this section served initially more as a vocal introduction than as a legitimate verse, it serves now as both a postlude and a transition to the next song, as the announcer introduces the Master of Ceremonies for the evening – Billy Shears. McCartney's opening song is marvellously successful on several levels, not the least because its stylistic diversity strongly suggests that all of the styles that the listener is about to encounter can in one way or another be effortlessly subsumed into the evening's entertainment.

'With a Little Help from My Friends', attributed primarily to McCartney (with Lennon traditionally given credit for the line 'I can't tell you, but I know its mine'), is most notable for its simplicity and sing-song quality, comparable in some respects to McCartney's 'Yellow Submarine'. But 'With a Little Help from My Friends' reflects not the simplicity of a pseudo-children's song but the simplicity associated with a non-singing Master of Ceremonies who has obviously been chosen for the job for his entertaining, self-deprecating manner rather than his voice. Ringo is cast perfectly for this role, of course, and his guileless singing voice fits the mood perfectly. Of course McCartney's song is not quite as guileless as it first seems. The primarily diatonic quality of the verse is in some ways (and in time-tested Beatles fashion) just a set-up for the introduction of the surprising subtonic chord in the refrain ('I get by with a little help from my friends'). The degree to which this song carries on the 'period' flavour introduced in the opening song is open for debate. Its simplicity and guileless quality does, at the very least, reinforce the notion of a music hall entertainment where the initial musical offerings would be unlikely to be the most 'serious' or artistic.

Having effectively established a framing device for a 'show within a show' concept, how does McCartney follow up? While Ringo later asserted that the show concept behind *Sgt. Pepper* 'went out the window' after the first two songs (Dowlding 1989, p. 160), it is hard to hear most of McCartney's other *Pepper* songs as not in some way related to his 'show within a show' concept, either in respect to musical style or in terms of their theatrical or narrative intent. Despite its placement as the ninth song on the album, McCartney's 'When I'm Sixty-Four', composed in the late 1950s as an affectionate tribute to his father and the antiquated popular musical styles he might have played in his youth, represents the most obvious example of an early music hall style in its melody, harmonic and rhythmic identity as well as in McCartney's vocal style (given a lighter, more vulnerable quality by having been transposed up a step electronically). Stylistically related to this is 'Getting Better' (which, as track No. 4, precedes 'Sixty-Four' on the recording), another McCartney composition with Lennon having provided some assistance with the lyrics. The chorus of the song is for the most part unabashedly cheerful, and the frequently bouncy, repeated note melody, which makes a prominent use of lower auxiliary tones in the brief vocal introduction, proceeds in a jaunty manner perfectly consistent with the music hall style from the 1920s and generally resembles the tune to 'With a Little Help from My Friends' in its simplicity and narrow range, although the reiterated pedal on the dominant stiffens the texture in a way not found in that earlier song.

The bridge is another matter, however, particularly in regard to the lyrics. Lennon's contribution ('I used to be cruel to my woman, I beat her and kept her apart from the things that she loved') picks up from the darker undertones of McCartney's verse and the ringing tones of the tambura (the second time through) dramatically distances the lyrics from the world of the music hall. So 'Getting Better' by no means epitomizes the show concept to the degree that either 'With a Little Help from My Friends' or 'When I'm Sixty-Four' does. Still, the song is stylistically related to both, and the primarily cheerful message communicated by the verse and refrain increases the degree of compatibility that listeners feel when experiencing the song in the context of the album.

McCartney's 'Fixing a Hole' also shows some kinship with 'When I'm Sixty-Four', less because of its jaunty rhythms and period-inflected melodic style than because of the song's wistful quality, manufactured largely by the prominent use of augmented chords and chromatic counterpoint, both of which underline the song's thoughtful, introspective lyrics. 'Lovely Rita' takes a much more extroverted, rock-oriented approach, but this quirky song about a parking-meter maid fits quite nicely into the show as the sort of rollicking, tongue-in-cheek novelty song with a 'period' inflected piano solo that might well have made its way into a music hall presentation.

Dramatically different in tone but equally appropriate to the music hall context is 'She's Leaving Home', a sentimental Victorian ballad complete with moral conveniently drawn in the last verse. McCartney's narrative, aided and abetted by Lennon's contributions to the refrain lyrics (primarily the parent's responses, for example, 'We gave her most of our lives ... Sacrificed most of our lives ...'), is sung to a melody as graceful and nostalgic as can be found in any sentimental song from the early decades of the twentieth century, and the lush accompaniment – although not strictly Victorian or even 'period-oriented' in style – successfully completes the picture. Both the sentiments and much of the language are dated, despite the fact that the message was widely interpreted as contemporary. Here, as in other McCartney contributions to the album, a 'modernist' perspective is combined with a 'historical' perspective, perfectly in keeping with the album's title song and the conceptual unity that most listeners were perfectly prepared to accept.

But was Lennon interested in contributing to this conceptual unity? Despite his subsequent eagerness to deny any interest in the *Sgt. Pepper* concept, many listeners read Lennon's contributions differently at the time. The same may be true for McCartney, who was the most enthusiastic proponent of the 'show within a show' concept, and Martin, who also contributed to the decisions regarding the ordering of songs on the album. Lennon's 'Lucy in the Sky with Diamonds' was given a prominent position, appearing third on the album after 'With a Little Help from My Friends'. Nevertheless, 'Lucy in the Sky with Diamonds' displays little to link it to the music hall style, unless one hears it as an exotic, electronically embellished 'magic act', an unlikely but not impossible addition to a music hall entertainment from the early decades of the twentieth century. After all, McCartney does refer to his intention to craft 'a good show' with this album (Dowlding 1989, p. 160). Still, Lennon's song appears to pursue its own agenda, which seemed to have more to do with producing another dreamily psychedelic song of the sort represented by 'Strawberry Fields Forever' in its original, unembellished version rather than capturing the spirit of an English music hall.

On the other hand, Lennon's 'Being for the Benefit of Mr. Kite!' embodies the circus aspect of *Sgt. Pepper* better than any other song on the album, the lyrics having been lifted almost directly by Lennon from a Victorian circus poster he had purchased in an antique shop, and the instrumental and tape sonorities heard in the song are evocative of an old-time circus in a number of ways. The verse itself is not without its interesting subtleties; the artful slippage between the keys of C minor and D minor in the verse and the dramatic contrast between the sinuous chromatic line that dominates the first section of the verse and the bolder, more assertive leaps that dominate the second half are particularly effective. But the song is probably best known for Martin's semi-random calliope effects achieved by juxtaposing unrelated tape fragments with harmonium and harmonica, based on Lennon's vague indications about summoning up a 'fairground' or circus atmosphere (Somach, Somach and Gunn 1991, p. 282). Lennon's disclaimers about his songs not contributing to the *Pepper* theme notwithstanding, there is no question that this song plays a major role on the album, recapitulating the festive show atmosphere of the opening number and encapsulating much of the jaunty music hall spirit that pervades many of the songs on side one by its incorporation of circus-music effects, while simultaneously reinvoking the magical atmosphere of 'Lucy in the Sky with Diamonds' by its fanciful use of tape effects. Nevertheless, Lennon expressed disdain for 'Mr. Kite' on more than one occasion after the fact, claiming that it was a poor thing, given life only because the album required more material at that point (Wenner 2000, p. 17). The song may have been his only contribution that clearly fits the emerging music hall/circus concept for the *Sgt. Pepper* album, but that fact did little to elevate it in Lennon's eyes.

Lennon's lack of enthusiasm for 'Good Morning, Good Morning' has also been well documented. Displaying more metric complexity than any other Beatles song to that point, the song may have been influenced by the cross-accents of McCartney's 'Good Day Sunshine' from the *Revolver* album and the Stax-Volt horn line of 'Got to Get You into My Life', while McCartney's virtuosic psychedelic guitar solo clearly echoes his earlier solo on Harrison's 'Taxman' from the same album. But there is little in the song, nominally inspired by a televised cornflakes commercial and replete with barnyard noises (perhaps the most direct reference to the Beach Boy's *Pet Sounds* album frequently cited by McCartney as an influence on *Sgt. Pepper*), to suggest much connection with the music hall theme. The opening verse lyrics ('Nothing to do to save his life, call his wife in') may be heard as a foreshadowing of the first verse of Lennon's contribution to 'A Day in the Life', but on the whole Lennon's song is aggressively independent in style and spirit from anything else on the album.

'A Day in the Life', which closes the album after the evening's entertainment has been formally brought to a conclusion by the reprise of 'Sgt. Pepper's Lonely Hearts Club Band', was one of the earliest of *Sgt. Pepper*'s tracks to be recorded, following only 'When I'm Sixty-Four' in the songs that were ultimately included on the record. Of course, two of the Beatles' most monumental pop-rock songs – McCartney's

'Penny Lane' and Lennon's 'Strawberry Fields Forever' – had been recorded first, at a point in which it appeared that the theme of the new Beatles album would be, at least in part, the Beatles' childhood, an idea usually attributed to Lennon. But the decision was made to issue the two songs as a single, eliminating them from consideration for the album. So now, starting from scratch conceptually and with only 'When I'm Sixty-Four' completed, Lennon and McCartney designed another epic song, one that would be destined to attract more attention than any other song on the album with the possible exception of 'She's Leaving Home'.

The Beatles stepped out of the Sgt. Pepper character for this song, even though it seems clear that it offers a moral every bit as cogent as the one delivered in the elegantly Victorian 'She's Leaving Home'. But the moral here is less direct and expressed in the form of a parable, with psychedelic and drug implications in abundance, about the tragedy of living a life of wasted opportunities and only a superficial awareness of self.

The song having been recorded so shortly after 'Strawberry Fields Forever', Lennon's creative juices were obviously flowing freely at this point as the album had not yet clearly taken the 'show within a show' direction for which he was to demonstrate little enthusiasm. His contribution begins casually enough with a gentle acoustic chord strum, but the song gains purpose as the texture is thickened and the first line is introduced ('I read the news today, oh boy, about a lucky man who made the grade'). There is nothing at this point to suggest that the song will develop into anything remarkable; the harmonies are based on a descending bass line of a sort Lennon and McCartney had both used before. But Lennon's vocal is breathy and sensitive and the lyrical, balanced melody features an unusually expressive use of non-harmonic tones, all of which suggest that the song will not remain on such a 'matter of fact' level. As the verse repeats, the mood begins to shift, becoming not so much sombre as ironic as Lennon refers to the 'lucky man' who 'blew his mind out in a car'. The instrumental accompaniment, marvellously embellished by Ringo's restrained yet masterful drum fills, increases the tension level with the piano dissonances becoming more strident even as the vocal remains unnaturally sedate. Both the second and third verses conclude with a climactic high G in the vocals, but after the third verse, a half-step melodic motive heard earlier is transformed into a slow, measured trill on the words 'I'd love to turn you on', a McCartney contribution that served as both a drug reference and a reminder that the parable has an urgent message to impart. A series of chords follows, an instrumental echo of Lennon's slow trill, and then a massive, semi-improvised glissando engineered by Martin with the enthusiastic coaching of McCartney, whose interest in the avant-garde music of Stockhausen and others had recently taken flight. The result of this elaborate manoeuvring is a modulation to the key of E and a fresh new context in which to hear McCartney's contribution.

His fragment, so artfully spliced onto Lennon's, is quite different in style, exuding an almost martial jauntiness, and may well have been intended as a parody of a 1930s pop song, similar to if somewhat more 'modern' sounding than 'When I'm Sixty-Four' (Everett 1999, p. 117). The lyrics ('Woke up, fell out of bed, dragged a comb across my head') can easily be heard as another reminiscence from childhood, comparable to those documented in his earlier 'Penny Lane' (Ibid.). The only real linkage to Lennon's fragment comes at the end, in another hallucinatory reference ('Found my way upstairs and had a smoke, and somebody spoke and I went into a dream'). Another wordless interlude (presumably the dream sequence to which McCartney refers) relocates the key back in E where Lennon makes his last statement, musing on the holes in Blackburn, Lancashire. There is no 'ending' to the song, the Beatles' call for their listeners to develop a heightened level of consciousness being, by its very nature, a continuous process. So the massive glissando returns, this time with epic force, and brings the song to its final, cosmic chord.

For this song, the collaboration between Lennon and McCartney seems as vital and exuberant as in the duo's most cohesive days between 1964 and 1965. But it is clear that the relationship between Lennon and McCartney was beginning to change prior to and during the recording of *Sgt. Pepper*. While both remained actively concerned about the recording process involved in the production of *Rubber Soul*, *Revolver* and *Sgt. Pepper*, they differed significantly in the degree to which they were invested in the themes or conceptual bases for these three albums. In the making of *Rubber Soul*, there was still to a large extent a unity of spirit, a compatibility of genre and style, and a shared desire on behalf of both Lennon and McCartney to create an album that was as coherent in its aesthetic as it was novel and unexpected. But the Beatles' next album, *Revolver*, presents a different situation. For this album, Lennon eagerly embraced the possibilities of the emerging psychedelic style while McCartney, though eager to display a new seriousness of tone in some of his songs, was less sure about the wisdom of the Beatles' new direction and worked to soften the edges of the record and make it more commercially palatable.

But when the time had arrived to put together the next major album, *Sgt. Pepper's Lonely Hearts Club Band*, the situation had changed. Buoyed by the great success – both popular and critical – of *Revolver*, McCartney now fully embraced the idea of experimentation, and in particular the possibilities of a sophisticated, multi-layered narrative approach. Lennon took a different lesson from the success of *Revolver*, choosing instead to focus on the refinement of his own, increasingly personal psychedelic style, combining it with traditional pop-rock elements without watering it down or softening its revolutionary edge. And, as always, Lennon's primary subject remained himself and his own, very personal experiences of the world. To Lennon, this was a future worth pursuing, while he retained serious doubts about McCartney's vision. As a result, Lennon's efforts to adapt his ideas to McCartney's 'show within a show' concept were half-hearted at best and frequently subject to harsh self-criticism after the fact. While it is always possible to hear Lennon's contributions to *Sgt. Pepper* as fully compatible with the album's innovative thrust, the fact remains that his aesthetic had diverged sharply from McCartney's by the conclusion of the *Pepper* sessions, never to converge completely again.

The Beatles were to combine their efforts with great success on a number of occasions after *Sgt. Pepper*, but the album nevertheless represents a critical point in their history in terms of the development of the unique and fully personal aesthetics of both Lennon and McCartney.

Chapter 3

Sgt. Pepper's quest for extended form

Thomas MacFarlane

Sgt. Pepper's Lonely Hearts Club Band is widely regarded as the first true concept album in popular music. However, *Sgt. Pepper* is not quite what it appears to be. Despite the recurrence of the title track, there is little evidence of the kinds of melodic or harmonic relationships one would normally expect in an extended form.[1] Instead, the group chose to employ an overarching thematic concept in an apparent effort to unify individual tracks.

It seems now that the Beatles were effectively saying, 'Look everyone! Concept albums are possible. This (*Sgt. Pepper*) isn't it, but it proves that it's possible'. In retrospect, this ingenious strategy helped them buy the time necessary to explore questions regarding formal space on a sound recording. The resulting album can thus be viewed as the first step in a two-year process of experimentation that culminates with the extended form of the *Abbey Road Medley*.

The following discussion will consider the music of the Beatles within the context of popular music and culture between 1962 and 1970, paying particular attention to the production of the album *Sgt. Pepper's Lonely Hearts Club Band*. The implications of this work will then be examined with regard to sound recording and emergent musical structures on subsequent Beatles albums.

In the town where I was born

The Beatles formed in the seaport town of Liverpool, England in the late 1950s. Following World War II, the prosperity Liverpool had enjoyed during the early part of the century was clearly on the wane. In an interview given on 5 August 2003,

---

1 'Extended form' corresponds to the term 'cyclic form', which the *New Grove Dictionary of Music and Musicians* describes as: 'Music in which a later movement reintroduces thematic material of an earlier movement … Beethoven (*An die ferne Geliebte, Piano Sonata in A*, Op. 101), Schubert (*Piano Trio in E♭, Fantasia in C for violin and piano*) and Berlioz (*Symphonie Fantastique*) laid the foundations on which Mendelssohn, Schumann, Liszt and Franck elevated cyclic principles to great importance, associated with the widespread application of thematic transformation and the desire for greater continuity between separate movements, all methods of establishing a tighter cohesion in multi-movement forms. Since the 19th century cyclic form has been adopted as a regular stock-in-trade of musical structure' (MacDonald 2001). The organic elements evident in a preliminary analysis tend to correspond to the *Grove* definition of cyclic form, and thus suggest the presence of a complex organizational structure at work within the *Abbey Road Medley*.

Peter Brown (personal assistant to Brian Epstein and the Beatles' de facto manager during the late 1960s) described the source of the distinctive Liverpool character:

> It was an amazingly successful English port. As the twentieth century went on, it became less and less so. And in our day[s], in the [19]50s and [19]60s, it was struggling a bit. But there was always an arrogance about the working class Liverpudlians like, 'Fuck you', you know, 'we'll manage on our own' … So there was always an attitude about Liverpudlians, and I think that the Beatles, because they came from that culture … learned to be very independent and that attitude became their thing. (Quoted in MacFarlane 2005, pp. 313–14)

In addition to fostering an innate toughness in the young Beatles, Liverpool also provided an ideal cultural environment for the development of their musical skills. As Brown points out,

> Also, the other thing about Liverpool was the fact that there was a lot of knowledge about American music that wasn't available in the rest of the country because of the sailors. A lot of the young, working class boys would go to sea initially. They would start going into the Merchant Marine when they were 16, 17, 18 years old. And they would go to sea to make some money. And, of course, a lot of them would go to America, and they would spend time in America, they would buy American records, because in those days of course the radio in Britain was very restrictive and there wasn't much going on. So we in Liverpool, and in the record stores that Brian [Epstein] and I worked in, were much more sophisticated about American music than probably the rest of the country. (Ibid., p. 314)

As a result of the availability that Brown describes, Liverpool musicians would learn American songs by rote and incorporate them directly into their stage act.[2] In time, this process spawned an original musical style known as Merseybeat. Although Liverpool artists such as Gerry and the Pacemakers, the Searchers and Cilla Black each achieved international success in the 1960s, the Beatles were the most pervasive practitioners of this style.

Lend me your ears and I'll sing you a song

During their early period (1962–64), the Beatles worked hard to consolidate the musical elements they had inherited from previous eras. They proceeded to integrate these elements into a distinctive musical approach that featured: unusual vocal harmonies ('Baby's in Black', 1964); the synthesis of rock and blues inflections with elements derived from country and western or folk styles ('You Can't Do That', 1964; 'She's a Woman', 1964); and distinctive studio-derived sound gestures ('Love Me Do', 1962; 'She Loves You', 1963; 'I Feel Fine', 1964).

The Beatles' middle period (1965–66) is distinguished by a marked increase in studio experimentation. This is particularly evident in several innovative tracks from the *Revolver* sessions:

---

2   Paul McCartney was very adept at this process and often learned the more obscure B-sides of various 45s in order to give the Beatles a more specialized, less typical set list (Lewisohn 1988a, p. 8).

- 'I'm Only Sleeping' (reversed guitar parts are featured throughout)
- 'Rain' (reversed vocals are prominent during the song's coda)
- 'Tomorrow Never Knows' (a series of tape loops form the backdrop of the song).

The idiosyncratic nature of these recordings combined with the groundbreaking sessions for 'Penny Lane' and 'Strawberry Fields Forever' in late 1966 helped pave the way for the increasing formal experimentation that would characterize the Beatles' late period (1967–69).

In the latter part of their career, the Beatles continually sought to expand the formal boundaries of popular music through an engagement of multitrack recording. In their early period, they had achieved a mastery of the musical forms inherited from previous eras. But by 1966, one can sense an increasing frustration with the limitations of the conventional pop song format. While *Rubber Soul* (1965) presents a near-perfect balance of form and content, *Revolver* (1966) seems to be the point at which the Beatles' content begins to overwhelm the limitations of their inherited forms.

Lennon raises the bar

During the Beatles' early period, John Lennon set the pace for the group's unique approach to musical form and content. At this point, Paul McCartney's work tended to provide stylistic relief to the rhythm and blues focus of his partner's early contributions. But during the Beatles' middle period, McCartney began to emerge as the architect of the group's subsequent musical direction. As a result of this shift, Lennon had to find a new role. In the wake of his partner's ascendancy, he began creating works that urged McCartney on to higher creative levels.

On *Revolver* (1966), Lennon seemed audibly frustrated with the folk-rock idioms he had been exploring since 1965. While McCartney was producing works in a variety of styles and genres ('Eleanor Rigby', 'Got to Get You into My Life', 'For No One'), Lennon presented material that seemed laboured by comparison. The notable exception is 'Tomorrow Never Knows', a work which actively explores avant-garde experimentation within the context of popular music. The finished track was augmented by a series of homemade tape loops assembled by McCartney. These were then fed into the recording console and 'played' during the final mix (Lewisohn 1988b, p. 72). This approach to multitrack recording helped pave the way for the formal experimentation that characterized the Beatles' late period.

Composing to tape with Sir George Martin

With the advent of sound recording, twentieth-century pop composers began to actively explore the possibilities engendered by the new medium. This development was addressed by Virgil Moorefield in *From the Illusion of Reality to the Reality of Illusion: The Changing Role of the Producer in the Pop Recording Studio,* with regard to the work of Brian Eno:

His approach to the studio as a fullfledged musical instrument was groundbreaking, and beginning in the mid-Seventies, his numerous interviews featured discussions of pop music in terms that were altogether new. A fan of 'roots' rock as well as reggae, he pointed out the implications of the techniques employed in the modern recording studio, and traced his own conceptual lineage as a composer back through Steve Reich and John Cage to Erik Satie. (Moorefield 2001, pp. 18–19)

The 'conceptual lineage' Eno sensed with Steve Reich, John Cage and Erik Satie foregrounds the connections that exist between sound recording and music composition. Similar connections can be found in the work of the Beatles. However, in their case, the links were not just conceptual; they were also very concrete, and due primarily to the influence of an EMI staff producer named George Martin.

Commonly considered the 'fifth Beatle', George Martin is the group's most important link with the musical traditions of the past. An accomplished instrumentalist and arranger educated at London's Guildhall School of Music, his skills were essential in attaining the professional lustre that became an indispensable aspect of the Beatles' music. But as the group's producer, he was also responsible for the technical innovations that characterized many late-period Beatles recordings. Working with engineer Geoff Emerick, Martin managed to turn the EMI Studios into a virtual laboratory of recorded sound (Lewisohn 1988b, p. 79).

Although it is not widely known, Martin also had direct experience with the creation of electro-acoustic music, albeit with an obscure and rather amusing pseudonym. As he himself recalled: 'Creating atmosphere and sound pictures ... that was my bag. I did a lot of it before the Beatles even came along. In 1962 Parlophone issued a single called "Time Beat"/"Waltz in Orbit", a compilation of electronic sounds, composed by a certain "Ray Cathode" – me' (Martin with Pearson 1994, p. 83). In *The Unknown Paul McCartney: McCartney and the Avant-garde,* Ian Peel describes how Martin's single '... mixed live musicians over a purely synthesized electronic rhythm track Martin had created with the Radiophonic Workshop' (Peel 2002, p. 22). 'It was a resounding flop', Martin later remembered, 'but an interesting flop ... something to learn from anyway' (Ibid.).

George Martin's experience with both traditional and progressive approaches to music composition explains his critical role in the Beatles' creative process. He clearly provided continuity with the musical traditions of the past, but he was also a viable link to contemporary music, which was becoming increasingly dependent on recording technology as the means for its realization.

'Wouldn't It Be Nice'

Between 1961 and 1965, the Beach Boys released a series of singles and long-playing records that exhibited an increasingly expansive level of musical sophistication. The architect of their sound, Brian Wilson, combined the jazz-based vocal harmonies of the Four Freshmen with the energetic sounds of Southern California 'surf music' to form a highly distinctive and original style.

As the group's producer, Wilson was also intrigued by the aesthetic possibilities of sound recording. With *Pet Sounds* (1966), he demonstrated a precocious mastery of composition, arrangement and production. 'Good Vibrations', a 45-rpm single that followed several months later, expanded on the formal development of *Pet Sounds*. It featured an elaborate series of tape edits that juxtaposed contrasting musical tempos and textures in a dazzling mosaic of recorded sound, which Virgil Moorefield describes as:

> ... a clear example of the use of the studio as a compositional device ... Listening to 'Good Vibrations' today, it is patently obvious that it is spliced together from recordings made in different spaces. Yet the music is powerful, a heady mix of exceptionally polished vocal harmonies and experimental instrumentation. (Moorefield 2001, pp. 32–3)

Although Wilson's efforts to build on the success of *Pet Sounds* and 'Good Vibrations' were abandoned in 1967 due to personal problems brought on by excessive drug use, his achievements had considerable impact on his musical peers. In *Many Years from Now*, Barry Miles describes how

> Paul [McCartney] regarded *Pet Sounds* as one of the greatest popular-music albums ever made and was effusive in its praise, particularly for the way in which it proved that the bass player need not play the root note of a chord but can weave a melody around it of its own. He recommended the album to everyone he met. (Miles 1997, p. 281)

Using *Pet Sounds* as a point of reference, McCartney set out to expand the focus of the Beatles' work with sounds and textures not normally associated with popular music.

Sgt. Pepper's Lonely Hearts Club Band (1967)

By late 1966, the Beatles had given up live performance, and thus had more time to devote exclusively to the studio. On 5 August 2003, Peter Brown pointed out that, '... prior to [19]66, albums were made between tours ... Once they stopped touring, there was nothing else to do. There was no other call on their time except recording, and so there was the freedom of time so they could experiment more ...' (quoted in MacFarlane 2005, pp. 308–9).

Sgt. Pepper, the first album that resulted from this shift in creative focus, is remarkably varied in both artistic ambition and technical execution. But it is not quite what it appears to be. Despite the reappearance of the title-track near the end of side two, there is no evidence of thematic or harmonic relationship between any of the album's 13 tracks. In his review on 29 May 1967, *The Times* music critic William Mann gently chided the Beatles on this very point:

> The one new exploration is the showband manner of the title song, its reprise, and its interval song 'Being for the Benefit of Mr. Kite!' These three give a certain shape and integrity to the two sides, and if the unity is slightly specious the idea is ... worth pursuing. (Reprinted in Thomson and Gutman 1988, p. 93)

It is interesting to consider the Beatles' own comments regarding the *Sgt. Pepper* concept. In *Many Years from Now*, McCartney described '... this idea of giving the Beatles alter egos simply to get a different approach ... I thought we can run this philosophy through the whole album … so we'll be able to lose our identities in this' (Miles 1997, pp. 303–4). However, this account was challenged in 1980 by John Lennon, who pointed out that 'Sgt. Pepper is called the first concept album, but it doesn't go anywhere. All my contributions to the album have absolutely nothing to do with this idea of Sgt. Pepper and his band; but it works 'cause we *said* it worked, and that's how the album appeared' (Sheff 2000, p. 197). Evidently realizing that a full-blown concept album was beyond their capabilities at that point, the Beatles wisely opted to present Sgt. Pepper as a more modest proposal.

Musical elements

Even if Sgt. Pepper does not exhibit the kind of organic unity one would expect from a bona fide extended form, there are still many noteworthy musical elements that should be considered in relation to the band's rapidly expanding compositional language. For instance, the album's exotic approach to instrumentation still challenges conventional notions of what is appropriate in the pop song format:

- 'Sgt. Pepper's Lonely Hearts Club Band' presents four French horns set in relief against a rock band that features distorted electric guitar and high-tessitura blues vocals
- 'Within You Without You' sets an authentic Indian ensemble (consisting of sitar, dilruba, tabla, suvar mandal and tambura) against Western classical instruments (violin, cello) for an elaborate duet in 5/4 time
- 'Getting Better' employs a pedal point on scale degree 5 that is reiterated throughout the track on electric guitar, pianette, sitar and bass to tremendous effect (Example 3.1).

Example 3.1 'Getting Better': electric guitar (intro)

These and other tracks on the album suggest an increasing awareness of timbre as an important compositional element.

Sgt. Pepper also exhibits a fascination with ostinato figures, and their use in the expansion of musical texture. On 'Fixing a Hole', McCartney plays a recurring pattern on bass guitar that reaches across the bar line to assert elements of both chords in a repeating i–IV progression (Example 3.2).

Example 3.2 'Fixing a Hole': bass figure (0'16"–0'23")

A similar line is heard during the coda of 'Lovely Rita' (Example 3.3), in which the bass underpins an extended improvisation that features piano, 'vocal percussion' and comb and paper (MacDonald 1994, p. 189).

Example 3.3 'Lovely Rita': bass figure (coda)

Note how each of these figures transcends the traditional harmonic function of bass to become a part of the overall textural fabric.

Recording strategies

Despite the significance of the preceding musical elements, *Sgt. Pepper*'s key innovation lies in the integration of recording technology into the compositional process. Such integration became viable following the premiere in 1958 of *Poème Electronique* (Grout and Palisca 2006, p. 926). This work, by composer Edgar Varèse, served to expand the definition of sound recording from archival documentation to the reification of the musical canvas. In this regard, the most significant track on *Sgt. Pepper* is 'A Day in the Life'.

40 years on, it is still remarkable to consider that the breathtaking aleatoric orchestral passages of 'A Day in the Life' – '… from nothing up to something absolutely like the end of the world …' (John Lennon, quoted in Martin with Hornsby 1979, p. 209) – were achieved by the synchronization of two four-track recording machines. In *Revolution in the Head: The Beatles' Records and the Sixties*, Ian MacDonald describes the origins of this effect:

> McCartney had decided that the 24-bar bridges would be filled by a full symphony orchestra going from its lowest to its highest note in an unsynchronised slide – a 'freak out' or 'aural happening'. Charged with realising this, George Martin halved the number of players and scored the glissando individually to ensure the right 'random' effect. Rather than a chaotic tone-cluster, each player was asked to finish on whichever note in the E major triad was nearest the highest note on his instrument. A second four-track machine was slaved to the one running the Beatles' own stereo track (the first time this had ever been tried in a British studio) and each orchestral glissando was recorded in mono four times before being mixed back to the master as a single monstrous noise (presumably remixed with ADT to take up the spare track). (MacDonald 1994, p. 183)

Since this account touches on elements of composition and orchestration, as well as the technical realities of sound recording, it suggests that the Beatles were continuing to integrate recording technology into their compositional process. The album can thus be viewed as the first phase in a two-year period (1967–69) of formal experimentation that culminates with the extended form of the *Abbey Road Medley*.

Mystery Tours to Abbey Road[3]

The Beatles' next release following *Sgt. Pepper's Lonely Hearts Club Band* was *Magical Mystery Tour* (1967). The six new songs included on this EP were written as the score for an original film in which the band members appear as wizards watching over a group of travellers on psychedelic holiday. Here, the Beatles elaborate on the *Sgt. Pepper* style by focusing on colour and texture as important compositional elements. But they also continue to explore the aesthetic possibilities engendered by the technology of recorded sound.

Mono vs stereo

In *The Beatles Recording Sessions*, Mark Lewisohn points out that until *Abbey Road*, all Beatles albums were released in mono and stereo. The Beatles themselves were only directly involved in the mono mix, while George Martin and EMI engineers would typically create the stereo version at a later date (Lewisohn 1988b, p. 108). However, evidence suggests that as early as *Magical Mystery Tour*, the Beatles

---

3   Mellers 1973, p. 107. As the title of an individual chapter, Mellers uses the phrase, 'A Magical Mystery Tour to Abbey Road'. I have adapted his title for the section of my discussion that creates an overview of the Beatles' late-period (1967–69) works.

and their collaborators were actively exploring the aesthetic possibilities of stereo mixing. Individual tracks such as 'Flying', 'Blue Jay Way' and 'Your Mother Should Know' each exhibit remarkable sonic qualities when one listens alternately to the right and left channels. In particular, the instruments that appear on the right channel of 'Flying' do not even enter until 0'13" into the song. In this context, the listener becomes decidedly more active, and thus has the option of choosing from various musical elements in the mix.

Remarkably, Lennon's 'I Am the Walrus' manages to combine both mono and stereo mixing techniques within the same track. As engineer Geoff Emerick explains, this effect was achieved by splicing two different mixes together:

> Ken [Scott] engineered the mono mix, but I was asked to do the stereo mix when I returned from vacation. We tried twiddling the radio dial that time, too, but the results weren't as much to John's liking as the Shakespearean play he happened to tune into during the mono mix, so we had to splice the end of the original mix in. We flanged it in order to spread the signal out in stereo, but avid listeners can still hear the image shift dramatically after the splice point ... (Emerick and Massey 2006, p. 215)

Effects to the fore

Although *Sgt. Pepper* gets most of the mainstream praise, it is *The Beatles*[4] that continues to inspire younger generations of musicians with its sprawling song sequence, its carefree approach to genre and style, and its blatant disregard for popular musical conventions (MacDonald 1994, p. 261). Here, the fundamental theme is incongruity, as the principle of organic unity itself is increasingly called into question. In an essay entitled 'The postmodern White Album', Ed Whitley asserts the presence of inter-textual processes at work within this album's widely varying and often baffling song sequence: 'By employing the disruptive aesthetics of postmodern art, the White Album calls attention away from itself as a source of meaning and instead clears a space where readers can engage the issues of what popular music is and what role it plays' (Whitley 2000, p. 122). On that basis, one could assert that *The Beatles* (1968) is a more fully realized conceptual statement than *Sgt. Pepper* since its central theme grows organically from within the work.

Building on the progressive recording strategies employed for 'Tomorrow Never Knows', Lennon presents the sound collage 'Revolution 9'. Here, tape loops similar to the ones used to 'colour' the earlier song are pushed to the fore to become this track's primary focus. As Mark Lewisohn describes:

> Just like the 7 April 1966 'Tomorrow Never Knows' session, there were people all over EMI Studios spooling loops onto tape machines with pencils. But instead of Geoff Emerick sitting at the console fading them in and out in a live mix, it was John Lennon, with Yoko closely by his side. (Lewisohn 1988b, p. 138)

Evidently taking inspiration from *Hymnen* (1967) by Karlheinz Stockhausen, 'Revolution 9' is still remarkable for its insight into the narrative potential of

---

4   Known through popular consensus as the White Album.

recorded sound (MacDonald 1994, pp. 233–4). At just under nine minutes, it is also the longest track the group had released to this point, and thus begins to prepare the listener for the sprawling multi-part structure of the *Abbey Road Medley*.

Audio vérité

The first project for 1969 was *Get Back*,[5] an album and film that attempted to foreground the Beatles' distinctive musical process. One might say that process itself is the unifying theme of *Get Back*. In the twilight of their career, the Beatles curiously chose to abandon all studio trickery and record every track live. This daring return to a recording aesthetic that existed prior to the appearance of *Poème Electronique* resulted in a remarkable audio documentary that certainly shed light on the Beatles' distinctive creative dynamic. Unfortunately, the accompanying footage that was used to create the film, *Let It Be* (1970), also reveals an emerging personal acrimony that would ultimately bring the Beatles to an end. In *At the Apple's Core: The Beatles from the Inside*, film producer Denis O'Dell (*A Hard Day's Night*, *Magical Mystery Tour*, *Let It Be*) describes the group's difficulties during this period:

> Communication – or the lack of it – was at the heart of the problem. Throughout my career as a producer I had seen many major creative disagreements; arguments between leading stars and actors, between stars and directors, directors and designers, designers and camera crews. I've even been involved in a few myself. Such clashes are usually resolved, often very quickly, to the mutual satisfaction of all concerned and mostly to the benefit of the film. In short, disagreements are frequently productive. But this wasn't the case with the Beatles. They would never thrash out their differences with each other (or anyone else for that matter) in any sort of constructive or reasonable way. Instead, they would simply stop communicating with one another. Nothing ever got resolved, and the awkward silences formed a breeding ground for hostility and resentment. (O'Dell 2002, pp. 140–41)

Extended forms and the music of chance

In the months that followed the abortive *Get Back* project, the Beatles recorded sporadically, while carefully considering their next move. Eventually, McCartney contacted producer George Martin and asked him about working together again on another album. However, Martin was reluctant:

> *Let it Be* [*Get Back*] was such an unhappy record (even though there are some great songs on it) that I really believed that was the end of the Beatles, and I assumed that I would never work with them again … So I was quite surprised when Paul rang me up and said, 'We're going to make another record – would you like to produce it?' My immediate answer was: 'Only if you let me produce it the way we used to.' He said, 'We will, we want to.' – 'John included?' – 'Yes, honestly.' So I said, 'Well, if you really want to, let's do it. Let's get together again.' (Beatles 2000, p. 337)

---

5   Released in 1970 as *Let It Be*.

By all accounts, the sessions for the album were peaceful and productive. Individual egos were subsumed for the sake of the music, and for the first time since the mid-1960s all four Beatles are featured on nearly every track.

Abbey Road concludes with a series of song fragments, which the Beatles and their collaborators deftly weave into a formal design predicated on double-tonic relationships between the tonal centres of A and C. This design facilitates the creation of a three-movement structure replete with sectional variation, thematic restatement, and inventive lyrical and harmonic development (table 3.1).[6]

Table 3.1   The three-movement structure of the *Abbey Road Medley*

Movement	Track(s)
Prelude	'Because'
Movement I	'You Never Give Me Your Money' 'Out of College'–'That Magic Feeling' 'One Sweet Dream'
Movement II	'Sun King'–'Mean Mr. Mustard' 'Polythene Pam'–'She Came In Through the Bathroom Window'
Movement III	'Golden Slumbers'–'Carry That Weight' 'The End'
Postlude	'Her Majesty'

In keeping with the Beatles' late-period compositional praxis, this work is realized by means of a thorough integration of recording technique into the compositional process. The most telling example of this integration concerns the album's final track, 'Her Majesty'.

In *The Beatles Recording Sessions*, Mark Lewisohn points out that 'Her Majesty' was originally intended as the midpoint between 'Sun King'–'Mean Mr. Mustard' and 'Polythene Pam'–'She Came In Through the Bathroom Window'. In fact, the album's initial running order featured the song in that position. Presumably reacting to its tendency to halt tonal motion, McCartney decided that 'Her Majesty' was not needed and asked engineer John Kurlander to dispose of it. Understandably reluctant to consign any Beatles material to the waste bin, Kurlander proceeded to splice 'Her Majesty' onto the end of the master reel, separating it from the end of the medley with leader tape. At a subsequent listening session, when the song serendipitously appeared at the end of the sequence, the group liked the effect so much they decided to keep it as the concluding track (Lewisohn 1988b, p. 183). With this Cage-like flourish, the Beatles brought the medley, the album and their entire career to a satisfying conclusion.

---

6   My dissertation, *The Abbey Road Medley: Extended Forms in Popular Music*, provides an in-depth analysis of the entire work (MacFarlane 2005).

Nothing has changed it's still the same

The preceding discussion has considered the significance of *Sgt. Pepper's Lonely Hearts Club Band* with regard to sound recording and emergent musical structures on subsequent Beatles albums. As we have seen, *Sgt. Pepper* should properly be regarded as the first step in a two-year process of experimentation that culminates with the release of *Abbey Road*. This process is evident in the works that followed in *Pepper*'s wake. *Magical Mystery Tour* (1967) explores the expressive possibilities of stereo sound, while *The Beatles* (1968) foregrounds technology itself in 'Revolution 9'. *Get Back* (1969) revisits an aesthetic prior to the creation of *Poème Electronique*, while *Abbey Road* (1969) offers a fascinating synthesis of composition and technology in a series of song fragments that are woven together to become the *Abbey Road Medley*. On their final recorded work, the Beatles fulfil *Sgt. Pepper*'s promise by presenting a genuine extended form in the popular style.

Although their true significance has yet to be properly assessed, it seems clear that the works of the Beatles' late period (1967–69) will continue to stand as a testament to the expressive possibilities of recorded sound. Whether or not subsequent generations of composers can adequately respond to the challenge inherent in these works remains to be seen. In *The Beatles with Lacan: Rock & Roll as Requiem for the Modern Age*, author Henry W. Sullivan writes:

> In all aspects of their creative activity and influence, they sent the message … that another kind of logic, or way of knowing, was to be sought and, perhaps, encountered. Inasmuch as these insights still remain to be articulated in a more communicable form, we have not as yet returned the Beatles a satisfactory answer to their message. (Sullivan 1995, p. 169)

Chapter 4

The sound design of *Sgt. Pepper's Lonely Hearts Club Band*

Michael Hannan

Although it is not a prime focus in studies of the Beatles' music, discourse relating to their sounds, instruments and effects is nonetheless extensive. Writers interested in discussing the audio production of the Beatles' recordings have been greatly assisted by the publication of *The Beatles Recording Sessions* (Lewisohn 1988b), as well as by Beatles producer George Martin's autobiography (Martin with Hornsby 1979) and his memoir on the making of *Sgt. Pepper's Lonely Heats Club Band* (Martin with Pearson 1994). The more recent memoir of Beatles principal sound engineer, Geoff Emerick, provides further insights into sounds and production processes (Emerick and Massey 2006). Amongst musicological researchers, Everett has paid great attention to specific instruments, sounds and mixing techniques alongside his interest in harmony and other aspects of the Beatles' music (Everett 1999; Everett 2001). Moore's monograph on *Sgt. Pepper*, although mainly focused on tonal structuring of the songs, is nonetheless attentive to timbre, instrumentation and production (Moore 1997). Studies on record production (Cunningham 1996; Moorefield 2005) invariably include short case studies of *Sgt. Pepper*.

The idea of sound design comes from theatre and film production where all aspects of sound (dialogue, atmospherics, music and sound effects) are used to support the narrative. As Sonnenschein puts it:

> The true sound designer must be immersed in the story, characters, emotions, environments, and genre of the film. With their contribution the audience will be led down the path in an integrated, yet most often subconscious manner towards an experience that is authentic and human, a metaphor for the life experience itself. Using all the tools of music, psychology, acoustics, and drama, the art of orchestration comes into play, selecting the right sound for the right moment. (Sonnenschein 2001, p. xix)

George Martin, whose background included doing sound design for radio and comedy records, illustrates this concept with a story about a pre-Beatles project:

> Irene Handl and [Peter] Sellers did a sketch together called 'Shadows in the Grass', all in the studio, with very little completed script, the basic idea being that a silly old woman walking in the park is gradually seduced by a wily Frenchman. I edited the fifteen minutes of their ad-libbing down to seven minutes, took out the pauses, then overdubbed things like the crunching of feet on gravel, the faint hum of traffic in the distance, a little bit of birdsong, a little bit of rustling of leaves. When we listened back to it, the illusion that we

were listening to two people walking through a park was remarkable, with just these few little touches. (Martin with Pearson 1994, p. 84)

The approach taken in the assembly of *Sgt. Pepper* lends itself to the notion of sound design in popular-music record production. Indeed, while not a particularly common term in the context of the pop song, 'sound designer' has gained a certain currency. The entry for 'sound design' in *Wikipedia* has a short section devoted to music: 'On certain ambitious and complex recording projects, artists and producers have relied on sonic consultants, often credited as "sound designer", to help them to create specific auditory effects, landscapes, or to ensure an overall consistency and quality of some of the (usually unconventional) sonic elements' ('Sound Design').

The idea of a 'sound designer' could legitimately be applied to an orchestrator or arranger, but it acquired great potency with the employment of multitrack tape machines and the development of electronic processing of sounds. It is obvious from the available documentation of the making of *Sgt. Pepper* that George Martin and Geoff Emerick, and indeed the Beatles themselves were constantly thinking in terms of sound design. Emerick clearly felt the pressure of the quest for new sounds:

> The onus had been on me all throughout the *Pepper* sessions. I was constantly wracking my brains trying to come up with ways to make things sound different. John and Paul's attitude, even more than on *Revolver*, was, 'We're going to play guitar, but we don't want it to sound like a guitar; we're going to play piano but we don't want it to sound like piano.' (Emerick and Massey 2006, p. 189)

Sgt. Pepper pushes the boundaries of the technology available at Abbey Road Studios, and is a breakthrough album in the history of popular music because of the inventive ways the studio equipment was used and of the new processes that were pioneered. The album was made on the cusp of the appearance of commercial analogue synthesizers, but does not include any 'synthesized' sounds: all the sounds were produced using acoustic instruments, electric guitars, electric organs, field recordings of sound effects and electronic processing devices available in the recording studio.

This essay advances the notion of sound design in the production of *Sgt. Pepper's Lonely Hearts Club Band* to encompass the timbres and playing techniques of instruments and voices, the processing used on these instruments, the use of recorded sounds to reinforce the narrative aspects of the songs, the noise elements resulting from the recording process, the texturing of sounds, the mixing of the sounds, and the structuring of all these elements over the whole recording. The stereo mix will be the version of *Sgt. Pepper* examined, mainly because it is most readily available on compact disc, and stereo is the mix that most listeners will have heard both on LP and CD. Consideration of structural elements will take account of the fact that the original releases were in LP format. Thus each side of the record would represent a distinct listening segment (similar to experiencing a two-act play perhaps).

Overall structure

George Martin gives a comprehensive account of his decision-making process for the running order of *Sgt. Pepper*. The initial decisions were driven by the album's 'concept': the title song had to be first; the title song reprise had to be placed second-last because the 43 second-long piano chord at the end of 'A Day in the Life' meant that that song had to be placed last; and 'With a Little Help from My Friends' needed to follow the title song because of the introduction of the character Billy Shears in the opening song. Martin's perception of the strength of each song drove most of the other running order choices: 'My old precept in the recording business was always "Make side one strong", for obvious commercial reasons' (Martin with Pearson 1994, p. 148); and 'Another principle of mine when assembling an album was always to go out on a side strongly' (Ibid., p. 149). Thus, ostensibly, most of the other decisions were not based on musical/structural considerations (keys, tempos, narrative links, sound contrasts) so much as on 'commercial' grounds. A case may be made, however, that sound design considerations played a major part in the ordering of the remaining songs. The two songs that end sides, 'Being for the Benefit of Mr. Kite!' and 'A Day in the Life', are 'strong' because they possess the most fulsome and unique orchestrations, while 'Lucy in the Sky with Diamonds' (a 'great song' in Martin's view), placed early on side one, is also sonically very distinctive (Ibid.). Martin admits that he placed 'Within You Without You' at the beginning of side two because it was so 'alien, mystical' (Ibid.), no doubt referring, at least in part, to the sound world of the north-Indian instrumentation. And there was one definite sound design-driven decision: Martin 'noticed that the chicken squawk on the end of ["Good Morning, Good Morning"] dovetailed, or rather could be made to dovetail, neatly with the sound of the guitar tuning up that begins the title song's reprise' (Ibid.).

A distinct aspect of the sound design of *Sgt. Pepper* is the way in which the individual songs were joined together on the album. As Lewisohn reports:

> Malcolm Davies had the task of assembling the *Sgt. Pepper's Lonely Hearts Club Band* prototype master tape, utilising George Martin's specification unique for a pop music album – it was to have no 'rills' or gaps between songs. The tape was compiled in such a way that either the merest split-second of silence separated the songs or they were 'crossfaded' ... (Lewisohn 1988b, p. 107)

Thus Martin was conceiving each side of the album as a continuous flow of sound rather than as a series of individual songs. The inclusion of sound effects to contribute to the narrative aspects of the album's concept probably informed this decision.

'Sgt. Pepper's Lonely Hearts Club Band'

At the start of the album, the listener is drawn into the make-believe of the Sgt. Pepper show. Martin explains his approach:

> By adding the sound effects of applause, tuning up, and so on, we tried to paint a tableau: of the curtain going up and seeing the band on the stage ... It meant overdubbing that wonderful 'hush' of an audience before the performance starts ... So I used a recording I

had made at a performance of *Beyond the Fringe*, a comedy review I'd seen at London's Fortune Theatre in 1961, starring Peter Cook, Dudley Moore, Alan Bennett and Jonathan Miller. (Martin with Pearson 1994, p. 65)

The recording of the orchestra tuning up was made in the famous orchestral session for 'A Day in the Life'. So here we have two recordings, the audience and the orchestra, mixed together to achieve the effect.

The line-up for the title song is two electric rhythm guitars (McCartney and Harrison), bass guitar (McCartney), drums (Starr), lead guitar fills (Harrison and then McCartney during the repeat verse), lead vocal (McCartney), backing vocals (McCartney, Lennon and Harrison) and four French horns. The bass guitar, according to Lewisohn, was recorded using direct injection, a new technique developed by EMI maintenance engineer Ken Townsend (Lewisohn 1988b, p. 95). Another track was devoted to audience effects.

The sound design of this song contrasts the hard-rocking combination of belted vocals and distorted electric guitars (in the verse and chorus sections) with an instrumental break of rather quaint contrapuntal head arrangements by McCartney for French horns. According to Martin, 'Paul liked brass bands, and he wanted one in' (Martin with Pearson 1994, p. 64), but oddly enough the choice of French horns is not characteristic of the sound of the English brass bands McCartney would have heard.

The Fender Esquire guitar used by Paul McCartney has a pickup close to the bridge, providing a bright treble tone. Some distortion has been added, probably a combination of 'cranking up' the amplifier's pre-amp and a touch of fuzz box. The guitar solo and fills have had their frequencies reduced by an equalizer. The sound has been compressed and a 'slap-back' echo added.

The fairly eccentric stereo mix is typical of the album. Lead guitar(s) and backbeat stab rhythm guitar are placed in the right speaker with another rhythm part and the French horns in the left once they enter. The verses have the lead vocal entirely in the right speaker but during the chorus and middle eight all the vocals move to the left. There is (understandably) a more subdued mix of drums and bass when the horns are playing in the break and in the middle eight. The surge of audience applause introduced to coincide with the entry of the horn break is clumsily mixed and thus narratively unconvincing.

Sonically, the standout features of the track are the warm recordings of the French horns, the interplay of the processed timbres of the rhythm guitars and lead guitars, and the high energetic belt quality of McCartney's vocal delivery. Martin is particularly enthusiastic about the latter: 'Paul sings his heart out on this one. Anyone who thinks that Paul McCartney is not a great singer of rock 'n' roll only has to listen to his voice on this track. You can hear the gravel in it' (Ibid., p. 66).

Everett hears the performance as 'Little Richard-styled' (Everett 1999, p. 101) and Moore as a Little Richard 'holler' (Moore 1997, p. 28), assessments which fit with McCartney's own estimation of his vocal development through imitation of other singers: '… if I sang high raucous stuff I thought I was being Little Richard' (quoted in Soto-Morettini 2006, p. 150).

'With a Little Help from My Friends'

To segue smoothly from the recording of 'Sgt. Pepper's Lonely Hearts Club Band' to the recording of 'With a Little Help from My Friends', a crossfade was employed and George Martin engaged in a little compositional sound design by recording a few bridging bars of ascending chords to move the tonality from the C7 (chord IV) final run-out of 'Sgt. Pepper' up to the key of E of the second song. Everett aptly labels this a 'fanfare progression' (Everett 1999, p. 103). Powerful quaver-triplet Hammond organ chords underscore a male choral setting (one syllable to each chord) of the words 'Bil-ly Shears'. Overlaid on this is the roar of the audience recorded at a Hollywood Bowl Beatles concert. It is in film sound-design parlance an example of 'monumentalizing', creating a grand effect by rich instrumental, choral and sound effect combinations (Huckvale 1990, p. 4). At the arrival of the triumphant E chord there is a tom-tom roll, simulating a dramatic timpani roll. Harrison's guitar lick has light phasing and delay effects applied to it. The audience applause, scattered throughout the title song, and often sounding more like background radio static than applause, disappears entirely with Starr's vocal entry.

By contrast to what has gone before, 'With a Little Help from My Friends' involves the straightforward rock band instrumentation of piano (McCartney), rhythm guitar (Harrison), drums (Starr) and cowbell (Lennon) with overdubs of lead guitar (Harrison), tambourine (Starr), lead vocals (Starr), backing vocals (McCartney and Lennon), and finally bass guitar (McCartney). The bright, stabbing rhythm guitar sound doubling the piano chords is similar to that of the opening track. Emerick recalls that for this track he recorded the tom-toms with their bottom skins removed so that the microphones could be placed underneath the drums to achieve a more direct capture of the unique sound of the slack-tuned top skins (Emerick and Massey 2006, p. 182). The drum mix is generally a lot more cohesive and solid than it appears to be on the title song, with good definition in the centre. The tom-tom fills are enhanced with reverb and other processing. During the choruses and the coda there is high-frequency emphasis in the right speaker from the jingles of the tambourine. Moore marvels at the variety of 'articulation' in the drumming (Moore 1997, p. 30). Certainly Starr peppers the basic closed hi-hat sound with unpredictable open hi-hat strokes and also occasionally moves from the shuffle feel into straight quavers; and in the third verse he replaces the hi-hat with ride cymbal strokes.

Emerick recounts the unique manner in which McCartney recorded the bass-guitar part. With the use of a long lead to his amplifier in the studio he sat in the control room working on it phrase by phrase, which he dropped in one by one until he felt it was perfected. The characteristically melodic bass part in the verses and middle eight features the upper range of his Rickenbacker (Emerick and Massey 2006, p. 183).

Starr's singing contrasts starkly to that of his colleagues. He projects a relaxed, dreamy, almost spoken vocal quality, which Everett explains as 'without diaphragm support' (Everett 1999, p. 103). In the chorus, the oh's and mmm's are expressively inflected with glissandos but otherwise it is a rather flat delivery. Starr's undeveloped vocal technique is exposed by the strained, high wobbly held tone at the end of the song. However, Lennon and McCartney provide well-blended support for Starr, adding firstly unison lines, then harmony vocals, then call-and-response harmonies. Automatic

Double-Tracking (ADT) is applied to the solo vocal line to enrich the sound, and the vocal mix is slightly to the left-hand side with delay added on the right-hand side.

'Lucy in the Sky with Diamonds'

The orchestration of 'Lucy in the Sky with Diamonds' presents the most unusual sound combination thus far on the album. The distinctive 'bell-like' sound (in the introduction and verses) comes from a Lowrey organ:

> ... the Hammond could not produce that spring-clear but slightly quavering note – the unique watery clarity we were looking for ... The great thing about the Lowry [sic] was that, whereas with the Hammond it was almost impossible to get any decay, with the Lowry [sic] it was easy. (Martin with Pearson 1994, pp. 101–2)

This sound blends seamlessly with the tambura drone used in the verses (and in the final chorus), almost as if it were coming from one sound-producing device. The organ sound playing backbeat chords in the choruses (and more varied rhythms in the final double chorus) is a different pre-set. The other instrumental sounds of 'Lucy' include cymbals (in verses and pre-choruses), bass guitar (throughout from the first verse), drums (in the chorus sections) and two different guitar sounds (one in the pre-choruses, the other in the choruses). Emerick recalls: 'We decided to route George Harrison's guitar through a Leslie speaker during the choruses' (Emerick and Massey 2006, p. 174). This gives an effect similar to flanging. The other guitar that follows the vocal line in the pre-chorus has a soft fuzzy quality and sounds as if the attack has been softened electronically. Harrison imbues these lines with Lennon's dreamy vocal characteristics including imitation of portamentos on the syllables 'head' and '-way'.

The complex manipulation of tape speeds during the tape transfer and the overdubbing of the lead and backing vocals gives Lennon's voice an almost feminine sound quality. Natural double-tracking of the voice is used at the end of each verse and echo is applied liberally to achieve a spacey hallucinogenic personality. The mix itself seems performed in the spirit of an acid trip, with a particular disconnection between right and left fields. Cymbals, drums, tambura, acoustic guitar (with ADT) and organ are entirely on the left and the two different electric guitar sounds are entirely on the right. Only vocals and bass guitar are spread across both sides to help marry the sounds together.

'Getting Better'

'Getting Better' is another stretched mix with the instruments spread across the stereo field. Drums, pianette (an electric piano), tambura and one of two electric guitars are entirely on the left, while the high electric guitar repeated note (in the intro and choruses) is on the right, along with touches of clapping (in the first interlude and second verse) and congas (from the second interlude through the last verse, final choruses and outro). Again only the vocals and bass are spread across the two sides.

The sonic feature of the track is McCartney's expressive lead vocal, displaying excellent diction and supported by cleverly arranged wispy falsetto backing vocals. Apart from these subtle elements, the arrangement and mix are sonically confronting. The aggressive repeated guitar notes which open the song and act as a treble pedal tone in the choruses sound as if they might be played on the 12-string electric Rickenbacker 360-12, an instrument known to have been in Harrison's collection (Everett 1999, p. 301). This sound also appears to be automatically double-tracked. It contributes to what is a very top-heavy frequency balance in the song, which focuses on 2–2.5 kHz for this guitar, 7 kHz for the cymbals and a general presence range of 4–4.5 kHz, but with little in the way of low frequencies to support the top. Even the bass-guitar part seems disembodied from the mix. Emerick remembers that he used 'the bathroom as an acoustic echo chamber' to add reverb to the overdubbed bass-guitar part, a technique he admits McCartney didn't like (Emerick and Massey 2006, p. 176). As a result, the bass sounds literally as if it were recorded in a different room.

An instrumental curio on this track is the pianette. As Martin recalls:

> I played a pianette, an early kind of electric piano, which gave us a funny kind of plucking sound, a cross between a harpsichord and a Fender Rhodes electric piano ... There is a particular point in 'Getting Better' ... where we all hit a bottom note, a suspended heavy pedal note, which is made up of guitars, [tambura] and me thumping the strings of the pianette. (Martin with Pearson 1994, p. 108)

Clearly, attacking the strings directly contributed to the distorted buzzy drone (dominated by the tambura) in the second interlude that Martin refers to, but when the pianette first appears in bar three played via its keyboard, it sounds more like a Wurlitzer electric piano.

The recording of 'Getting Better' is remarkably free of noise elements considering it involved three (or possibly four, depending on whose account is to be believed) four-track tape transfers. Electronic processing used to enhance the top end of the frequency range during the transfers probably contributes to the 'in-your-face' quality of this mix.

'Fixing a Hole'

'Fixing a Hole' is a relatively straightforward recording made at Regent Sound Studios. The most distinctive aspect of the arrangement is the use of harpsichord (performed by George Martin) as the principal rhythm instrument playing the tightly voiced chord progression on each beat of the bar throughout with some backbeat variations. Lewisohn is vague about the tracking for the initial session on 9 February 1967 and for the reduction and overdubbing session on 21 February (Lewisohn 1988b, pp. 95, 99); and the tracking details supplied by Martin (Martin with Pearson 1994, pp. 86–7) indicate that harpsichord, drums and bass were all on one track and vocals and rhythm guitar were on another 'together!' (the exclamation mark surely indicating he felt this was an unconventional method of tracking), but in the final stereo mix there does not appear to be any rhythm guitar. This leads one to suspect that rhythm guitar was not played on the take that was used. Interestingly, Everett, who draws on Martin's account of the session, avoids mentioning a rhythm guitar (Everett 1999, p. 107).

The other standout feature of the arrangement is the distorted lead guitar part. Harrison plays descending two-part chordal licks at the ends of the verses, a single-line chordal decoration during the bridges and a guitar solo over the chords of the verse, a solo memorable not only for its unique timbre but also because it ends up in the depths of the guitar range. To achieve the guitar timbre, Martin recalls that 'George had his guitar volume and both bass and top tone controls up very high' (Martin with Pearson 1994, p. 87). The guitar sounds heavily compressed and gated, with significant equalization and flanger/chorus effects added.

Unlike many of the tracks on *Sgt. Pepper* where the bass guitar was recorded as an overdub and/or was mixed to stand out, on this recording it is dull-sounding and back in the mix (constrained by the sub-mix of harpsichord, drums and bass).

McCartney shows off his highly flexible tenor range voice in this song, particularly his skilfully produced detached speech quality in the high register and his seamless transition into falsetto on the word 'go' (although at 0'35" there is some vocal distortion in one of the double-tracked parts). Typically for the album, the voice is heard across the stereo image with echo added to the right-hand side. McCartney saves the backing vocals for the final bridge and verse sections, consisting mostly of harmonies on the syllable 'oo' mixed entirely to the right. Moore suggests these backing vocals fix a hole in a somewhat unbalanced mix (Moore 1997, p. 37). Before this, all the rhythm instruments (bass, harpsichord and drums, and possibly rhythm guitar) had been placed predominantly on the left and the only forceful instrumental presence on the right was the relatively intermittent lead guitar.

'She's Leaving Home'

The appearance of harpsichord on 'Fixing a Hole' can serve as preparation for the next song, 'She's Leaving Home', the first song on the album to depart entirely from the use of rock-music instruments in favour of the classical music combination of string nonet (four violins, two violas, two cellos and one double-bass) with the addition of a chromatic harp. George Martin was clearly peeved that McCartney chose to hire another arranger for this song:

> Mike Leander did a good workmanlike job on the score of 'She's Leaving Home'; I did not change it a great deal. Twenty-odd years of hindsight make me wish I'd been tougher on it, though. At the risk of being accused of sour grapes, I find that on hearing it today, the harp part is a little bit too tinkly, the voicing of the strings a shade too lush. Could it have been a little more astringent? (Martin with Pearson 1994, p. 134)

The recording of this song was also relatively straightforward. The strings and harp were all recorded on the first four-track tape, which was reduced to two tracks on a new four-track tape, leaving two tracks for the vocals. One of these was devoted to McCartney's lead vocals and the call-and-response vocals of McCartney and Lennon (singing together) in the chorus, and the other track saved for the overdubbed double-tracking of these call-and-response vocals.

McCartney's and Lennon's singing here represents the *tour de force* of vocal performance on *Sgt. Pepper*, particularly the expertly laid double-tracking of both performers and McCartney's high falsetto lines. Unfortunately, the fussy string arranging (especially towards the end of the song) detracts from the grace of the singing and vocal arranging. In addition, the stereo mix of the strings is disturbing if one is used to hearing performances and recordings of classical string music where the high instruments are on the left and the low ones on the right. Here this tradition is strangely (perhaps perversely) reversed.

MacDonald considers 'She's Leaving Home' 'pursues the cinematic style' of 'Eleanor Rigby' and 'For No One' in its 'generation gap' theme, and believes the 'poignant' arrangement captures the song's 'heart-tugging sentiment' as it might in a film music cue (MacDonald 1994, pp. 194–5). In other words, this song may be seen as making the connection between sound design in narrative media and sound design in popular music.

'Being for the Benefit of Mr. Kite!'

The same might be said of 'Being for the Benefit of Mr. Kite!', although the intention here is somewhat different. Rather than tug at the heartstrings with emotionally charged string group underscore, the approach is to create a soundscape one would associate aurally with a circus or fairground environment. George Martin interpreted John Lennon's narrative brief with the idea of employing the calliope (steam organ) sounds associated with fairground carousels. As this bulky instrument was virtually impossible to bring into a studio, he decided instead to use the reedy organ sounds available in the studio combined with a collage tape made up from existing commercial recordings of calliopes and other organs (Martin with Pearson 1994, pp. 90–92). Two-track tape dubs of different recordings were then cut into 15-inch segments and 19 of them were randomly reassembled for future use on the track, some of them respliced backwards if they were considered too structurally coherent when the tape was played forward (Lewisohn 1988b, p. 99). A pedal-powered harmonium (played by George Martin), as well as bass guitar (McCartney) and drums (Starr) were used on the initial backing track, and during the subsequent tracking sessions a variety of other reedy sounds were overdubbed. In the sung verses, only drums, bass guitar, some kind of jingling percussion and harmonium (playing crotchet oom-pah chords) accompany the voice. In the organ break, a crotchet triplet oom-pah-pah organ part (played by Lennon) provides the backing for the rapid and mostly descending chromatic scales recorded by George Martin at half speed (an octave below the required pitch) because he was unable to play them accurately at normal track tempo. The piecing organ timbres in this section are those of the Lowrey organ. McCartney's five-bar, mostly ascending guitar solo line in the first organ break (at 1'18") sounds very un-guitar-like (more like a digital synthesizer sound yet to be invented), and is likely to have been palm-muted and played with either precise up-and-down plectrum strokes or treated with slap-back tape echo as well as with other effects.

The second organ break (coda) is created over the chord structure of the verse (played by harmonium mostly in swung quaver oom-pah style), with the addition of Hammond organ playing the verse tune, the calliope collage tape, plus a hint of the chromatic Hammond swirling lines at its outset, a new repeated melodic line in its last seconds (derived arguably from the melody of the introduction) and a furious metallic percussion flourish to end the track. The numerous short segments of the collage tape are quite varied in timbre and texture and are rhythmically out of phase with the backing groove, although there are some uncanny synchronizations. The effect of this extraordinary sound design is to conjure up the giddy experience of a hallucinogenic carousel ride.

Other instruments used in this track are four harmonicas (including a bass harmonica) that add block-chordal reinforcement to the harmonium in the introduction and the interlude between verses one and two, and a piano used to play a chordal fanfare-like rhythmic pattern in the bridge between the organ break and the start of verse three. Unlike some of the previous tracks, and despite its tendency towards shrill timbres, 'Being for the Benefit of Mr. Kite!' has a better spread of low frequencies, courtesy of the low harmonium part. There is a vivid contrast between the dryish sung verses and the organ breaks which are soaked in reverb. Lennon's double-tracked vocals are mixed entirely to the far right and compete with the centred open hi-hat splashes for the listener's attention.

'Within You Without You'

From the chaos of the end of side one, we recommence at the beginning of side two with 'Within You Without You', which transports us to the serene world of north-Indian classical music. Martin reports that George Harrison may have experienced some reincarnation flashbacks: 'What appealed to George was the sound – the unique sound the instruments made when used in this very ancient tradition. In some mystical way, he told me, he recognized that sound; it was as if he had heard it before' (Martin with Pearson 1994, p. 126). As is the case with many sacred music traditions of the East, the complexity of the sound colour of voices and instruments can be a focus for achieving deep meditative states. Harrison's composition is a richly textured combination of complex timbres. The basis for all Indian compositions and improvisations is the drone (sruti) over which the melodic material unfolds. Rather than use a single specialist drone instrument, three tamburas were combined to create a denser-than-usual, pulsating jivari, the characteristic buzzing sound, rich in harmonics, which is a feature of many Indian lutes, but particularly the tambura. Indian music is based around a single melodic line heard against the drone with drums (tabla or mridangam) providing the metrical/rhythmic support. If multiple melodic instruments and voices are used, they all follow the same melody with slight variations, creating a heterophonic texture. In Harrison's song, the vocal line is doubled by two dilrubas,[1] and, at certain points, by a (Western) string ensemble (eight violins and three cellos) and, at other points, sitar. Martin based a lot of

---

1   The dilruba is a bowed lute with a buzzy, nasal, hollow-sounding timbre.

his string ensemble arrangement ideas upon a transcription of the dilruba part. His arrangement does however deviate from traditional heterophonic practice. According to Reck: 'The role of Martin's little string orchestra is particularly interesting, echoing phrases, taking short bits of melody, working in [unobtrusive] melodic counterpoint, or marking the 5/8 metre pizzicato theka-like "drum beats"' (Reck 1985, p. 109).

In the central instrumental section, Harrison has overdubbed some sitar licks in the gaps of the previously recorded main melody (played either by the dilrubas or the violin and cello string ensemble), giving the impression of live performance interplay. Reck likens this passage to the 'rapid "questions and answer" alternation of phrases common in Indian classical music performance' (Ibid.). The short introductory section and the interlude between the instrumental section and the last verse employ the distinctive resonant metallic timbre of the suvar mandal, a plucked zither resembling the Western autoharp in shape (but without the chord-enabling damping mechanism). In these sections, which serve the function of alap (an introductory free-form exposition of the main melodic characteristics of the raga), it plays a charismatic ascending flourish, representing the main tones of the raga's parent scale.

A feature of the production of 'Within You Without You' is the capture of the tabla sound. Consisting of small main drum (dayan) and larger secondary drum (bayan), the tabla playing style involves a variety of drum strokes producing different timbres (bols), some precisely pitched and others subject to pitch manipulation by the application of heel-of-the-hand pressure. Emerick 'decided to close-mic them and add signal processing to make things a bit more exciting sonically' (Emerick and Massey 2006, p. 180). Lewisohn quotes Emerick: 'The tabla had never been recorded the way we did it. Everyone was amazed when they first heard a tabla recorded that closely, with the texture and the lovely low resonances' (Lewisohn 1988b, p. 103).

George Harrison's vocal sound is mantra-like, sitting in the back of the mix, dominated by the elaborate tabla playing. The singing style closely follows the dilrubas' sliding ornamentations (meend) that are a feature of Indian performance practice. George Martin's string lines also aim to imitate the portamento playing style of the dilruba, although the British string players lack the subtle languid quality of Harrison and his Indian musician colleagues. The intense unison and octave doubling aspect of the arrangement was further emphasized by applying ADT (Martin with Pearson 1994, p. 129; Lewisohn 1988b, p. 104).

George Harrison's songwriting and George Martin's arrangement and production of this song represent a successful attempt to bring a mystical musical tradition into the contemporary music domain, forming an engaging interplay of Eastern and Western musical ideas. 'Within You Without You' contains a serious message for the turbulent times, but George Harrison was worried it might be interpreted as too serious, as explained by Martin: 'George wanted to dub some laughter at the end of the song. He didn't want people to think he was being over-earnest' (Martin with Pearson 1994, p. 129). The requested laughter recording, mixed into the tambura drone coda, was sourced from the Abbey Road Studios sound effects collection – Volume 6: 'Applause and Laughter' (Lewisohn 1988b, p. 104).

'When I'm Sixty-Four'

Harrison need not have worried about the reception of his song because Martin chose to shatter its ethereal mood by placing the light-hearted 'When I'm Sixty-Four' next. This nostalgic ditty has been variously described as 'a whimsical, music-hall number' (Martin with Pearson 1994, p. 34), 'Paul's vaudeville charmer' (Lewisohn 1988b, p. 89) and a 'genuine ragtime … pop synthesis' (Moore 1997, p. 47). Its production called for some kind of sound design that would contemporize its period quality. Martin describes the breakthrough: 'Paul got some way round the lurking schmaltz factor by suggesting we use clarinets on the recording, "in a classical way" … This … pushed it firmly towards satire' (Martin with Pearson 1994, p. 34).

The instrumental combination for 'When I'm Sixty-Four' is bass guitar (McCartney), piano (McCartney), drums (Starr), orchestral chimes (Starr), electric guitar (Lennon), two clarinets and one bass clarinet (orchestral session players). The bass guitar sound is dampened. The finger-picking guitar playing is very much backgrounded in the mix and only used in the last verse. The chimes are an unusual addition to a pop album as much as they are to a music hall number, and thus add to the satirical mood. The drumming concentrates on a swung quaver feel played with brushes on snare, but there are some occasional cymbal decorations and a kick drum (featured four-on-the-floor in the bridge sections). Martin outlines his approach to writing for the clarinet trio: 'The arrangement of this song is deceptively simple, but in a way it underlines my constant belief in simplicity in orchestration. By restricting ourselves to three instruments … we could hardly be lush' (Ibid., p. 35). Even so, Martin's inventive clarinet arrangement dominates the backing track. As Emerick explains: 'The clarinets on that track became a very personal sound for me; I recorded them really close up, bringing them so far forward that they became one of the main focal points' (Emerick and Massey 2006, p. 137). The sound is warm, and a wide variety of timbres and vibrato effects are evident. The rich timbres of the clarinets give the mix a fuller, fatter sound than many of the other tracks on the album.

During the mix, the tape was significantly sped up to make the song sound a semitone higher than recorded. According to Emerick, McCartney asked for this so that 'his voice would sound more youthful, like the teenager he was when he originally wrote the song' (Ibid.). This piece of sound design makes the clarinets (in particular) more vibrant in timbre than they would normally sound. It may also have emphasized the higher-than-usual level of tape hiss evident on the original snare drum track in the verses (a legacy of the tape transfer process), which is masked effectively by the high-frequency rat-a-tat-tat of the snare sound itself.

'Lovely Rita'

'Lovely Rita' signals a return to the guitar-based rock band format. It is significant in the structuring of the album that the last two tracks of side one and the first two of side two have virtually no guitar presence. There's no guitar in 'She's Leaving Home', only five bars of guitar that doesn't sound like a guitar in 'Being for the Benefit of Mr. Kite!', no audible guitar in 'Within You Without You' despite Lewisohn reporting the overdubbing by Harrison of acoustic guitar (Lewisohn 1988b, p. 104), and backgrounded guitar in the last verse only of 'When I'm Sixty-Four'.

Moore refers to the 'treble-rich strummed guitar' in the introduction of 'Lovely Rita', but notes that it is thereafter 'relegated somewhat' (Moore 1997, p. 49). Indeed, the introduction of drums at the start of the verse seems to make the acoustic guitars in the guitars-piano-drums backing track combination, disturbingly mixed entirely to the left, sound rather amorphous. The fact that the bass guitar, piano solo and vocals were overdubbed later, and centred, gives them greater clarity and dominance in the mix.

'Lovely Rita' is characterized by its backing vocal antics. Emerick notes that McCartney wanted the vocal arrangement to be approached like the Beach Boys (Emerick and Massey 2006, p. 171). To make his vocal sound much brighter in timbre, McCartney recorded his lead vocal at a slower speed. He and Lennon then recorded their impressive high backing vocal harmonies with heavy echo (Martin with Pearson 1994, p. 96). In addition to these straight vocals, some comical devices were added. The most distinctive is the unison comb-and-paper loud humming glissandos (once at 0'27" and four times at 0'50", where the ending pitches of the glides follow the I-vi-ii-V bass line). There is imitation of a champagne cork popping (on the phrase 'over dinner' at 1'27") using cheek finger popping, and imitation of a repeated hi-hat semi-quaver shuffle pattern using the vowel-less sound, 'chit' (at 0'41" and in the corresponding position at 1'30"). In the last chorus, another repeated percussive sound ('a-duh') is added to the groove. Finally, in the piano vamp coda, a variety of vocal sounds with extreme echo is employed: a short repeated 'uh', slow exhaling breaths, rapid inhaling and exhaling (panting), a contented sigh, groaning and melodicized moaning. Moore interprets this coda section as Lennon 'undermining ... the song's geniality' (Moore 1997, p. 49), but Emerick remembers the mood of the session as extremely jovial: 'On that ... night, they overdubbed the heavy breathing at the end of the song, with John looning about and sending the others – and Richard [Lush] and me up in the control room – into fits of laughter' (Emerick and Massey 2006, p. 171).

Emerick explains his method of recording George Martin's honky-tonk piano solo, that is, by placing a piece of 'sticky editing tape on the guide rollers of a tape machine that was sending signal to the echo chamber, causing the tape to wow and flutter' (Ibid.). The piano solo was also recorded at a slower tape speed in order to facilitate Martin's performance and, in the process, it changes the piano timbre slightly. There is so much echo on this solo that (when listening to it isolated with the bass guitar in the right speaker) it sounds as if it is being doubled by distant high-pitched Hammond organ chords.

'Good Morning, Good Morning'

'Good Morning, Good Morning' continues the zany humour of the backing vocals of 'Lovely Rita' by its use of animal sound effects, but its overall sound design is rooted in electronic processing. It is worth quoting Emerick at length to get a good sense of this:

'Good Morning, Good Morning' ended up with the dubious distinction of being the *Pepper* track with the largest number of overdubs, hence the most four-to-four reductions ... Despite that, it still sounds good, albeit a bit strident due to all the compensatory top end we had to add during mixing. There's a lot of ADT on John's voice, and on Paul's lead guitar – in one spot, there's a huge 'wow' on the guitar where the effect almost makes it sound like the note was bent. One reason why our Automatic Double-Tracking worked so well was that it had a sweep oscillator control that you could actually play like a musical instrument, allowing you to constantly vary the delay time in response to the performance.

During that mix, I also enjoyed whacking the faders all the way up for Ringo's huge tom hit during the stop time – so much so that the limiters nearly overloaded, but it definitely gets the listener's attention! Add in the flanged brass, miked in an unorthodox way, and it's all icing on the cake; take those effects off and the recording doesn't have the same magic. That song serves as a good example of how simple manipulation can improve a track sonically. (Emerick and Massey 2006, pp. 178–9)

'Good Morning, Good Morning', another satirical song, was inspired by a Kellogg's breakfast cereal advertisement. It charts the banality and sameness of everyday middle-class existence. The highly compressed confronting mix reminds one of the widespread practice of broadcasting media advertisements significantly louder than the surrounding programmes. There is a distinct lack of lower frequency content, a piece of sound design suggesting the music is coming from a tiny speaker in a portable radio. Fittingly, the track possesses a frenetic rat-race quality, bolstered by the frequent changes of metre and groove, the strident timbres and rough ensemble of the saxophone-dominated Sounds Incorporated horn section, the aggression, distortion and wild 'outside' quality of McCartney's guitar solo and licks, the busyness of McCartney's bass line, and the comedy of Starr's machine-gun snare fills and theatrical accents. There is an appropriate cynical, sneering affect in Lennon's vocal delivery. The only thing staid about this track is Harrison's perfunctory rhythm guitar contribution, mixed right back on the left side (with the bass and drums). Everett identifies a vibrato-guitar effect by McCartney on the tonic note in the introduction (it's also heard in the outro), but it sounds more like a microtonal French horn trill (Everett 1999, p. 115).

Using a cockerel crowing was an obvious effect to introduce a song called 'Good Morning, Good Morning', but Lennon decided to expand on the idea by creating a sequence of different animal calls in the song's outro. According to Emerick, Lennon's 'idea was that ... each successive animal ... would be ... capable of chasing or frightening the next animal in line' (Emerick and Massey 2006, p. 178). Lewisohn indicates that the sounds (assembled by Emerick) came from the EMI sound effects collection as follows: '"Volume 35: Animals and Bees" for the lion, elephant, dog, sheep, cow and the cat, and "Volume 57: Fox-hunt" for the bloodhounds chasing the fox, the tooting and the galloping' (Lewisohn 1988b, p. 105). The use of this sound collage fits with the Beatles' attraction to postmodern artistic experimentalism, but it is possible to interpret it simply as a piece of inventive sound design, reinforcing the narrative thrust of the song. Perhaps the sequence of animals symbolizes the pecking order of human society and the fox-hunt is emblematic of English upper-class dominance over the middle and lower classes. Martin refers to an 'imaginary landscape' (Martin with Pearson 1994, p. 75) conjured up in the stereo mixing session: 'As the Beatles sang and played, and the animal sounds came in, I was watching the story unfolding in my mind' (Ibid.).

Given the often bizarre stereo mixing practices of *Sgt. Pepper*, it is odd that the animal calls sequence involves the only instance of stereo panning on the album. It begins on the right but is panned to the left during the fox-hunt segment to give the impression of the hunting party passing by.

'Sgt. Pepper's Lonely Hearts Club Band (Reprise)'

Sound design of a different nature was called for in the recording of 'Sgt. Pepper's Lonely Hearts Club Band (Reprise)', made in the large reverberant Studio One at Abbey Road as Studio Two was unavailable. Designed for orchestral recording, the space was not at all suitable for an amplified rock band. To solve the problem, Geoff Emerick and his crew fashioned a room within a room using sound baffles. Emerick claims that the sound they achieved was 'tight and ballsy' and with natural reverberation (Emerick and Massey 2006, pp. 184–5). The other natural aspect of the track was its manner of recording: only one four-track tape was used and the song was performed 'live' by all four Beatles. McCartney's guide vocal was wiped as all four Beatles performed the final vocals as an overdub (also adding tambourine). A vestige of the guide vocal can be heard in the final chorus and coda, as picked up by the overhead drum microphone (Ibid., p. 185). The high-energy up-tempo version of the title song undergoes an upward key change (at 0'44"), adding to the build-up, but designed primarily to bring the song into the key of the previously recorded final song, 'A Day in the Life', thus facilitating a smooth crossfade between the two tracks. The mix of the reprise is the most sonically integrated on the whole album, probably as a result of the live performance context, the lack of track bouncing and the more traditional spread of instruments and voices across the stereo field.

The sound design of the lead-in to the reprise is worth examining. Following the sound of the hen clucking (the final sound of 'Good Morning, Good Morning'), the matching electric guitar motif is stated (as described earlier), precipitating a percussive quaver metronomic beat. McCartney's 'one, two, three, four' count-in is then heard, followed by Lennon's cheeky 'bye-ee' interjection (coinciding with the third count). The audience crowd murmur is mixed up just before the four-bar drum groove introduction begins. Once the song starts the audience noise disappears, but a simulated spontaneous burst of audience applause lasting about two bars is added following the line 'We hope you have enjoyed the show'. Any further crowd applause is delayed until the final tumultuous moments of the reprise, and it is cleverly continued for one bar into the suddenly soft introduction of the final song, to give the impression of a live performance segue from a rocker to a ballad and the expected audience reaction to this scenario.

'A Day in the Life'

After the predominance throughout the album of mixes with high-frequency emphasis, it is refreshing to hear the warm combination of acoustic guitar and piano at the start of 'A Day in the Life'. This song contains some outstanding examples of sound design relating to the vocals, the drums, the orchestra and the final piano chord.

Martin recalls that for 'A Day in the Life' Lennon wanted his voice to sound like Elvis Presley on 'Heartbreak Hotel': 'So we put the image of the voice about 90 milliseconds behind the actual voice itself' (Martin with Pearson 1994, p. 53). Emerick reports that Lennon would 'sing to the echo, which would in turn cause him to approach the song differently. The way he'd pronounce his d's and t's – really spit them out – actually triggered the tape echo better than anyone I'd ever heard' (Emerick and Massey 2006, p. 147). McCartney took a different approach in his middle section of the song:

> ... he wanted to sound all muzzy, as if he had just woken up from a deep sleep and hadn't yet gotten his bearings, because that was what the lyric was trying to convey. My way of achieving that was to deliberately remove a lot of the treble from his voice and heavily compress it to make him sound muffled. (Ibid., p. 152)

A feature of the arrangement of the verses is Starr's flamboyant drumming. Rather than just keeping the groove, he interpolates inventive fills that feature the tom-toms. Emerick's method of recording the tom-toms, with top skins slackened and the bottom skins removed allowing for close-miking, has been described above. Further to this, Emerick indicates that he 'added a lot of low end at the mixing console', making the toms 'sound almost like timpani' (Ibid., p. 149).

One of the most ambitious elements of the arrangement is the famous orchestral climb. Martin relates McCartney's concept:

> He had told John he would like to include an instrumental passage with this avant-garde feel. He had the idea to create a spiralling ascent of sound, suggesting we start the passage with all instruments on their lowest note and climbing to the highest in their own time. (Martin with Pearson 1994, p. 56)

A small symphony orchestra of 40 players was recorded four-times (thus making 160 individual parts) on a separate four-track tape. These kinds of indeterminate textures were common during the 1960s in the orchestral works of composers such as Penderecki and Lutoslawski, but unheard of in pop music. Even so, as Moore points out, 'The link between popular music and dance has not been severed at this historical point' (Moore 1997, p. 52), because the beat continues under the dissonant multi-layered texture. The climbing crescendo idea (aided by fader manipulation) is used twice following the line 'I'd love to turn you on' which ends both the third and last verses.[2] Depending on whether this lyric is meant to refer to sex or drugs (or both), the musical sound design can be interpreted as depicting the build up to an orgasm or the onset of a bad acid trip. As the lyrics 'Woke up, fell out of bed' follow the first climax, another possible interpretation is the representation of a nightmare.

---

2   The orchestra is also used conventionally to powerful effect in the octave doublings of the roots of the chords which accompany Lennon's dreamy 'ah' vocalize, heard prior to the final verse.

The final sustained piano chord is an ingenious piece of creative sound design. This was again McCartney's idea following the limited success of another of his ideas involving massed humming, but it was left to Geoff Emerick to sort out the details of its realization. Emerick lists the instruments involved: two grand pianos, an upright piano (with two players, McCartney and Starr), a Wurlitzer electric piano, a blond-wood spinet and a harmonium (Emerick and Massey 2006, p. 161). The 43-second sustain was created by a variety of techniques. There were a series of staggered overdubs of the chord allowing for cross-fading between them: as one recording started to die out, the next could be made to kick in. Emerick describes how he used 'a compressor, cranked up full' (Ibid., p. 160) and manipulated the faders on the mixing console: 'If I set the gain of each input to maximum but started with the fader at its lowest point, I could then slowly raise the faders as the sound died away, thus compensating for the loss in volume …' (Ibid.). The outcome is a sound-object with a complex, ever-changing timbre. It is literally a final chord but it is also a technologically created drone in the spirit of the tambura of 'Within You Without You'. There is a definite element of naturally distorted buzzing as with the tambura, and the tonal emphasis seems to shift from the tonic to the third and then to the fifth and finally to the octave as the harmonics of the various overdubs interact and the amplification is applied. The contemplative spell is broken by a noise at 5'50" which, according to Emerick, was Ringo's shoe squeaking (Ibid., p. 161).

Once the chord finally fades, there are two more bonus pieces of sound design. A noisy 15 kHz tone (requested by Lennon to stimulate any dogs that might be listening) leads to a two-second piece of gibberish which was cut into the run-out groove of the LP. The making of this fragment is described by Emerick in the following terms: 'They [the Beatles] made funny noises, said random things; just nonsense. We chopped up the tape, put it back together, played it backwards and threw it in' (quoted in Lewisohn 1988b, p. 109).

Conclusion

In discussing *Sgt. Pepper's Lonely Hearts Club Band*, traditional aspects of musical analysis such as tonal structuring, chord progressions and melodic design have been consciously downplayed in favour of discussion of instrumental and vocal timbre, sound effects, sound processing and sound mixing. An effort has been made, where appropriate, to relate these to the narrative aspects of the conception of the album and its component parts. The thinking here is to honour the long-standing idea that in the musicology of popular music more emphasis should be given to timbre and timbre combinations, and that the approaches traditionally used in the analysis of Western classical music may indeed be largely inappropriate when applied to popular music genres.

Sgt. Pepper has proved to be a fruitful vehicle for such an approach to analysis. The album is made up of a broad variety of musical and theatrical genres reflecting the varied interests of the Beatles and their production team, and resulting in an extraordinary richness of instrumental and vocal timbres and other sounds. Reflected in this stylistic mix is Harrison's profound engagement with Indian classical music; McCartney's and Lennon's attraction to the avant-garde; McCartney's family roots in the English music hall; the general immersion of the band in American popular musical traditions such as the blues, Motown and the Beach Boys; Martin's classical music training as a performer, composer and arranger, and also his experience making comedy records. On the technical side, Geoff Emerick's flair for capturing and manipulating sounds is brilliantly supported by the technical innovations of maintenance engineer Ken Townsend, including direct injection, Automatic Double-Tracking (ADT), frequency changing (varispeeding of tape machines) and ambiophonics (manipulation of room acoustics as used in the orchestral recording session of 'A Day in the Life').

The notion of sound design, taken from theatre and film, is apt in popular music research when considering the way that specific instrumental and vocal timbres and specially selected field recordings of natural and man-made sounds are used to support the narrative intentions of particular songs, and, in the case of a concept album like *Sgt. Pepper*, of larger structural entities.[3]

---

3   Thanks to colleagues Leigh Carriage, Peter Martin and Mic Deacon for their comments on certain aspects of the sound design of *Sgt. Pepper*.

Chapter 5

The Beatles and Indian music

David Reck

When the nasal twang of the Indian sitar first appeared playing John Lennon's mesmerizing tune in 'Norwegian Wood' (*Rubber Soul*, 1965), few realized – perhaps least of all the Beatles – that here was an unprecedented event, unique in pop music history, one which was to have ramifications in perhaps as many as 20 songs over the years spanning the mid- to late 1960s.

'Norwegian Wood', we all know, is autobiographical: a one-night stand disguised (he was married at the time) in Lennon's lyrics' caustic wit and the evocative and succinct scene-painting. In our mind's eye we (at least anyone who has lived through the 1960s) can almost imagine a video to the song: the 'bird' with long straight hair à la Joan Baez, black turtleneck, mini skirt; the pickup at a club fuelled by Lennon's storied gift of the gab; turning the key to the girl's 'pad'; the camera scans the mattress in a corner on the floor, no furniture, pillows on a rug in front of a fireplace, a bookcase comprised of planks on stacked bricks containing Sartre, McLuhan, Kerouac, maybe Allen Ginsberg, the *I Ching*, Hesse's *Siddhartha*, certainly the *Tibetan Book of the Dead* as interpreted by Timothy Leary. There is no doubt that the 'bird' is cool in a 1960-ish sort of way. The sharing of a joint, the obligatory Buddhist-Hindu-existentialist philosophical pre-coital dialogue (they 'talked until two' – don't believe the 'slept in the bath' part). And on the stereo we imagine... a recording of Ravi Shankar with Alla Rakha pattering away on tabla.

The sitar, then, in 'Norwegian Wood' is not just a gimmicky exotic guitar. It is, first, a recognition (perhaps intuitive) by Lennon that his repetitive tune with its major/minor interplay and modal harmony shares sonic qualities with the north-Indian classical music which he, his band mates and millions of other young listeners in the West heard as Ravi Shankar began his meteoric ascent from ethnic Asian musician to international superstar. Secondly, the sounds of Hindusthani instrumental music, primarily that of Shankar's sitar, but to a lesser extent the sarod playing of Ali Akbar Khan as well, became associated in the collective mind of the counterculture, European and American – and despite Shankar's protestations – with the spaced-out alternative consciousness state induced by drugs ranging from marijuana to LSD, peyote and other hallucinogenics. North India's classical music with its expanded time-sense, perceived repetitiveness and hypnotic harmonics of the tambura drone made it, as Lillian Roxon has pointed out, 'background sounds for the drug experiences of that period' (Roxon 1969, p. 168). Elements of classical Indian music in Beatles songs – drones, scales, instruments, rhythms, ornaments, timbre – became a code for 'trippiness'. The sitar in 'Norwegian Wood' thus must be interpreted as part of a soundscape with very 1960-ish associations, essential both to Lennon's storyline and in establishing the mood and setting of the song.

Indian music shared its connections with drug states in various countercultural (mis)readings of Eastern religions from Zen to Tibetan Buddhism, from the 'Hari Krishnas' (ISKON or the International Society for Krishna Consciousness) to various jet-set gurus, such as the Maharishi Mahesh Yogi, who was to entice the Beatles themselves to his ashram in Rishikesh in India (February 1968). Both the fad for Eastern religion and for Indian music were part of a much larger infatuation with the East that included Indian clothes and fabric, artefacts (such as clay chillums, posters of deities, Tibetan thangkas and incense), interest in myths and art, and even the expansion of everyday vocabulary to include Sanskrit technical terms such as chakra, asana, dharma, nirvana or karma. While based upon real civilizations that are without doubt also rich in history and tradition, the West's perceptions of the East – and the 1960s are no exception – have tended to be filtered through what the celebrated scholar Edward W. Said has labelled 'Orientalism': the East (a region stretching from north Africa to China and Japan) is viewed as a pastiche of fantasies, stereotypes, half-truths and generalities. It is an exotic Other which contrasts with the 'normal' Self of the West (Europe and the Americas). As Said has written: 'The Orient was almost a European invention, and has been since antiquity a place of romance, exotic beings, haunting memories and landscapes, remarkable experiences …' (Said 1978, p. 1). '… Oriental despotism, Oriental splendor, cruelty, sensuality … Eastern sects, philosophies, and wisdoms …' (Ibid., p. 4).

There is no room in this vision for massive cloth and steel mills, factories, nuclear power plants, dams, railways, computers and cell phones, or normal people (much like us) going through the pursuits of their lives and loves in a workaday world. The 'India' of the 1960s was not only a tourist poster of exotic temples and Moghul forts and tombs like the Taj Mahal. It was a hippy destination (Goa, Banaras, Kathmandu) of unlimited opium and hashish, and a land of gurus sitting under every tree who could guide devotees into the magical world of an Alternative Reality and an exploration of the Inner Self. It was a fantastic vision of a world much more pleasant than the relentless pursuit of money and power by the Western 'Establishment' in their corporate suits and offices, or the horrific barbarism of America's Vietnam war.

The genealogy of 'Norwegian Wood' leads directly back to *Help!* (1965), the Beatles' second movie. An Orientalist romp, the film contrasts sharply with director Richard Lester's acclaimed first Beatles film, the pseudo-documentary *cinéma vérité* in black and white, *A Hard Day's Night* (1964). The plot of the Technicolor *Help!* concerns an Indian cult led by a bloodthirsty guru who needs to retrieve a sacred ring from Ringo's finger in order to complete a human sacrifice.[1] At one point in the movie the scene moves into a London Indian restaurant. Amid chaos in the kitchen and as the Beatles dine, a ragtag Indian band plays Beatles hits on sitar and tabla. Seeing this sitar, George Harrison bought one in London for himself, practised on it and played it on 'Norwegian Wood'.

It was also during the filming of *Help!* that the Beatles began perusing books on Indian religious philosophy. During the shoot of a scene in the Bahamas, an Indian

---

1   The fact that the goddess of the film is a thinly-disguised version of Kali, worshipped by millions of Hindus, particularly in Bengal, seems to have bothered no one in those less politically sensitive times.

swami, Vishnu Devananda, suddenly rode up on a bicycle and presented each of the group with a small book with the sacred syllable 'Om' on the cover. In the madcap confusion of shooting, during which most of the participants were stoned and India jokes came fast and furious, no one knew if the incident was part of the film or not. Still, the book – and others like Paramahansa Yogananda's *Autobiography of a Yogi*, which although originally published in 1946 had become a cult classic in the 1960s – became part of the Beatles' library.

On 5 July 1966, on the way back from their Asian tour and the near disaster in the Philippines, the Fab Four finally found themselves in Delhi for several days (they had been bumped from a KLM flight). This was their first actual physical experience of India. Besides shopping for sherwanis and kurtas and munching on curries, they made their way to the famous music store, Rikki Ram's, which had become something of a pilgrimage site for international travellers, where they all purchased quality Indian musical instruments.

Revolver (released on 5 August 1966) included two songs which take a giant leap forward from the sitar of 'Norwegian Wood' to indisputable Indian music influences. Harrison's 'Love You To' is the first song in the Euro-American pop music canon that is scored predominantly for Asian musical instruments, sitar, tabla and tambura replacing the usual rock band guitars, (keyboard,) bass and drums. There are no chord changes; melody and drumming are set against an incessant tambura drone in the Indian fashion, fortified by electric guitar. Structurally, the song proper is placed between a few seconds of sitar 'alap', an introduction in free time which in Indian classical music can last up to an hour, an instrumental break in the middle for sitar and tabla, and a sitar/tabla coda which fades out, the former and latter two sections relating obliquely in style to Hindusthani music improvisations. The sitar and vocal melodies, like those in other Indian-influenced songs, could be connected to raga sources, as well as to the modes of English folk music, although it is doubtful if Harrison could have had any substantial knowledge of the intricacies of the raga system at that time. It is therefore irrelevant if the basic scale is called natural minor, dorian or raga kapi, although the occasional sharp fourth scale degree hints at an Indian influence. Ostensibly a love song, there are touches of the philosophical and a curious turn towards bitterness in the last verse (people who will 'screw you in the ground').

The Psychedelic Experience: A Manual Based on the Tibetan Book of the Dead by Timothy Leary, Ralph Metzner and Richard Alpert had appeared in 1964 and quickly shot to the top of the charts in the counterculture. Based on the authors' experiments with LSD at Harvard, the book contends that LSD hallucinations and the visions of the soul on its journey between death and rebirth as described in the Tibetan Buddhist sacred text are connected. Leary and his fellow researchers thus made a crucial link between drugs and Inner Consciousness, the experience of an Alternative Reality as described by various Eastern gurus, seers and Hindu and Buddhist scriptures over the centuries. No longer was it necessary to undergo years of training, austerities or meditation – a pill, a sugar cube or a puff on a chillum would do the trick. Everyone could now take the journey into the Inner Self which would change perceptions of Reality and lead one towards moksha, nirvana, enlightenment. It is known that the Beatles first smoked pot with Bob Dylan. But it was George's dentist who introduced them to LSD.

Lennon's masterwork 'Tomorrow Never Knows' is one of a number of songs from the Beatles' oeuvre ('A Day in the Life', 1967, is another) which seem to jump out from classification as a pop song and into the realm of the creation of fine art, a composition. A booming drone of electric guitars and tambura along with Ringo Starr's hypnotic driving drumbeats provide the bedrock for a complex texture of backward tapes ('seagulls') and electronic effects. Lennon's original idea of including a thousand chanting Tibetan monks was muzzled by George Martin, the group's producer and collaborator, as impractical. Even without the monks there is an Otherness about the soundscape that transports the listener into a helter-skelter, swirling, nightmarish, hallucinogenic world of the unconscious, or the transitory journey from death to rebirth as described in the *Tibetan Book of the Dead*, or both. Lennon's unearthly voice (said to have been sung through a length of drainage pipe) is like that of a lama in the flickering candlelight and incense of a Tibetan monastery. The words are ritualistic and Buddhist ('Turn off your mind ... float downstream', and later, 'surrender to the void'). The instrumental break in the middle resembles a sitar solo from hell more than the sped-up backward guitar tape which gave it birth. Here readings in Buddhist scripture, absorption of Indian music, first-hand LSD experiences and, perhaps, familiarity with recordings of the electronic music of Karlheinz Stockhausen and the European avant-garde combine in a unique and unprecedented approach to song. Like a chant, the minimalist melody has only two parts: the outline of a major triad and a movement up from the lower fifth through flatted seventh to tonic (Example 5.1).

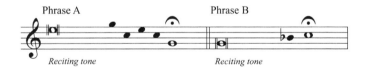

Example 5.1   The two phrases of the melody of 'Tomorrow Never Knows'

'Love You To' and 'Tomorrow Never Knows' illustrate two basically different approaches both to song composition and to the utilization of oriental elements. Harrison transfers Indian instruments and musical textures verbatim into an English pop song context with lyrics that are increasingly transcendent. Lennon moves towards the complex, into musical collage, electronic manipulations and linguistic puzzles, through Dada and Surrealism towards the avant-garde. Indian music references, particularly tambura drones and nasal or buzzing timbres, create associations of trippiness, part of a toolkit of elements used to put in his songs '... the Technicolor imagery, the stream of consciousness, random associations and abrupt change, the sense and nonsense, and the dreamlike peace and euphoria induced by LSD' (Reck 1985, p. 105). Both songs were part of the well-documented extraordinary changes in the subject, structure and scoring of Beatles songs in this middle period. As Paul

McCartney said: 'We can make a bridge ... between us and Indian music, or us and electronic music, and therefore we can take people with us' (Ibid., p. 103).

It is essential to note the role which George Martin played as the Beatles' songs became more unorthodox and experimental. As head of Artists and Repertoire at the Parlophone division of EMI he had discovered the Beatles, but functioned hands-on as producer, arranger, recordist, editor, a conductor, and sometimes keyboard player for the group. Trained as a classical musician, there was little in his background to precondition his approach to pop song. Through the years he nurtured the growth and development of the group through all their iconoclastic turns and eclecticism, executing stunning potpourri orchestrations, realizing electronic sounds, mixing musical collages and sound effects, and shaping each song and album with sharp musical instinct and thorough professionalism.

Lennon's 'Rain', released as a single in early June 1966 with McCartney's 'Paperback Writer', illustrates a more subtle absorption of Orientalism. Here in the lyrics were, as Nicholas Schaffner notes, '... the first articulation of a philosophy John and George were to expound repeatedly in their work over the next few years: that the outward manifestations of the material world are all nothing more than "a wall of illusion"' (Schaffner 1977, p. 55). While there are no Indian instruments in this exquisite song, Harrison's distorted guitar, Starr's inventive drumming and the backward tape effects give it an Indian music sound (and the requisite trippiness). In the refrain where the words 'rain' and 'shine' are each stretched out for 13 beats, Lennon's flat vocal timbre and the sliding ornamentation reference the singing and ornaments (gamaka) of Hindusthani vocal music, despite the harmonizations.

It is not clear precisely when Harrison met Ravi Shankar (b. 1920), but it seems to have occurred after the Beatles' final concert at San Francisco's Candlestick Park on 29 August 1966 and before his second trip to India later that fall with fiancée Pattie Boyd. The meeting was at the home of a Mr Anghadi who headed the Indian Music Circle in London. Shankar later came to Harrison's home in Esher where he initiated him as a disciple on sitar. This and later lessons on sitar were the only music lessons which the self-taught rock star was ever to have!

By 1966, Shankar was already an established international virtuoso. Although a disciple of the legendary Allauddin Khan, he did not come from a musical family. As a boy he had grown up in an unorthodox manner as a member of the troupe of his brother (dancer Uday Shankar) in Paris and had toured Europe and the United States. The release of filmmaker Satyajit Ray's celebrated *Apu Trilogy* (1955 to 1959), for which Shankar composed and played the music, had spiked his career in the West. By 1963 Shankar had played in the prestigious Edinburgh Music Festival, the first Indian musician to do so, and he was regularly concertizing in New York, London and Paris. Shankar's sophistication allowed him to move with ease in the West, and he quickly collected a circle of important admirers and collaborators like the violin virtuoso Yehudi Menuhin and the flautist Jean-Pierre Rampal. Largely through his efforts, he came to represent Indian classical music in the United States and Europe, not only for the growing cadres of listeners drawn from the intelligentsia, but also alongside the musical superstars of the counterculture – Jimi Hendrix, the Beatles, the Jefferson Airplane and the San Francisco acid-rock bands whom he had influenced in their rambling psychedelic improvisations. His fame was to peak at the

Monterey Pop Festival where he appeared as the first performer on the third and final day, Sunday morning 18 June 1967.

At Shankar's invitation, Harrison and Boyd travelled to India in the fall of 1966 for an extensive stay. Despite the persistent hordes of fans, both had a fairy-tale visit, travelling to Bombay, Banaras and Kashmir, studying Indian classical music (Pattie studied the bowed dilruba), meeting Shankar's guru and absorbing the country, its landscape, its culture and its people. Back in England the pair were married in December. The band had gone back to Abbey Road Studios to work on a new album.

On 17 February 1967, a remarkable double-A side single was released containing McCartney's 'Penny Lane' and Lennon's 'Strawberry Fields Forever'. Although the latter gained a reputation as a drug anthem, there is little significant Orientalism evident. By now drones, unusual scales, extended improvisation and Indian-like timbres played on guitars had moved into the pop mainstream.

The much-anticipated *Sgt. Pepper's Lonely Hearts Club Band* was released on 1 June 1967. The album cover, created by Robert Fraser and designed by Peter Blake, includes a number of Indian elements. Along with a figurine of the Buddha, a pop art-like multi-armed idol of Lakshmi, Hindu goddess of wealth and good fortune (sometimes incorrectly identified as a 'four-armed Indian doll'), smiles from the greenery on the bottom centre, reminiscent of the immense statue of goddess Kali which oversaw the chaotic final battle on the Bahama beach in *Help!* Four Indian gurus peer out from among the iconoclastic gaggle of movie stars, musicians, authors, actors, boxers, comics, thinkers and celebrities surrounding the Fab Four and their wax effigies. The four gurus are:

- Swami Vivekananda (1863–1902), chief disciple of Ramakrishna, known for four books on yoga in English and his celebrated speech at the World Parliament of Religions in Chicago in 1893
- Paramahansa Yogananda (1893–1952), one of the earliest gurus to settle in the West, who came to the United States in 1920, settled in Los Angeles in 1925, and wrote *The Autobiography of a Yogi* (1946), which became iconic in the 1960s
- Sri Yukteswar Giri (1855–1936), the guru of Paramahansa Yogananda, described in his book as the originator of kriya yoga
- Mahavatar Babaji (birth date and biography unknown), a legendary yogi and saint said to be 1,800 years old, also described by Paramahansa Yogananda in his book.

A fifth Indian saint, Mahatma Gandhi (1869–1948), was also to have been on the album cover, but like Elvis, Hitler and Jesus he was eliminated from the final version. Sir Joseph Lockwood, chairman of EMI, recalls that after much trepidation he gave approval to the album cover: 'All right, I said, but take Gandhi out. We need the Indian market. If we show Gandhi standing around with Sonny Liston and Diana Dors, they'll never forgive us in India' (Norman 1981, p. 286).

Harrison's 'Within You Without You', which opens side two of the original LP, is another purely Indian song. London-based Indian musicians playing sitar and tabla, the bowed dilruba, the suvar mandal (often incorrectly called the 'sword mandal')[2] replace guitars and drum set. A constant tambura drone replaces Western chord progressions. The tunes are in raga-like scales. A violin section, scored and trained by George Martin to do slides and ornaments recalling those of Bollywood cinema orchestras, emerges from time to time, notably in an instrumental break in 5/4 (or 5/8) time, a nod to Indian tala cycles where units of five (and seven) are common.[3] This time around the lyrics are decidedly Indian philosophical with references to introspective meditation, the 'wall of illusion' (maya), the oneness of life (advaita), perceiving truth (satya) and universal love ('With our love we could save the world').

Lennon's Indianisms are relegated to the timbral backgrounds of hallucinogenic trippiness ('Lucy in the Sky with Diamonds', where a tambura appears), the cascading backward tapes describing not a Tibetan Buddhist ritual journey, but the (child's? tripping adult's?) experience of a calliope and the dizzying aural/visual/emotional overload of a circus ('Being for the Benefit of Mr. Kite!'). In contrast with Harrison's unabashed Indian songs with their sitars, tablas and Eastern textures, Lennon has, as earlier noted, absorbed Indian components into his vast compositional toolkit. These are just a few of many elements which his substantial creativity can infuse into the texture of his songs in which the musical elements are predominantly Western.

In February 1967, Pattie Harrison had become a follower of the Maharishi Mahesh Yogi's Spiritual Regeneration Movement. The Maharishi (1917–2008), with his flowing shoulder-length hair and beard, twinkling eyes, saffron robes and easy laughter, looked the part of an enlightened Hindu holy man fresh out of Central Casting. His teachings came from the Hindu mainstream with its ultimate goal of experiencing sat-chit-ananda (ultimate truth, supreme intelligence, spiritual bliss). But the Maharishi marketed his movement as a Western science, free of the baggage of Hindu polytheism, ritual, sacred texts and temple worship, austerities and monastic life. Transcendental Meditation (TM) could be pursued conscience-free by the European or American devotee without changing profession or affluent lifestyle. And it was easy, requiring only a 15- to 20-minute commitment twice a day – as easy, a cynic might say, as popping a pill, sucking on a sugar cube or puffing a funny cigarette. The benefits were also marketed in a non-religious way: better health, increased concentration, happiness and success.

The TM movement was organized along the lines of a multi-national corporation, and there were fixed fees ranging from that for getting your own secret mantra, to those for special seminars in advanced meditation, culminating in a tithe of one tenth of one's yearly salary – which in the case of a movie actress or a rock star might be considerable.

On 24 August 1967, the Beatles attended a lecture by the Maharishi at the London Hilton Hotel, with a private darshan (or face-to-face) afterwards. Three days later, the most famous new members of the Spiritual Regeneration Movement along with their spouses and girlfriends and a group including Mick Jagger and Marianne Faithfull

---

2   The sword mandal is a small bow harp with a dragon's head at one end and a fish's tail at the other.

3   South-Indian khanda chapu tala (five beats, 2+3), north-Indian jhaptal (ten beats, 2+3+2+3).

took the 3.05pm train to Bangor for a weekend retreat with the Maharishi at the campus of the University of Wales. But the news of their manager Brian Epstein's sudden death brought the meditations to a halt. Shocked and grief-stricken, the group returned home. However, their new discipleship continued unabated.

On their own for the first time, the Beatles made an improvised movie, the hour-long *Magical Mystery Tour* which premiered on BBC television on Boxing Day (26 December) 1967. Scriptless and plotless, the film was universally panned, '... a glorified and progressively irritating home movie' (Norman 1981, p. 312) which the *Daily Express* labelled as 'blatant rubbish' (Ibid., p. 313). Considering that the group was in its first flush of involvement with the Maharishi, there is relatively little evidence of Orientalism in the songs introduced in the movie, with two exceptions.

As a song, Harrison's 'Blue Jay Way', named after a street in Los Angeles, is a throwaway. Set for Hammond organ, bass guitar, drums and tambourine, the sound is nonetheless Indian throughout. A constant echoey background drone supports a rambling repetitive tune set in a scale unlike those of Western music, but familiar to any Indian musician conversant with the raga system: a diminished triad (C, E♭, F♯, E♭, C, E♭) resolving to a major third (E natural). The phrase is then transposed up a minor third (resolving to G natural). The resulting raga-like scale has a parallel in the south-Indian mode known as raga ranjani (Example 5.2). The lyrics evoke a foggy dream-state of disorientation and confusion, with one phrase ('Don't be long') repeated no less than 21 times. In *Magical Mystery Tour*'s visualization of the song, Harrison sits cross-legged on an oriental rug playing an imaginary harmonium to multi-lens cinematic effects.

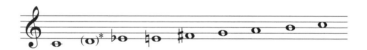

* With D natural rare (alpa).

Example 5.2   The scale of 'Blue Jay Way' (south-Indian ranjani raga)

The rap-like madcap surrealism of Lennon's 'I Am the Walrus' also contains a couple of references to things Indian. It is possible that the opening lines of the song ('I am he as you are he as you are me ...') could be an irreverent comic reference to one of the linchpins of Hindu religious thought: the advaita vedanta theology of Adi Sankara (mid-eighth century CE). Sankara, a southerner and prolific writer, rationalized that ultimately everything is one, there is no other, even atma (self) and God (brahma) are the same. Less hypothetically, later in the song Lennon refers to a 'penguin singing Hari Krishna', the latter a part of a popular Vaishnavite devotional chant (bhajan) brought to Western airports and street corners from Bengal with missionary zeal by saffron-robed, sneaker-clad European members of the International Society of

Krishna Consciousness. ISKON members later were to record with Harrison and hang out with Lennon and Yoko Ono during their bed-ins for peace.

In January 1968, Harrison made his third trip to India to record musicians at the EMI Studios in Bombay for an independent project, the soundtrack for the film *Wonderwall*. He also found time to record 'The Inner Light', released later in the year as the B-side of a single with McCartney's 'Lady Madonna'. The song, with lyrics based on a translation of an ancient Chinese sacred text, has an interesting history. Juan Mascaró (1897–1987) was a Sanskritist at Cambridge University. He had taught for a time in Sri Lanka, and although his native language was Catalan, his translation of the *Bhagavad Gita* into English (1962) was long considered one of the best. Impressed with Harrison's interest in Indian religious philosophy, Mascaró had sent him a fan letter along with a passage from the *Tao Te Ching* as possible song material. Amazingly, the letter got through to the reclusive superstar, who basically accepted the text intact, only changing parts of it to the first person. The lyrics describe a Chinese scholar in his study who understands the universe through introspection and scholarship, without walking through his door or even looking out the window ('The further one travels, the less one knows'). With its haunting melodies and Indian instruments (including tambura, harmonium, bamboo flute, the double-reed shehnai and the santur), 'The Inner Light', more than its predecessors ('Love You To' and 'Within You Without You') lives in a unique musical world floating somewhere between Indian song in tropical Bombay and the trans-Himalayan metaphysics of ancient China. Quite a trip for a boy from Liverpool!

After many delays and changes of plans, on 6 February 1968 the Beatles finally travelled with spouses and girlfriends, along with actress Mia Farrow, the folkie Donovan and Mike Love of the Beach Boys, to Maharishi Mahesh Yogi's ashram (hermitage) in Rishikesh in the Himalayan foothills north of Delhi for an extended course in TM. The accommodations were hardly those of the simple forest retreats described in ancient Indian texts. A Gurkha guarded the walled compound. The posh bungalows were equipped with English-style furniture and electric heat. A host of servants scurried about, serving tea in bed and even providing massages for the devotees. The group recollected the ashram as something like a summer camp, and – besides meditation – they had little to do aside from enjoying the Maharishi's occasional reward of rides in his helicopter. Ringo, worried about a steady diet of vegetarian curry and rice, had travelled with several cases of English baked beans.

Remarkably, the Beatles, who had brought along acoustic guitars, composed most of the songs of the so-called White Album (1968) in India, songs which signalled the end of experimentation and innovation and a return to the forms and styles common in pre-Beatles Euro-American pop music. It was as if an extended stay on Asian soil brought the group back musically to the sounds and forms of Western pop music traditions, to classic rock 'n' roll, ballads and blues. In sound and form almost all the Rishikesh songs are occidental. But a number of the songs reflect the Indian experience in their lyrics: the satirical 'The Continuing Story of Bungalow Bill', the seductive 'Dear Prudence', possibly the exquisite 'Blackbird' or the rocking 'Everybody's Got Something to Hide Except Me and My Monkey'. Ardent believers in the Maharishi and TM for five months, one by one the Beatles became disillusioned and fled, first Ringo after a few weeks, then Paul and John, and finally, most reluctantly, George.

Two autobiographical Lennon songs, neither of which has an Indian sound, illustrate the extremes of euphoria and disillusionment of the Maharishi caper. 'Across the Universe', which did not appear until the much tinkered-with album *Let It Be* (1970), is a gentle and earnest paean full of poetic images drawn from Sanskrit religious literature (for example, 'Limitless undying love which shines around me like a million suns'). The chorus includes a Sanskrit phrase: *jai guru deva om* ['victory to the guru-god' plus the sacred syllable 'Om']. It is rumoured that this was Lennon's favourite song, though the assertion may be apocryphal.

The second song is 'Sexy Sadie' (White Album). At first glance the bitter lyrics make little sense, until one learns that the song's villain has undergone a gender and name change at the insistence of corporate lawyers. 'Sexy Sadie' is none other than the Maharishi. It is the Maharishi with his seductive smile ('the world was waiting for a lover'), his devotees vying to sit at his table, who 'broke the rules', 'made a fool of everyone', and ultimately will 'get yours yet'. With Sadie identified as Maharishi, Lennon's autobiographical references become startlingly lucid.

Harrison's four songs are among the strongest on the White Album. All are within the musical parameters of Western pop styles, but 'While My Guitar Gently Weeps' has an oriental origin. As he writes:

> … I had a copy of the *I Ching* – the (Chinese) *Book of Changes* – which seemed to me to be based on the concept that everything is relative to everything else, as opposed to the Western view that things are merely coincidental … I decided to write a song based on the first thing I saw upon opening any book … I picked up a book at random – opened it – saw 'Gently weeps' – then laid the book down and started the song. (Harrison 1980, p. 120)

It is in this song that Eric Clapton's scorching guitar solo brings to an ear trained in Indian music an interesting question: how far apart, really – or how close – are blues guitar and Indian sitar?

Traces of India can also be found in some of Harrison's later songs; in 'Here Comes the Sun' (*Abbey Road*, 1969) the recurring instrumental riff organized rhythmically in its first occurrence after the chorus as 3+3+3+3+2+2 (Example 5.3) has unmistakable Hindusthani music origins – the tihai which closes improvisations. And about the lyrics of the angry, hard-rocking 'I Me Mine' (*Let It Be*, 1970), he writes:

> 'I Me Mine' is the 'ego' problem. There are two 'I's: the little 'i' when people say 'I am this' and the big 'I', i.e. OM … the little 'i' is like a drop in the ocean. Swami Vivekananda says, 'Each soul is potentially divine' … [so] get rid of the little 'i' by the drop becoming merged into the big 'I' (the ocean) … the truth within us has to be realized … (Ibid., p. 158)

Post-Beatles, Harrison continued to display his south-Asia connection in the triple album *All Things Must Pass* (1970). The ecumenical 'My Sweet Lord', where Christian 'Alleluias' morph into Hindu 'Hari Krishna, Hari Ramas', is an example, as was his philanthropic Concert for Bangla Desh in Madison Square Garden (1971), the granddaddy of pop music charity events.

Where were Paul McCartney and Ringo Starr in all of this, as John Lennon and George Harrison soaked up the Orient? Certainly they were active and often essential participants, if not co-creators. McCartney, after all, was busy building up his own remarkable catalogue of masterful songs. Though the Indian musical trip was not for him, he went along with his band mates for the ride, a willing fellow traveller. Starr, whose personal taste tended towards the genre of country music, nonetheless provided the perfect drumming whatever, whenever called for.

Example 5.3   The tihai-like riff in 'Here Comes the Sun'

For Lennon, the involvement in Orientalist doings was certainly a part of his complex creativity which, sponge-like, soaked up diverse elements, collaging them into his own experiences and his explorations of an inner reality, the other psychic worlds opened up by hallucinogens as well as by his wild imagination. But Harrison's Oriental connection was a lifelong endeavour. His love of India itself, his interest in Hindusthani classical music and his interest in Hindu philosophical thought were part of what he was. His friendship with Ravi Shankar outlived his brief discipleship. Time and his post-Beatle musical activities have given Harrison at least some of the recognition as a songwriter denied to him as a Beatle. After his death in 2001, it was noted with great pride by the Indian press that his ashes were to be taken to be immersed in the Ganges at Banaras by his wife Olivia, joining those of generations of Indians before him. In many ways he had returned home.

Chapter 6

The Beatles' psycheclassical synthesis: psychedelic classicism and classical psychedelia in *Sgt. Pepper*

Naphtali Wagner

The first sounds heard on the album *Sgt. Pepper* – a mixture of tuning instruments and the noise of an audience – create the impression that this is a live recording from the concert hall. I assume that many fans who had been waiting impatiently for the Beatles' new album thought for the first few seconds that the clerk had accidentally wrapped up a classical album.[1] The distraught listeners must have been reassured 12 seconds later by the sound of traditional rock 'n' roll, until a contrapuntal interlude (0'43"–0'55") suddenly brought them back to the classical world. Moreover, this interlude is not just an instrumental episode in a standard popular song; it appears too early to be so (just 22 seconds after the entrance of the singer) and precedes the chorus. In the first verse the singer acts as an announcer whose entire job is to introduce that fictional band whose virtual performance is documented here: 'So may I introduce to you the act you've known for all these years, Sgt. Pepper's Lonely Hearts Club Band'. Hence it is the entrance of the horns that marks the start of the 'real' performance. The horn episode is tied to the preceding vocal verse by a modulation that is not just a transition from one scale to another but a transformation from one genre to another: the C7 chord, which just a moment before functioned as a blues chord, turns into a traditional applied chord and is resolved to an F chord in accordance with the rules of the classical theory of harmony. The note B♭ turns from a rebellious blue note of the youth culture into the learned, elderly note of the seventh, which demands and is given proper resolution (Wagner 2003, pp. 362–4).

When George Martin reaches this episode in his discussion of the making of the album, he says: '… and then a bit of classical work, bringing in four French horns' (Benson 1992). But the classical image conveyed by the passage is not unequivocal: when the producer plays the horn track by itself (without the rhythm section), we seem to find ourselves in an eighteenth-century atmosphere – but where exactly? A consort of horns does not belong to any standard instrumental ensemble or specific genre in that period. Under the influence of the programmatic context of the frame song, the percussion accompaniment and the uniforms and brass instruments on the

---

1   More precisely, the opening sounds convey an ambiguous message: the string instruments in the background suggest a classical orchestra preparing for a performance, but the sounds of the audience hint at a different kind of show (for details, see Benson 1992). This very ambiguity may confuse listeners.

record sleeve, we can hear the passage differently: as a military band or perhaps a firemen's band playing light classical music in a pavilion in a London park to entertain the people out for a stroll.

This would seem to be an extremely surprising start for an album that is supposed to represent the Beatles' psychedelic phase! After all, classical and psychedelic music express two diametrically opposed aesthetic ideals: classical music is perceived as rational and has clear form, tone and texture, with the music splitting clearly into distinct units and subunits and relying on regular phrase rhythm. Any deviations from these properties attract attention because they stand out against the backdrop of the normative environment. The music revolves around intelligible texts with a logical narrative and a definite beginning and end. Thus classical music reflects lucidity and sobriety. Psychedelia, in contrast, is associated with altered states of consciousness – hallucinations, dreams, or the supernatural. It is manifested in music in various strange elements that produce a sense of detachment from reality – such as distorted sound and fusion of successive musical units on the macro and micro levels – and sometimes of tonal disorientation as well. The psychedelic fantasy relies on surrealistic, nonsense, and enigmatic texts, frayed at the edges, usually based on free association and constituting a broad ground for hermeneutic analysis.

Classical and psychedelic music delimit the eclectic, multistylistic and multigenre nature of *Sgt. Pepper*. But they are not only endpoints; they also interact in an interesting manner within the songs themselves. Ostensibly, there is no symmetry: psychedelia is spread over the entire album whereas the classical influence is just one of many stylistic influences in it, including traditional rock 'n' roll, vaudeville, big band, old-fashioned piano jazz, classical chamber music, light classical music, circus music, musical avant-garde and Indian raga. We have to distinguish between the Beatles' 'classicism' as a range of influences originating in Western art music and its more abstract meaning as an aesthetic ideal. Both meanings are discussed below: first, I will briefly survey influences of art music in the Beatles' albums, in an effort to show the simultaneous attraction and repulsion. Then I will return to the contrast presented at the start of this paper with the help of two diametrically opposed songs: 'Lucy in the Sky with Diamonds' (the most psychedelic song on the album) and 'She's Leaving Home' (which can be thought of as 'classical'). Let us see whether and how the Beatles manage to reconcile the aesthetic contradiction between classical and psychedelic and achieve 'psycheclassical synthesis'.

Bach, Beethoven and the Beatles

In 1963, the Beatles began the second side of their second album – *With the Beatles* – with Chuck Berry's song 'Roll Over Beethoven', which calls for the dying classical music to retreat in favour of the up-and-coming world of rhythm and blues.[2] Six years later, towards the end of the band's career, Lennon composed

---

2   It is worth pointing out for the benefit of the younger readers that once every record had two sides. The first song on the second side, due to its positioning, was especially prominent and was therefore carefully chosen. Today, such a song appears somewhere in the middle of the CD and loses its advantage.

'Because' under the inspiration of Beethoven's *Moonlight Sonata*. The key of C♯ minor, the arpeggio figuration in the accompaniment, the entrance of the melody and a few harmonic elements (such as the strong presence of the Neapolitan chord) all confirm the association between 'Because' and the latter sonata. The pattern of the accompaniment is somewhat reminiscent of the first prelude in Johann Sebastian Bach's *Well-Tempered Clavier* (to show how similar they are, I invite readers to play the figuration of the first prelude transposed to C♯ minor). It seems, then, that in the end, though not for the first time, the Beatles were reconciled with Western art music and joined with two of the other great 'Bs' – Bach and Beethoven. But did they really? According to a well-known anecdote, John asked Yoko to play the *Moonlight Sonata* for him from the end to the beginning, and it was this backward playing that inspired him to compose 'Because'. The reverse Beethoven, along with the nonsense text that undermines the seriousness of the tune, negates the great classical tradition, attesting that Lennon at least was not entirely reconciled with highbrow music.

Harrison, who was the lead singer on the cover version of 'Roll Over Beethoven', also made his way to art music, but it was a different kind of art music – classical Indian music – that attracted him, and it was with this that he opened side two of *Sgt. Pepper*. He committed the 'offence' of writing Western classical music only once – his later Orwellian song 'Piggies'. There the classical texture, with strings and harpsichord, takes on a very negative connotation when it connects to the piggish, cannibalistic, petty bourgeois lifestyle (the pigs eat bacon).

Of the three composers in the group, McCartney seems to have had the least difficulty with the classical tradition and adopted elements from it as needed. It is interesting to compare (or juxtapose) statements by Lennon and McCartney in the *Anthology* regarding their musico-poetic turnaround around the time they recorded *Rubber Soul* and *Revolver*: Lennon said that the Beatles had been exposed to 'contemporary influence' at that time; the impression is that he was referring to the zeitgeist of the mid-1960s. McCartney, in contrast, said that the Beatles had been listening to classical and other kinds of music that diverged from their own musical background: 'It was just around that period, when we were all getting into various different kinds of music ... [We] were all listening to sort of classical and various types of music other than our own and our rock 'n' roll ... roots' (Beatles 2003a). The image of Paul as the classical Beatle is manifested most saliently in the *Anthology* in the discussion of what the Beatles were doing while on vacation before getting together to record *Sgt. Pepper*: first, we hear about Lennon's involvement in making a film in Spain (where Ringo Starr joined him), then we hear about Harrison's stay with Ravi Shankar in India. At this point the background music becomes baroque, and Paul recounts his involvement in writing music for a film together with George Martin. In spirit and atmosphere, the music is reminiscent of 'She's Leaving Home'.[3]

But it turns out that McCartney also had his 'classical complexes'. In his biography, we discover the trauma of his first encounter with 'serious' music: a few piano lessons that stopped soon after they started and did not lead to anything.

---

3   Even though the score to 'She's Leaving Home' was arranged not by George Martin but by Mike Leander.

I did then take lessons, but I always had a problem, mainly that I didn't know the tutor, and I wasn't very good at going into an old lady's house – it smelt of old people – so I was uncomfortable. I was just a kid. I quite liked what she was showing me, but then she started setting homework: 'By next week I want you to have learnt this.' I thought it was bad enough coming for lessons, but homework! That was sheer torture. I stuck it for four or five weeks, and then the homework really got difficult so I gave up. To this day I have never learnt how to write or read music; I have vague suspicion now that it would change how I'd do things. (Beatles 2000, pp. 18–19)

We see a certain attraction ('I quite liked what she was showing me') but also repulsion ('it smelt of old people'). Interestingly, Paul never felt repulsed by jazz-like old music, the sort his father played (for example, music from the glory days of Paul Whiteman).

Classical touches

Ultimately, none of the band members was raised on classical music – not even Paul, whose father was a jazz trumpet player and a self-taught pianist. But there is no doubt that 'classical' influences seeped into their work. These diverse influences can be summed up in the following categories:

Instrumentation

The Beatles used musical instruments and ensembles associated with the classical world.[4] It is interesting to follow their use of string instruments since *Help!*, because this album required overcoming a huge obstacle: in the rock world of the mid-1960s, the sound of strings might be considered reactionary, not to mention a betrayal. It meant a return to the kind of American musical entertainment that had preceded rock 'n' roll and expressed everything that rock 'n' roll was rebelling against. Lush strings are associated with the world of musicals on the one hand and with pre-rock 'n' roll pop stars such as Frank Sinatra on the other. The string quartet on 'Yesterday' is a solution that is brilliant in its simplicity: the quartet does not evoke a regressive association; rather, it is identified with the loftiest, purest musical expression in Western art music. From then on, the Beatles added more and more strings at a time, but without losing the chamber-music character: in 'Eleanor Rigby' the quartet is doubled to form an octet, and in 'She's Leaving Home' we have a string nonet plus a harp. This gets dangerously close to orchestral kitsch and demands a cautious, delicate arrangement. Perhaps it was already the edge of the slippery slope that would ultimately lead to the orchestral accompaniment full of strings in the later Beatles' songs 'Good Night' and 'The Long and Winding Road' (an arrangement made over Paul's objections). Another type of classical instrumentation is the use of the obbligato such as the French horn in 'For No One' and the $B\flat$-piccolo trumpet in 'Penny Lane', but this necessarily diverges from the instrumental aspect on its own and connects to the stylistic aspect.

---

4   The kettle drums in 'Every Little Thing' from the album *Beatles for Sale* set a precedent of borrowing instruments associated with the classical symphony orchestra.

'Classical' stylistic elements

The use of the obbligato brings us back to the eighteenth century not only in terms of the instrumental colour but also in terms of the counterpoint that the instrument gives the tune. In the two examples mentioned above, the instrument appears first in the instrumental interlude in the middle of the song, but 'surprisingly' it also appears as a perfect counterpoint to one of the vocal sections. This is reminiscent of the obbligato horn in 'Quaniam' from Bach's *Mass in B minor* or the trombone in 'Tuba Mirum' from Mozart's *Requiem*. The selection of instruments and the presence of classical soloists in the Beatles' recording studio have led to an abundance of oft-repeated anecdotes; this is not the place to mention them. The first distinctive baroque element – composed or perhaps improvised by George Martin – was inserted as an interlude in John Lennon's 'In My Life'. Since this is a 'nostalgic' song, sounds from the past are appropriate, despite the absence of any direct connection between John's childhood and baroque music.[5] Other baroque elements in various songs involve ostinato, interlude, texture, accompaniment and so on. The bass line in 'Penny Lane', for instance, is reminiscent of baroque bass lines such as that in the 'Air' from Bach's *Third Orchestral Suite* or rapidly descending bass lines, as can be found in a few fast movements by Handel, Vivaldi, Marcello and others.

Lieder

Do some of the Beatles' songs cross the line between popular music and art songs? The root of the problem is that the term 'art song' is so hard to define unless we use extra-musical criteria such as social function, the record stores that sell it and the shelves on which they display it, the radio stations that play it and other genres represented in the composer's repertoire. But these criteria do not interest us here. We would like to define the term according to criteria that relate solely to the song itself (the music, the text and the relationship between them), but these are elusive. It is hard to come up with a list of essential features of art songs: sometimes it is the complexity that is accentuated but sometimes it is the simplicity; sometimes a song is praised for its extensive internal expansions and development and sometimes for its succinctness and minimalism. Even deviations from simple metric and hypermetric regularity are not a solid basis for a definition, since the many lieder are perfectly regular, strophic and repetitive. In contrast, many tunes that are unquestionably popular music are based on some irregular gimmick. Interestingly, all these troublesome questions are relatively easy to resolve intuitively: some combination of lyricalness, sophistication and beauty may cause us to listen to a song from a rock album as if it were from a song cycle by Schumann, Schubert, Mendelssohn, Brahms or Hugo Wolf. Such a combination can perhaps be found in songs like 'Julia', 'Here, There and Everywhere', 'For No One' and 'Fixing a Hole'.

---

5   In cheerful songs in a nostalgic vein, the past is marked by old-fashioned, light musical styles such as the vaudeville style of 'When I'm Sixty-Four' and 'Your Mother Should Know'. (In the former there is an interesting paradox: although the text refers to the future, the music suits the tastes of old people in the present, as if they were already 64.)

Abstract principles of classical music

Such principles are discovered only through exacting musical analysis, which tries to uncover structural levels under the musical surface and to find a hidden parallelism (where the same features are found in different magnitudes on different structural levels). All these may attest to an 'organic' quality of the sort common in art music. Such features are discovered through a Schenkerian-style linear analysis. Many of the Beatles' songs were found to be 'Schenkerable' (subjectable to Schenkerian analysis), as Walter Everett and I have shown, and they are referred to in the analytical discussion that follows. This criterion is completely independent of categorization as a particular genre or style.

Musical avant-garde

Towards the end of the Beatles era, John preferred to connect to Western art music through the musical avant-garde. Bear in mind that electronic music and *musique concrète* were developed in modern art music before being adopted by and becoming associated with popular music. 'Revolution 9', on the White Album, is a pioneering attempt by Lennon to incorporate an entire segment of *musique concrète* in a rock album, but it was preceded by the use of backmasking and other electro-acoustic tricks in the Beatles' songs. This brings up another dimension that reflects the Beatles' attempt to adopt elements of Western art music. But let us not forget that modernity per se is to a large extent aimed at rejecting tradition. A prominent representative of the musical avant-garde is John Cage, who in his most radical statements rejected music entirely and proposed directly aestheticizing the surrounding world without the mediation of artists. It was Cage who influenced John Lennon through Yoko Ono. Hence the friction between Lennon as a composer and radical modern music is more consistent with the spirit of the rock rebellion than with a reconciliation with classical music.

Psychedelia in a classical guise

Of all the songs on *Sgt. Pepper*, 'She's Leaving Home' is the most classical in that it fits into most of the categories listed above: in terms of the instruments, it is accompanied by a string nonet and harp and no rhythm section; in terms of style, it is unfocused but slightly reminiscent of nineteenth-century chamber music with a mildly French fragrance; in terms of the genre, it has a bit of art song about it because it presents a fine-tuned – sometimes almost madrigalian – relationship between lyrics and music; even the distribution of parts (the narrator and the parents) has precedents in lieder; and the song is to a large extent Schenkerable (see Figure 6.1) even though it deviates drastically from the dictates of the standard Schenkerian *Ursatz*, as will be explained below.

Figure 6.1ab An interrupted ascending *Urlinie* and its twisted realization in 'She's Leaving Home'

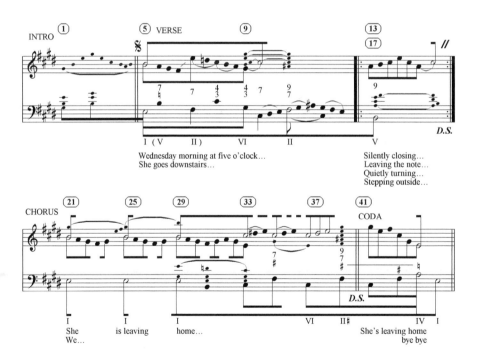

Figure 6.1c A detailed voice-leading graph of 'She's Leaving Home'

The main deviation from the standard Schenkerian formulas is manifested in the ascending fundamental line, from which a somewhat unusual interruption form is derived.[6] Moreover, even if we legitimate the ascending *Ursatz* for the purpose of our discussion (Figure 6.1a), its specific realization in the song will look very strange (Figure 6.1b). Figure 6.1a introduces an interruption form of the ascending *Ursatz* (assuming there is such an animal). Despite the ascent in the fundamental line, the graph shows the standard relationship between the two wings of the interrupted structure: a half-cadence in the left wing and a perfect authentic cadence in the right wing. Figure 6.1b shows a synoptic graph (on two levels of detail) of the structure of the song, which deviates significantly from this outline. Here the left wing ends on a dominant ninth chord, while the right wing is a plagal cadence. The retreat from A♯ to A (which occurs here during the movement from 7̂ to 8̂) is idiomatic of the Beatles (it is manifested in a contraction in the left wing and in disalteration in the right wing). Despite the numerous deviations from what was considered standard, the song is subject to linear analysis, as can be seen in Figure 6.1c: this detailed graph of the entire song shows a multilevel structural hierarchy and linear progressions. There is also a hidden parallelism: the bass progression in the coda (starting in bar 41) is nested in an identical but broader bass progression (beginning in bar 37).

The song is fairly modular (Figure 6.1c) and consists of several distinct musical units, each of them well defined and with its own musical content:

Intro (bb. 1–4)

The harp arpeggios that precede the entrance of the narrator conjure up the stereotype of the troubadour. They can remind us, however, of the piano figures that open Schubert's song cycle *Die Schöne Müllerin*, where they imitate the flow of water and here, perhaps, the sunrise.

First half of the verse (bb. 5–9)

The melody is simply a descending Hypo-Mixolydian mode, with a transfer of register an octave higher. The transfer occurs on a dissonant note, E, which stands out as a peak note. Under the surface, a bold counterpoint forms between an ascending trichord in the bass (E–F♯–G♯) and an arpeggio in the upper voice (B–E–G♯). On the surface, there is a sequence of ascending fifths in the bass, causing a harmonic sequence of regressive steps (as opposed to descending fifths, which are considered progressive). Interestingly, there is incomplete synchronization between the sequential bass, which extends over five notes (E–B–F♯–C♯–G♯), and the harmonic sequence, which includes only four chords (I–V–II–VI). Only in bar 9 do the harmonic steps become progressive (VI–II–V) and lead to the point of interruption. Regressive sequences are a sort of musical oxymoron: the regression causes disorientation, whereas the sequential nature conveys regularity and indicates direction. In the present case, the direction is blurred by the partial non-concurrence between the bass and the harmony. The internal contradiction inherent

---

6   An argument in favour of the existence of ascending *Urlinie* may be found in Neumeyer 1987.

in the impact of the sequence corresponds to the emotional state of the daughter, who is determined but also distraught (she is 'clutching her handkerchief', implying crying). The sequence thus goes along with the daughter's actions more than the parents'.

Second half of the verse (bb. 13–20)

The internal harmonic movement within a dominant ninth chord always reminds me of the opening bars of César Franck's *Sonata in A major*. The static nature of the situation rips the dominant away from its inherent dissonant tensions and turns it into a sort of impressionist chord that extends outwards both vertically and horizontally (the melodic notes are all derived from the notes of the chord as it appears in bars 13 and 17). Again we get a somewhat ambivalent musical message: on the one hand a tense chord, on the other a non-evolving situation that stems partly from cyclic repetition of the melodic fragment. The paradoxical message of the music beautifully suits the text, which is full of silent action taking place on tiptoe. The daughter's actions (see the lyrics under the graph) correspond to the short melodic fragment that is repeated on a static chord, while the dissonant tension latent in that chord reflects the internal tension to which it is subject. We have here a rare moment of static impressionist music that supports a dynamic text and is full of activity.

Chorus (bb. 21–40)

The dialogue between the narrator and the parents is actually a pseudo-dialogue; the two alternating texts are not listening to each other. The graph shows that the melodic line of the anguished parents is the main line, attached to the structural note B, whereas the melodic line of the narrator hovers over it. In bars 21–32, the melody is nested in the lower major pentachord (E–F♯–G♯–A–B), which is extended to form a complete octave in bars 33–40, where the upper trichord (C♯–D♯–E) is repeated persistently and gets rid of the Mixolydian impression that formed during the verse.

Coda (bb. 41–4)

The coda concludes with a pentatonic line that covers the entire ambitus of the song. The direction of the melodic curve is the opposite of that at the beginning of the intro.

'She's Leaving Home' is full of ambivalent situations that evoke conflicting feelings: harmonic and contrapuntal retreat, internal motion within a static block of harmony and a distorted superstructure (at least from an orthodox Schenkerian perspective). The ambiguous musical environment is amazingly appropriate for the ambivalence that emerges from the text: the scenario is dawn twilight, no longer night but not yet really day; mixed feelings (the girl's sense of liberation mixed with extreme distress; the parents' discomfiture as they wonder, 'What did we do that was wrong?'). These are threshold states that are easily assimilated to the psychedelic concept of the album. Although the sound is not distorted, the texture includes episodes of contrapuntal distortion (for example, the passage with the string instruments, 1'25"–1'30"). However, the classical framework encompassing all these occurrences is not in doubt, this framework is manifested not only in the chamber instrumentation but also in the clear division into musical units and subunits, each of which focuses on the development of its own raw material (that is, its notes).

What is the significance of the classical feel of the song? It would seem to be connected to the old, dusty world of the parents' generation, that world from which the girl is trying to escape. But paradoxically, classical chamber ensembles became the latest thing in rock music, associated with the young generation (by virtue of precedents that the Beatles themselves had created). Thus, while rock was undermining the heritage of 'serious' music, it was also trying to connect to this heritage. These attempts did not always succeed, as we can see in many of the products of 'progressive rock'. But in the present song McCartney managed to put the typical Beatles idiom (manifested, inter alia, in regressive steps, disalteration and pentatonicism) under an outer classical umbrella. Whereas the content of the song depicts an intergenerational conflict, the musical synthesis ultimately embodies a certain reconciliation. Even the offended parents eventually achieve insight and 'repent'.

The classicism behind the psychedelia

If 'She's Leaving Home' is a sort of 'classical' song that passes through the psychedelic prism of the album, 'Lucy in the Sky with Diamonds' is an extremely psychedelic song with classical elements. When George Martin comes to 'Lucy' in his survey, he plays the intro on the piano and says, 'I'd say it is a most wonderful phrase. I think if Beethoven was around he wouldn't have minded one of those' (Benson 1992). Indeed, the most psychedelic song on the album emerges from the 'classical' core in the intro. It may be said that here Lennon exchanged the rock riff for a quasi-baroque ostinato (see Figure 6.2).

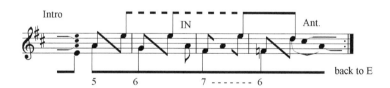

Figure 6.2   A hidden counterpoint in the compound 'ostinato' of 'Lucy in the Sky with Diamonds'

We have here a repetitive figure that first appears in the intro and afterwards carries the melody. Thus it functions as a riff, but it is very different from the typical riff patterns of rock music:[7] it is slow, with a triple metre and monotonous rhythm, whereas the typical riff has a diverse rhythmic, sharply turning profile in a quadruple metre and a vigorous, assertive tempo. Essentially, we have here a cross between

---

7   Typical riffs can be found, inter alia, in 'Drive My Car', 'Day Tripper', 'What You're Doing', 'Paperback Writer' and 'Rain'.

the principle of the riff and the principle of passacaglia. The compound figuration includes a descending chromatic line that interacts contrapuntally with the notes above it (see the numbering under the staff in Figure 6.2), bringing us back to the baroque period. However, the 'cooked' sound of the electric organ prepares us for the dominant psychedelic atmosphere of the song. The latent syncopation resulting from peak notes on weak beats and the zigzagging melodic curve bridge the gap between the two worlds.

Testing the Schenkerability of 'Lucy' requires first classifying the song from a tonal perspective, but this classification is not easily done. Tonal ambiguity is one of the main effects of psychedelia in the song. The listener oscillates between various tonal feelings that exist not only in succession but also side by side simultaneously. This is true both of the tonal instability in the song as a whole and of the separate sections. We can get an indication of the lack of tonal clarity by taking a quick look at various published transcriptions of the song. Table 6.1 presents a comparison of the key signatures as they appear in two more or less reliable publications (Beatles 1993; Beatles 1983).

Table 6.1   The key signatures of 'Lucy in the Sky with Diamonds' according to Beatles 1993 and Beatles 1983

	Intro	Verse	Pre-chorus	Chorus	Coda
Beatles 1993	♯♯	♯♯	♭♭	♯	♯
Beatles 1983	♯♯♯	♯♯♯	♭♭	♭♭	♯♯♯

Based on the 1983 edition, we can conclude from the first and last key signatures that the tonality of A major prevails in the entire song whereas according to the 1993 edition the song ranges from D major to G major. Disagreement exists not only among publishers but among scholars as well:

- Steven Porter believes that the main tonality is A major, surrounded by tonicized structural neighbour notes (B♭ major and G major), as a sort of substitute for the absence of a structural dominant (Porter 1979)
- Walter Everett asserts that the song is in G major, as manifested in the voice-leading graph that opens with the hypothetical notes G and B in the outer voices. Thus the Schenkerian *Ursatz* appears in its traditional form, extending from the start of the verse to the start of the chorus (Everett 1999, p. 105)
- Allan Moore presents a totally ambivalent graph: the scale steps in the upper voice correspond to G major, but the key signatures suggest D major. The bass line, as Moore draws it, does not support the tonal classification as G major either (Moore 1997, pp. 32–4).

The lack of agreement regarding the classification of the song in a particular key is evidence of tonal ambiguity. To illustrate this, I would like to present the song according to three rival tonal interpretations: in A major, D major, and G major.

Figure 6.3abc Three rival tonal interpretations of 'Lucy in the Sky with Diamonds'
(A major, D major, G major)

Each is consistent with the Beatles' harmonic style and has precedents in many other songs. The graphs show the song without the coda.

Figure 6.3a presents an A major (or, more precisely, Mixolydian) interpretation of the entire song. This understanding is based on an expanded plagal cadence. Its advantage is that the tonality at the start of the song is indeed the correct tonality for the entire song. Its weakness is that the chorus is merely interposed in the plagal cadence that encompasses the song. This leads to the absurd conclusion that the song can exist even without the chorus, which in fact is its peak!

Figure 6.3b shows a D major interpretation that attributes a cyclic structure to the song (a sort of infinite loop in potentia). Therefore the fundamental structure does not have to start at the beginning of the song (as in the A major version); its starting point can be anywhere on the time axis. According to Figure 6.3b, the *Ursatz* starts at the end of the chorus (part C) and ends in the pre-chorus (part B). The chorus is perceived as an auxiliary cadence (IV–♭VII–I), with the ♭VII functioning as a dominant substitution.

Figure 6.3c rests approximately on the upper line as drawn by Allan Moore, but differs from Moore's version in the harmonic interpretation. Here, too, we perceive the song as being cyclic. All the notes in the fundamental line correspond to the notes of the scale, without chromatic or modal deviations. But despite its originality, the picture obtained is not satisfying. Whereas in the previous versions one basic progression dominates the entire song, here there are two progressions: one (V–II♯–V, beginning at the end of C and ending at the end of B) exists entirely in the realm of the dominant, with no real connection to the tonic (paradoxically, following Walter Everett, the chord supporting $\hat{3}$ is not a true tonic); the other, which starts at the tonic, ends with a half cadence (I–IV–V). Thus it turns out that the G major tonic is never the end point of a musical unit, and it is very hard to hear the G chord as a tonic chord.

We could suggest other hypothetical interpretations, such as abandoning the idea of monotonality and viewing the song as oscillating between two centres – A in the verse and pre-chorus, G in the chorus. This version could be defended with the argument that oscillation between tonal centres separated by a major second is found in other Beatles' songs, such as 'Doctor Robert', 'Good Day Sunshine' and 'Penny Lane' (see Wagner 2001, pp. 94–5).

We can compare how well each of the tonal explanations works in light of the structure of the chorus, which constitutes the peak of the entire song. The harmony of the chorus, as it appears in the repetitive, fading coda, is formulated here in the three possible keys:

Coda (repeat & fade out)

A major:	♭VII	♭III	IV	IV	I
D major:	IV	♭VII	I	I	V
G major:	I	IV	V	V	V/V

Lucy in the Sky with Diamonds   Ah————————

————————x3————————

To begin, let us look at the first three chords that accompany the key words: of the three options, the G major version produces the most conventional harmony – a routine half-cadence. In D major, an authentic auxiliary cadence is obtained, with ♭VII functioning as the dominant. Although ♭VII is so common in the Beatles' music that it can be seen as their trademark, it rarely comes between IV and I.[8] In A major, a strange cadence is obtained that ends on the subdominant and does not touch the tonic. This observation would seem to favour the G major interpretation, but the last two chords turn the picture on its head. Now the D major cadence is the most conventional, flowing to the dominant when the latter leads, as is customary, to a repetition of the entire phrase. Slightly less probable is the A major cadence, which proposes a plagal ending on the tonic; this does not encourage repetition of the phrase. The G major version is now the least likely of the three, since it is terminated on the dominant of the dominant.

My inclination is therefore to decide in favour of D major, and I drew the more detailed graph of the song accordingly (Figure 6.4). The figure is a 'close-up' of figure 6.3b and does not apply to the coda. It shows section A in abridged form, as heard when it is repeated after section C. The figure discloses the parallel among the different tetrachords, which constitute a framework for many of the linear progressions. We can see from the graph that the descending tetrachord G–F♯–E–D, which is so prominent in section C, is interwoven in a comprehensive system of tetrachords that includes major, Mixolydian and Lydian tetrachords, all descending. The notes G, D, A and E constitute starting notes for the various tetrachords.

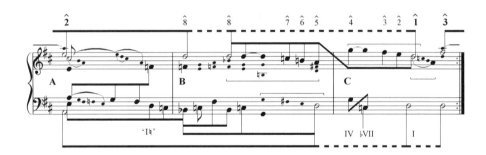

Figure 6.4   A detailed voice-leading graph of 'Lucy in the Sky with Diamonds' according to the outline given in Figure 6.3b

Although the song satisfies the criteria for Schenkerability in its unique way, if anything in the world is a psychedelic Schenkerian graph it is this graph. We have already noted that according to the D major interpretation of the song the *Ursatz* starts at the end of the song and ends in the middle. Furthermore, the coupling that descends from 8̂ to 1̂ is a sort of musical Moebius strip. It is also reminiscent of the

---

8   The flatted seventh is most common in the Beatles' music in the following combinations: ♭VII–IV–I (hyperplagal cadence), ♭VI–♭VII–I, I–♭VII–I, ♭VII–V–I.

monks in M.C. Escher's famous picture 'Ascending and Descending'; in this case, the monks are going down the steps of the octave only to find themselves where they started (compare with the transfer of register in Figure 6.1c, bb. 5–9).

So far we have examined the two most extreme representatives that delimit the expressive spectrum of the album: Lennon's psychedelic fantasy and McCartney's classical lied. We saw, however, that at each pole there are reflections of the opposite pole. Thus, the entire album may be seen as embodying the psycheclassical synthesis.

Additional pairs

McCartney is less associated than Lennon with psychedelia, but his songs do frequently explore ambiguous, elusive and altered states of consciousness (as in 'I've Just Seen a Face' from the album *Help!*, 'Got to Get You into My Life' from *Revolver* and 'Fixing a Hole' from *Sgt. Pepper*). There are pairs of songs in which Lennon demonstratively leads the strangeness and McCartney leads the sanity. The most salient example is the pair formed by Lennon's 'Strawberry Fields Forever' and McCartney's 'Penny Lane'. They are both nostalgic songs belonging to the *Sgt. Pepper* recording wave (even though they were ultimately left out of the album because they were sold as singles). Ostensibly, 'Strawberry Fields' is purely psychedelic,[9] whereas 'Penny Lane' is the epitome of classicism, inspired by Bach's *Second Brandenburg Concerto* (Benson 1992). However, the psychedelic synthesis is built into both songs. Lennon's use of four-six chords in the intro comes from the world of classical music, but a series of successive parallel four-six chords is not consistent with the traditional rules of harmony and creates a sense of instability associated with the psychedelic world (Wagner 2006).[10] McCartney's harmonic progressions in 'Penny Lane', despite their classical appearance, diverge substantially from the classical tradition. Interestingly, the first exceptional chord in each of these songs is the same one: the minor dominant (Bm7 in bar 4 of section A in 'Penny Lane' and Fm7 in bar 3 of section A in 'Strawberry Fields'). We would expect Lennon's enigmatic text to welcome the psychedelic strangeness, but McCartney's childhood memories, too, include surprising and even surrealistic details (such as the fireman with an hourglass). McCartney sums up his impressions with the words 'very strange', which conclude two of the verses. It turns out that poetic inquiries into threshold states of consciousness can be found in both Lennon's and McCartney's songs. These states, which are not connected solely to drug experiences, are the programmatic trigger for Lennon's externalized psychedelia. Although McCartney expresses them more traditionally, just addressing them sometimes leads him into what can be called 'soft psychedelia'.

A similar but earlier pair of songs can be found on the album *Revolver*: Lennon's 'I'm Only Sleeping' and McCartney's 'For No One'. The two songs were recorded

---

9   George Martin called 'Strawberry Fields Forever' 'our first psychedelic track', even though many people regard 'Tomorrow Never Knows', recorded more than half a year earlier, as the first (Benson 1992).

10   There is a precedent for successive parallel four-six chords in Brahms' 'Immer leiser wird mein Schlumer', Op. 105, No. 2 (bb. 16–21 and 43–8). Interestingly, this song is also about a hazy state of consciousness (sleep).

around the same time (late April and early May 1966). McCartney was looking for a musico-textual way of expressing a sense of alienation and emptying the words of their meaning. His song begins with the stupor of a morning hangover – 'Your day breaks, your mind aches' – and contains a 'classical' response to Lennon's psychedelic stupor upon awakening 'in the middle of a dream'. Here the contrast between Paul's 'lieder' character and John's psychedelia is sharper than in the previously mentioned pairs. If the songs on *Revolver* constitute a sort of psychedelic-classical mixture, on *Sgt. Pepper* the psycheclassical synthesis is already at its best. This synthesis, which reached its peak with *Sgt. Pepper*, attests to the creative interaction between artists with compositional orientations as different as Lennon's and McCartney's.

Outro

The analysis above made free use of the terms 'classical' and 'psychedelic'. These terms were stripped of their narrow stylistic definitions and were used to denote diametrically opposed 'aesthetic ideals': the 'classical' extreme covered everything that contributes to clarity of form, tonality and text, whereas the 'psychedelic' was represented by the negation of all of these. We found that in the Beatles' music 'classical' and 'psychedelic' are not separate entities but interactive ones. Their interaction results in the psycheclassical synthesis, which reaches maturity on the album *Sgt. Pepper*.

Another way of classifying *Sgt. Pepper* from a musico-poetic standpoint is to look at the songs on the album in terms of their proximity to or distance from the here and now. The here and now were all that could be expected of a conventional rock album in the mid-1960s. The distance from the 'here' was manifested most prominently in the turn to a foreign (Indian) musical culture. The distance from the 'now' is more complex, as it includes musico-poetic journeys along the time axis. Among these journeys are nostalgic voyages to styles of the recent past (as in 'When I'm Sixty-Four'), 'historical' voyages to styles of the distant past (baroque and classical), and voyages backwards in biographical time – to personal childhood memories – in search of original, personal musical expression (as in 'Strawberry Fields'). This search is one of the catalysts for the emergence of the Beatles' psychedelia.

From this perspective, the classical and the psychedelic are both aimed at creating distance from the conventional rock 'n' roll of the late 1950s and early 1960s. They both contribute to eclectic pluralism in terms of styles and genres, which today can be termed postmodern. The postmodern impression is enhanced by the concept of a live performance by a fictional band that is hard to anchor in any real musical or dramatic framework: it's somewhere between a rock 'n' roll band, a firemen's band, a big band, and a hybrid of all these and more. The elusive musical experience of the album is consistent with the fascinating historical fact that the Beatles produced a recorded simulation of a live performance just when they had removed themselves from the stage and the spotlights and barricaded themselves in the recording studio. In this way they 'virtualized' themselves and situated themselves somewhere in a fictional world outside their contemporary cultural reality while also constituting it.

Chapter 7

Cover story: magic, myth and music

Ian Inglis

Sgt. Pepper remains the only album within popular music whose cover has attracted as much attention and debate as the music it contains. Despite the musical innovations, commercial transformations, and proliferation of styles and related cultural practices that had redirected the production and consumption of popular music since the birth of rock 'n' roll in the mid-1950s, the art of the album cover had remained largely untouched. The principal pre-war album design strategies – painterly covers, poster-like covers, graphic covers (Jones and Sorger 2000, pp. 72–3) – had gradually converged to produce a post-war adoption of 'the personality cover' (Thorgerson 1989, p. 10) on which a positive, attractive image of the performer(s) was presented alongside their names and the album title. With very few exceptions and little variation, this approach had persisted unchallenged. Indeed, the Beatles' first six albums (*Please Please Me* to *Rubber Soul*) had broadly confirmed the practice, and it was not until the whimsical photograph-and-illustration design of *Revolver* that the group had attempted to consider any other possibilities.

In fact, the success of *Revolver* – its designer, Klaus Voorman, won the Grammy Award for Best Album Cover of 1966 – was instrumental in persuading the Beatles to contemplate alternative ideas for the cover of their next album, *Sgt. Pepper*. While the recording of the album continued from December 1966 to April 1967, agreement developed within the group that the cover should not be separate from, but an integral part of, the album itself. Art and music were to be equally significant components; the Beatles' intention was to create a record whose musical impact would be complemented by its visual impact.

> Paul [McCartney]: This album was a big production, and we wanted the album sleeve to be really interesting. Everyone agreed. When we were kids, we'd take a half-hour bus ride ... to buy an album, and then we'd come back on the bus, take it out of the brown paper bag and *read* it cover to cover ... you read them and you studied them. We liked the idea of reaching out to the record-buyer, because of our memories of spending our own hard-earned cash and really loving anyone who gave us value for money. (Beatles 2000, p. 248)

That the Beatles were so determined to participate in the design of the cover – at a time when such decisions were routinely made by the record companies' marketing executives – was in itself indicative of the growing presence in popular music of cohorts of young people for whom art was a legitimate avenue of expression. McCartney had taken Art and English at A level, with the intention of going on to train as a teacher; and Lennon (and Stuart Sutcliffe, who had left the group in June 1961 to attend Hamburg State School of Art) had studied at Liverpool College of Art.

They were not at all unusual; the list of successful migrants from the classrooms of British art colleges to careers in popular music included Keith Richards, Jeff Beck, Pete Townshend, Eric Clapton, Jimmy Page, Cat Stevens, Eric Burdon, Syd Barrett, Sandy Denny, Ray Davies. Far from being unrelated, their individual histories were to have a profound effect on the trajectory of popular music for the rest of the decade: 'they inflected pop music with Bohemian dreams and Romantic fancies, and laid out the ideology of "rock" – on the one hand a new art form, on the other a new community' (Frith and Horne 1987, p. 73).

McCartney's original suggestions had consisted of nothing more than some pen-and-ink sketches of the Beatles, suitably dressed, in various settings from the Victorian/Edwardian era – in a sitting room lined with photographs and trophies, in front of a floral clock, at a civic ceremony with the Lord Mayor. His ideas should not be seen as surprising, since a preoccupation with the popular culture of the past has been a perennial component of much of Paul McCartney's music, from Beatles' songs such as 'Honey Pie', 'Martha My Dear', 'When I'm Sixty-Four', 'Your Mother Should Know', 'Rocky Raccoon', 'Maxwell's Silver Hammer' to his later solo songs including 'Hands of Love', 'You Gave Me the Answer', 'She's My Baby', 'Famous Groupies', 'Baby's Request', 'Average Person'. All draw on, and reflect, a wide-ranging tradition of 'family entertainment' which encompasses the singalong conventions of music hall/vaudeville, the show tunes of Fred Astaire and Jack Buchanan, the seaside postcard humour of Donald McGill, the communal excitement of the mystery tour, the ukulele expertise of George Formby and the mannered lyrics of Noel Coward. In this context, the Sunday afternoon brass-band concert in the park, which the cover of Sgt. Pepper so freely recalls, also serves as an appropriate indicator of routine activities in the northern, working-class environments where the Beatles grew up.

On the advice of gallery owner Robert Fraser (famously arrested in May 1967 with Mick Jagger and Keith Richards on drugs charges), McCartney contacted British pop artist Peter Blake and his American wife Jann Haworth to discuss developments of the group's initial design ideas.

> … I think my contribution was to talk a great deal to them about the concept and try to add something visual to it. Paul explained that it was like a band you might see in a park … with a crowd of people around them. I think my main contribution was to decide that if we made the crowd a certain way the people in it could be anybody … a life-sized collage incorporating real people, waxworks, photographs and artwork. I kind of directed it and asked the Beatles and Robert … to make a list of characters they would like in a kind of magical ideal film. (Peter Blake, quoted in Taylor 1987, pp. 32–5)

For the Dartford-born Blake, whose own working-class roots had exposed him to similar cultural experiences as the Beatles, it was a significant opportunity to acquaint new audiences with the connections between consumerism, popular culture and fine art that had characterized his output since the mid-1950s. That an established and influential artist should undertake to design a popular music album cover was in itself remarkable, and a striking demonstration of the challenge to existing cultural boundaries that characterized much intellectual activity through the 1960s. Blake later went on to create or contribute to the artwork of albums by a variety of performers, including Eric Clapton, The Who, Brian Wilson, Ian Dury, Band Aid and Paul Weller, but he has described his association with the Beatles as 'the moment when everything changed' (Blake 2006).

Freed from any restrictions (other than having to gain, at EMI's insistence, the legal consent of the characters involved), the Beatles were able to construct a list of cast members whose participation was not determined by their material presence, and which accurately reflected not merely the group's personal interests, but also the shifting intellectual climate of the 1960s, marked by 'a new wind of essentially youthful hostility to every kind of established convention' (Booker 1969, p. 33).

In this sense, the figures (57 photographs and nine waxworks) collected for the tableau acted as a guidebook to the cultural topography of the decade – or, as Melly has described it, 'a microcosm of the Underground world' (Melly 1970, p. 151) – and indicated, above all, an ongoing process of democratization, in which traditional barriers between 'high' and 'low' culture were being effectively eroded. Thus, movie stars (Marilyn Monroe, Marlon Brando, Tony Curtis) stood with artists (Richard Merkin, Aubrey Beardsley, Larry Bell); sportsmen (Sonny Liston, Johnny Weismuller, Albert Stubbins) with gurus (Sri Yukteswar Giri, Sri Mahavatar Babaji, Sri Paramahansa Yogananda); comedians (Issy Bonn, Tommy Handley, Laurel and Hardy) with writers (Oscar Wilde, H.G. Wells, Dylan Thomas); singers (Bob Dylan, Dion, Bobby Breen) with philosophers and scientists (Karl Marx, Albert Einstein, Carl Jung). And some characters were hidden from view (Bette Davis, Sigmund Freud) while others were rejected (Adolf Hitler, Jesus Christ, Mahatma Gandhi).

The motivations for the group's choices have been clarified in George Harrison's explanation that 'we were trying to say we like these people, they are part of our life' (quoted in Martin with Pearson 1994, p. 117). In passing, his comment does much to confirm the identity of the 'friends' whose presence and support are acknowledged in the album's second song, 'With a Little Help from My Friends'. It is not, as has often been alleged (Noebel 1982, pp. 60–62; Martin 1996, pp. 157–8) a song about drugs; it is a song about the companions, teachers and friends whose images appear on the album cover.

> In making their selection, the Beatles were understandably drawn to figures who promote the idea of other possible worlds or who offer literary and cinematic trips to exotic places … the cover suggests that the Beatles to some extent live the past in the present, live in the shadows of their own as well as of other people's past accomplishments, and that among the imaginative creations that fascinate them most, the figures closest at hand on the cover, are their own past selves. (Poirier 1969, pp. 178–9)

By surrounding themselves with their heroes and mentors (past and present, living or dead) in an unprecedented way, the Beatles thus displayed their ability to transgress the normal barriers of time and space, and demonstrated that they 'had changed from rock musicians into magicians' (Assayas and Meunier 1996, p. 46). The fact that they appear twice (as the Fab Four and as the members of Sgt. Pepper's Lonely Hearts Club Band) adds to the viewer's recognition that these are not ordinary men, but persons possessing unusual, even supernatural powers; not only are they able to conjure up figures from history, but they also have the apparent ability to exchange their own identities at will.

It is often overlooked that this belief in a multiplicity of selves is seen at its most striking in the position occupied by Ringo Starr. While he too exists as a Beatle and as a bandsman on the front cover, his true identity is further complicated by McCartney's introduction of him, on the album's opening track, as 'the one and only Billy Shears' – exceptional, unique, and greeted by a crescendo of applause. More importantly, the bandsmen's uniforms reveal that, of the four, it is he who wears the stripes, he who is, in fact, Sgt. Pepper. The elevation of Ringo Starr – the one Beatle who played no part in the selection of characters for the cover (Martin with Pearson 1994, p. 115; Miles 1997, p. 336), who was to describe his role in the album's creation as 'a bit like being a session musician' (Clayson 1991, p. 114) and who was commonly perceived as 'the lonely outsider, the non-intellectual of the group, who ... gets by with a little help from [his] friends' (Peyser 1969, p. 131) – to the position of band leader is central to the imagery and ideology of Sgt. Pepper. It makes it absolutely clear that, in the world favoured by the Beatles, all of us have the ability to be magically transformed into whomever and whatever we may choose, whenever and wherever we may desire.

And, of course, the group's exploration of its roles as surrogate magicians was to be revisited explicitly in two subsequent screen projects. In *Magical Mystery Tour* (1967), the group members appeared as Beatles and as wizards:

> Away in the sky, beyond the clouds, live four or five magicians. By casting wonderful spells they turn the most ordinary coach trip into a magical mystery tour. If you let yourself go, the magicians will take you away to marvellous places. (Barrow 1967, p. 1)

And in *Yellow Submarine* (1968), the Beatles again manipulated their twin identities from the cover of *Sgt. Pepper* in order to free the oppressed inhabitants of Pepperland:

> Once upon a time, or maybe twice, eighty thousand leagues beneath some far-off ocean, stood a huge rainbow gate. Inside the gate was a magic land called Pepperland, where flowers grew, butterflies flew, and the people were all happy. (Brodax 1968, p. 2)

In each case, the association between the Beatles and the transformative power of their musical/magical capacities is the central element in the film's narrative, and both draw directly from the characterizations of *Sgt. Pepper*.

The perception of the Beatles as magicians or shamans provided an apt contemporary illustration of Weber's comments on the attribution of charismatic powers by devoted followers to their leaders. The concept of charisma refers to 'a certain quality of an individual personality by virtue of which he is set apart from ordinary men and treated as endowed with supernatural, superhuman, or at least specifically exceptional powers or qualities' (Weber 1947, p. 358). It was a perception, and a treatment, emphatically endorsed in the increasingly frequent assessments that identified the creators of *Sgt. Pepper* as magical rather than musical characters:

> *Sgt. Pepper* quickly became all things to all people. To the budding counterculture, it was ... an advance report from some magical plane of existence. (Kozinn 1995, p. 160)

Rumours spread that there actually *was* a Pepperland, an emerald city of rock and roll. Someone would come and spirit you off to Pepperland ... and when you got there all your friends would be there waiting for you, all your friends and most especially your old friends the Beatles. (Garbarini, Cullman and Graustark 1980, pp. 62–3)

As pop musicians they are simultaneously magicians (dream-weavers), priests (ritual celebrants), entertainers (whiling away empty time), and artists (incarnating and reflecting the feelings ... and perhaps the conscience of a generation). (Mellers 1973, p. 183)

I declare ... that the Beatles are mutants. Prototypes of evolutionary agents sent by God with a mysterious power to create a new species – a young race of laughing freemen ... They are the wisest, holiest, most effective avatars ... the human race has ever produced. (Timothy Leary, quoted in Norman 1981, p. 287)

Once the final montage had been assembled, it was supplemented by additional accessories and ornaments. The bass drum behind which the Beatles stood was painted by fairground artist Joe Ephgrave. The satin uniforms worn by the group were made for them by theatrical outfitters Berman's. The musical instruments they held were (in place of guitars and drums) a French horn, a trumpet, a cor anglais and a flute. The plants, foliage and flowers were supplied by Clifton Nurseries in London. In front of the cast, and around the floral display in which the word 'Beatles' is prominent, are a number of other items, some brought in by the Beatles themselves, others spontaneously added during the final stages of construction – a television, a Mexican candlestick, various dolls, a tuba, a hookah, a toy car, several busts and stone figures.

The set had been assembled over two weeks at the Chelsea studio of photographer Michael Cooper, and his photo session took place there on 30 March 1967. The session also produced two other images for the album: the picture of the Beatles that would appear on the back cover, in which Harrison, Lennon and Starr face the camera while McCartney faces the other way; and the centre-fold spread of the four Beatles in close-up. While apparently endorsing the conventions of the 'personality cover' through its reproduction of four smiling faces, there is an obvious and immediate warmth to this picture which distances it from the sterility and artifice typical of such images.

Paul [McCartney]: One of the things we were very much into in those days was eye messages ... So with Michael Cooper's inside photo, we all said, 'Now look into the camera and really say "I love you!" Really try and feel love, really give love through this! It'll come out, it'll show, it's an attitude.' And that's what that is, if you look at it you'll see the big effort from the eyes. (Miles 1997, pp. 344–5)

Before the decisive theme of bandsmen had been adopted, other ideas for the album's artwork had been considered. Manager Brian Epstein had suggested a plain brown paper bag (Martin with Pearson 1994, p. 167) and Dutch design team The Fool (Simon Posthuma and Marijke Koger) had, at McCartney's invitation, submitted various psychedelic paintings for the centre spread, which were ultimately rejected, largely at the insistence of Robert Fraser (Beatles 2000, p. 248). However, The Fool was permitted to design the paper sleeve that would contain the actual record. Its abstract wave pattern, moving through shades of maroon, red, pink and white, thus became the first album sleeve to depart from a simple, white format. Moreover, The

Fool's contribution to *Sgt. Pepper* did result in its designs appearing on several other albums, including the Incredible String Band's *5000 Spirits*.

The most remarkable feature about the back cover lies, however, not in its artwork, but in the fact that it reproduced the printed lyrics of the album's 13 songs. The idea was suggested by graphic designer Gene Mahon (who later provided the image of the apple that became the symbol of the group's Apple project). Initially greeted with alarm by EMI, who feared legal repercussions stemming from arguments about copyright infringements, the practice quickly became commonplace and effectively ended the automatic inclusion of informative/promotional 'sleeve notes' that had been standard for more than a decade. In fact, while the group's first four albums – *Please Please Me*, *With the Beatles*, *A Hard Day's Night* and *Beatles for Sale* – had contained conventional sleeve notes (written by Tony Barrow or Derek Taylor), the custom had been abandoned on *Help!*, *Rubber Soul* and *Revolver*. Given the Beatles' insistence that the album should contain as many extra features as possible – 'we wanted it to be very very full of value … we wanted to pack it with goodies' (Miles 1997, p. 340) –, Mahon's proposal was enthusiastically adopted. And by presenting song lyrics as poetic texts to be studied and assessed, it formally acknowledged that (along with other contemporary songwriters, including Bob Dylan and Paul Simon) the Beatles had shifted the function of popular music from music-as-entertainment to music-as-communication.

Drawing on their memories of childhood surprises, the Beatles had hoped to include a free gift – 'a little magic presentation … a packet of things inside the record sleeve' (Paul McCartney, quoted in Taylor 1987, p. 37) – but this was rejected for financial reasons (EMI was concerned about the mounting cost of the cover's artwork and production) and logistical reasons (the group recognized the difficulty of inserting a bulky package inside a flat sleeve). The agreed compromise was a cardboard sheet of cut-outs, designed by Peter Blake and Jann Haworth. It included a postcard-size portrait of Sgt. Pepper (inspired by the statue from John Lennon's house which sits next to the bass drum), a moustache, two sets of sergeant's stripes, two lapel badges and a stand-up likeness of the Beatles in their satin uniforms.

When the album was released in June, the cover excited critical debate in a way that no other album cover had done before. Its enormous expense – its final costs were almost £3,000, compared to a norm of around £50 – was forgotten, as it quickly became evident that 'Beatles album sleeves, in the opinion of fans and critics, had assumed the status of Works of Art' (Evans 1984, p. 96). It was honoured: repeating the success of *Revolver*, it won the Grammy Award for Best Album Cover of 1967. It was copied: the Rolling Stones' *Their Satanic Majesties Request* borrowed not only the same concept, but the same photographer. It was parodied: most famously, by Frank Zappa for the Mothers of Invention's *We're Only in It for the Money*. And at the end of the century, the BBC placed it in its list of British twentieth-century masterpieces of art and design, ahead of such national icons as Mary Quant's mini skirt, Gilbert Scott's red telephone box and Alec Issigonis's Mini car.

One of the undoubted strengths of the cover is its unspoken familiarity. While the content of the design is radical and innovative, the form it takes is implicitly reassuring. The cast of characters on the front echoes the tradition of the annual school or team photograph; the reliance on bold primary colours (the blue backdrop to the front cover, the bright red of the back cover, the yellow of the centre spread) evokes the simplicity of childhood painting experiments; the sheet of cut-outs reintroduces us to the delights of dressing-up and play; the printed lyrics mimic the song sheets given to audiences at open-air concerts at the seaside or in the park. In all of these facets, the group knowingly exploited the concept of nostalgia for themselves and their listeners. Like the music it contained, the cover demonstrated 'a kind of selective filtering back from one generation to another' (Peter Shrag, quoted in O'Grady 1983, p. 120).

If an important part of nostalgia is a feeling of 'belonging', of membership in a community of peers, there was an additional way in which the design of the album cover permitted its audience to be participants rather than spectators:

> Not only did we have the gatefold sleeve and printed lyrics (inviting us into what was portrayed as a closed coterie) but the badges, the false moustache and Sgt. Pepper stripes that were supplied as cut-outs suggested we could all the more easily pretend to be in the band. (Moore 1997, p. 57)

And these nostalgic connections are amplified when it is noted that the two additional tracks intended for inclusion on *Sgt. Pepper* but removed in order to satisfy EMI's desire for a new Beatles single in February 1967 were 'Penny Lane' and 'Strawberry Fields Forever' – both of which celebrate specific locations in Liverpool, and their place in the childhood memories of Paul McCartney and John Lennon.

But set against this overall mood of familiarity was the unfamiliarity of the Beatles themselves. *Sgt. Pepper* was the first album cover to allow the Beatles to move away from the distinctive image of clean-shaven, look-alike 'mop-tops'; instead, they had moustaches (a conventional sign of maturity) and, in a frank rebuttal of contemporary expectations about the appearance of 'pop stars', Lennon was happy to be seen wearing glasses. The explanation for these changes went back to the group's final performance – at Candlestick Park, San Francisco, in August 1966 – following which George Harrison had famously concluded 'Well, that's it, I'm not a Beatle any more' (Clayson 1990, p. 139). With no more touring commitments to fulfil, the Beatles were free to embark on individual projects outside the group, and in September 1966, John Lennon flew to Germany and Spain to begin filming the satirical comedy *How I Won the War* for Richard Lester, who had directed *A Hard Day's Night* and *Help!* For his role as Private Gripweed, Lennon was required to look like a typical British soldier of the Second World War: '... he was shorn of all his long Beatles hair, and ... he adopted wire-framed National Health spectacles – "granny glasses" as they became known' (Coleman 2000, pp. 431–2). The retention of his changed appearance after filming had finished, and his and the other Beatles' gradual rejection of similarities of clothing, identification and hairstyle were clear indications of the distance that they wished to place between the group's former image and its new reality. Indeed, between their final tour performance and the release of *Sgt. Pepper*, the Beatles consciously embarked on a series of individual enterprises: McCartney had composed the musical score for Roy Boulting's *The Family Way*; Harrison had travelled to India for several weeks' sitar tuition with Ravi Shankar and (with his wife Pattie) had attended his first lecture by the Maharishi Mahesh Yogi in London; Lennon had made another solo acting appearance in Peter Cook and Dudley Moore's *Not Only But Also* television series and had met Yoko Ono. (And in December 1967, Ringo Starr was to make his solo acting debut

– alongside Richard Burton, Marlon Brando, John Huston and Walter Matthau – in Christian Marquand's *Candy*.) The idiosyncrasies of *Sgt. Pepper*'s cover were therefore a continuation of these new directions and a public announcement, of the most deliberate kind, that the Beatles, and their music, had undergone significant changes.

The patterns, themes and associations discussed above are plausible inasmuch as they approach *Sgt. Pepper*'s cover as an active partner of the music inside. Perhaps the songs are composed by those on the cover, perhaps the songs are composed about those on the cover; perhaps the cover contains clues to the songs, perhaps the songs contain clues to the cover. Either way, there is a tangible relationship between music and art, mirrored in the subsequent searches – which continue today – for 'hidden meanings'. Musical investigations have included repeated attempts to discover the true identities of the young girl in 'She's Leaving Home' or the meter maid in 'Lovely Rita' (Turner 1994, pp. 144–71), to ascertain the presence of pro-drug sentiments in 'Lucy in the Sky with Diamonds' or 'Fixing a Hole' (MacDonald 1994, pp. 187, 190–91) and to offer conclusions about the philosophies expressed in 'Good Morning, Good Morning' or 'Within You Without You' (Hertsgaard 1995, pp. 203–21).

At the same time, investigations of its art 'sparked a massive cult following, a kind of cover-cult that grew and grew … despite all the attempts at demystification, myths about the cover sprang up, fully formed, from thin air' (Martin with Pearson 1994, pp. 113–14). The most notorious of these myths, which began to circulate freely in autumn 1969, claimed that Paul McCartney had died in a car crash in 1966, that the group had continued with a replacement (an actor named William Campbell) and that copious clues to the affair had been provided by the Beatles in the lyrics of their songs and on the covers of their albums including, crucially, *Sgt. Pepper*.

Popular music is, of course, a familiar territory for the proliferation of urban myths or legends – sensational or dramatic narratives initially transmitted, often by word of mouth, within recreational, occupational and regional communities, which go on to achieve a much wider circulation. Other performers to have been the subject of such tales include Elvis Presley, the Rolling Stones, Bob Dylan, Led Zeppelin and Pink Floyd (Barron and Inglis 2005). The significance of this example – which quickly became known as the 'Paul is dead' story – was not only that it was the first such story, but that the protagonists (the Beatles) were alleged to have deliberately provided the evidence themselves, rather than have attempted to conceal it. A careful inspection of the album cover would thus reveal, according to the myth, an abundance of clues.

On the front cover:

- The Beatles are standing around a grave
- The yellow hyacinths display a left-handed guitar (McCartney's instrument) and/or the word 'Paul'
- The drum was painted by Joe Ephgrave, an anagram (of sorts) of 'epitaph' and 'grave'
- The open hand above McCartney's head is a symbol of death
- The toy car resting on the 'Rolling Stones' doll is the Aston Martin in which McCartney died
- Lennon, Starr and Harrison are turned towards McCartney, as if supporting him
- McCartney's musical instrument is black.

On the centre spread:

- McCartney's black armband reads OPD (Officially Pronounced Dead)
- His medal signifies a heroic death.

On the back cover:

- McCartney's back is turned towards the camera, indicating the presence of an impostor
- The words 'without you' are printed alongside McCartney's head
- Harrison's right hand points to the words 'Wednesday morning at five o'clock' – the time of the car crash. (Reeve 1994, pp. 153–5; Patterson 1996, pp. 130–31)

Added to the dozens of other clues scattered through the Beatles' singles and albums in the late 1960s, these details from the cover of *Sgt. Pepper* were thus co-opted into an elaborate narrative which not only related the circumstances of McCartney's death, but also revealed the location to which he had been transported – Pepperland itself.

Urban myths, of all kinds, are told and retold by a variety of storytellers to accomplish a wide range of social and personal objectives (Barron and Inglis 2005, pp. 62–4). Nevertheless, 'it has always been the prime function of mythology to supply the symbols that carry the human spirit forward, in counteraction to those other constant human fantasies that tend to tie it back' (Campbell 1949, p. 11). In order to comprehend the role that the 'Paul is dead' story might play in these processes, it is important to examine both the *Sgt. Pepper* cover and the Beatles themselves as such symbols.

The search for a system of meaning via the imposition of order on chaos lies at the heart of much social, political and intellectual activity. The 'meanings' of those texts produced by the Beatles had, by the time of *Sgt. Pepper*, become more elusive:

> The Beatles had, over the years, moved from the straightforward comprehensible statements of the 'I Want to Hold Your Hand'/'I Saw Her Standing There' period of 1963 to the confusing and seemingly unintegrated verbal streams that are characteristic of many of the 1967 songs. The 'absurdity' of the songs was reflected in the style of the album cover decorations ... typically designed as collages of apparently unrelated and randomly selected items. (Suczek 1972, p. 70)

From this perspective, the absence of a 'straightforward' reading thus encouraged subjective, idiosyncratic, even bizarre explanations of the images on the album cover. Attempts to supply meaning could, and did, range from 'the Beatles in fancy-dress' to 'the development of a new musical direction' to 'Paul is dead'. Freed from any restrictions, boundaries or guidelines by the group itself, audiences were able to construct a complex modern myth that combined elements of collective excitement, religious ecstasy and personal involvement (Ibid., pp. 73–4).

And just as the *Sgt. Pepper* cover possessed symbolic as well as material properties, so too did the Beatles. Indeed, far from being pop stars,

... the Beatles are mythical figures, with the individual members combined in the public mind into a mythical unity. A myth is something large numbers of people believe and, more importantly, believe in ... the citizens of the 'industrialised' West still look to mythical heroes for that which they psychologically need but cannot find in everyday life. As they live on in music and image, the Beatles continue to provide vicarious fulfilment of many of these needs. (Burns 1987, pp. 170–71)

This was no less true at the time of *Sgt. Pepper*'s release than it is today. Against a background of increasing hostility to US involvement in Vietnam, greater sexual and personal liberation, an expanding Civil Rights movement, rapid technological and economic change, the emergence of feminism, wider availability of drugs, the growth of the student movement and the counterculture, the Beatles seemed to symbolize the freedoms and opportunities so many desired: 'In the years 1965–67 it had all come together astonishingly coherently. There were clear catalysts whose hold on spiritual values kept the thing on track. Dylan was one ... the Beatles ... were another' (Taylor 1987, p. 110).

Confronted by a text with no single meaning, and authors who seemed to be more mythical/magical than real, audiences' constructions of alternative accounts therefore became not only intelligible, but inevitable. The 'diligent investigation, priestly interpretation and blind faith' (Burns 1987, p. 173) needed to decipher the clues on the album cover was a small price to pay for the acquisition of knowledge and information, and the rewards (particularly the promise of salvation) they might bring to the chosen few who correctly solved the mysteries of the text. On two previous occasions in their career, the Beatles had been characterized – rightly or wrongly – as individuals with miraculous powers. First, on the tours of 1963–64, handicapped children, often in wheelchairs, would be routinely brought to their dressing room (against the group's wishes) in search of comfort or cure (Wenner 2000, pp. 103–4; Taylor 2001, pp. 121–2). Secondly, John Lennon's (largely misunderstood) remark in 1966 that the Beatles were more popular than Jesus Christ had led to media condemnation and organized demonstrations against the group, especially in the United States (Davies 1992, p. 287; Goldman 1988, pp. 245–7). Unlike those occasions, however, *Sgt. Pepper*'s elevation of the Beatles may well have suggested a spiritual transformation, but possessed no formal religious significance. To state this is not to deny the relevance of the myth, but to place it in its appropriate context:

[This is] the myth of the Beatles – a quasi-religious force more powerful than most religions in the secularized West. It is common knowledge that the Beatles are important, but few have taken the time to notice just how important. To many people, Pepperland is more important than heaven. To this extent, it becomes heaven, albeit a secular one. Pepperland is the counterculture equivalent of Disneyland. (Burns 1987, p. 180)

And the cover of *Sgt. Pepper* was thus revealed as the map that could lead the enlightened explorer to his or her intended destination.

However, it has to be recognized that, in other ways, *Sgt. Pepper*'s cover can be justifiably approached as a conventional, and highly effective, example of album marketing and promotion. After all, one of the principal tasks of any album cover is to act as an advertisement for the music within and, in this respect, an album cover that stands out from its competitors and which succeeds in attracting attention is performing its task efficiently. This requirement, as Jones and Sorger have explained, developed in post-war years after the introduction of self-service selection at record stores that allowed potential purchasers to browse through the records: 'shelves that displayed only the spines of records were replaced by racks that brought customers face to face with covers. Slowly the importance of the cover as a "silent salesman" was noticed by record company executives and marketing personnel' (Jones and Sorger 2000, p. 73). To confront customers with startling and colourful artwork, as *Sgt. Pepper* did, was to demonstrate the persuasive powers that such distinctive images possess.

In addition, the details on the cover made it very clear what it was that the customer was looking at. The Beatles appear, not once, but twice; they are explicitly named in the floral arrangement; the title of the album is prominent on the drum. There is thus little doubt that this is a named album by the Beatles. This strategy is in contrast with some of the albums by, for example, Led Zeppelin (*Houses of the Holy*, Untitled Album/*Four Symbols*, *Presence*) and Pink Floyd (*The Dark Side of the Moon*, *Atom Heart Mother*, *Wish You Were Here*) whose covers are devoid of information and contain no references (pictorial or textual) to the group, the music, or the album (Inglis 2001, pp. 94–5). In this sense, it might be argued that the cover of *Sgt. Pepper* was, despite its radical design and sophisticated execution, a conservative text that succeeded in fulfilling familiar commercial imperatives. And, in a perfect illustration of the routine incorporation of the innovative into mainstream styles (Melly 1970), its themes and vocabularies were quickly adopted by others, for whom the marriage of a complex creative aesthetic and a powerful commercial presence was irresistible:

> By the end of the 1960s, sleeve designers were roaming across the history of modern art, film and fashion as knowingly (and for much the same reason) as advertising agencies – the sleeves, like the rock posters and group images, at first glimpse the most obvious sign of a high art presence in rock, were, in fact, designed to sell the product. (Frith and Horne 1987, p. 108)

Yet, however effective the cover of *Sgt. Pepper* may have been as an advertisement for its music, the overwhelming response at the time of its release – and in the years since – has been to applaud its ability to provide an accompaniment to the music. In the majority of cases before *Sgt. Pepper*, this task had usually been reduced to little more than a photograph on the front and some perfunctory notes on the back. *Sgt. Pepper* redefined this activity; for the first time, an album sleeve was not a superfluous thing to be discarded during the act of listening, but an integral component of the listening, that assisted and expanded the musical experience. The unprecedented correspondence between music and art, time and space, that the cover announced, has been emphasized in almost every account of its significance: 'a collage as colourful, imaginative and intriguing as the record itself' (Schaffner 1978, p. 81); '[the] artwork on the sleeve complements the music inside it perfectly: both are types of collage' (Martin with Pearson 1994, p. 116); 'a monument to the sixties, it glows with the excitement of an age that felt it had the whole world at the tip of its ... fingers'

(Goldman 1988, p. 308); 'it perfectly personified the incense-laden, rainbow-coloured, psychedelic sixties themselves' (Brown and Gaines 1983, p. 213).

In view of this, it is hugely ironic that the cover of the Beatles' next album (released in November 1968) should eschew any kind of association with its music and opt instead for a completely blank design, empty of all details save for the name of the group and a serial number. The contrast between the kaleidoscopic indices of *Sgt. Pepper* and the tabula rasa of *The Beatles* could not appear greater, and yet there is, in both cases, a similar challenge to the reader to supply some kind of explanation. In one, we are faced with a surfeit of extravagant visual clues, in the other there is a complete absence of clues; but both invite inspection, discussion and analysis. Herein lies, perhaps, an indication of the real legacy of *Sgt. Pepper*. Over the past 40 years, album covers – whatever their design characteristics – have become legitimate texts for critical attention. To see them merely as attractive wrappers is to go back to a time before *Sgt. Pepper*, when the idea that the structures and cultures of popular music could attract a 'serious' or 'intellectual' discourse would have been regarded as a fanciful conceit. With *Sgt. Pepper*, the Beatles effectively removed that prejudice. Its cover has been regarded as groundbreaking in its visual and aesthetic properties, congratulated for its innovative and imaginative design, credited with providing an early impetus for the expansion of the graphic design industry into the imagery of popular music, and perceived as largely responsible for the connections between art and pop to be made explicit. What *Sgt. Pepper* has also provided, and continues to provide, is a source of excitement and delight at the real or imagined places – magical, mythical and musical – to which its audiences can be taken.

Chapter 8

Within and without:
Sgt. Pepper's Lonely Hearts Club Band
and psychedelic insight

Russell Reising and Jim LeBlanc

To make this trivial world sublime,
Take half a gramme of phanerothyme.
Aldous Huxley to Dr Humphrey Osmond

To fathom hell or soar angelic,
Just take a pinch of psychedelic.[1]
Osmond's response (1957)

Psychedelic vision is reality to me.[2]
John Lennon

The term 'psychedelic' was born as a result of the above-quoted exchange between two early LSD pioneers, before Paul McCartney joined John Lennon in the Quarrymen, also in 1957. Fortunately Osmond's coinage prevailed, as Huxley's proposed 'phanerothyme' does not have quite the same mellifluous cachet. The Beatles had all soared angelic since the recording of *Revolver* and especially in the months preceding and during the recording of *Sgt. Pepper's Lonely Hearts Club Band*, and although what John Lennon calls 'psychedelic vision' might not always have been reality for Paul, George and Ringo, it provided the astonishing glue that resulted in two of the greatest creations in rock history. *Sgt. Pepper's Lonely Hearts Club Band* synthesized the contemplative monologues, the razor-sharp social critiques and the bracing psychodrama of *Revolver* with an even more lavish attention to sonic detail and adherence to the pop tradition. Looking within themselves and looking without at the often lonely wastes of the Cold War West, the Beatles suggest some possible ways of fixing holes, making things better, and soaring in Technicolor beyond the mundane greys of Liverpool, London, New York or California. Through the alter egos of their colourful Victorian-era band, the Fab Four guarantee a splendid time for those willing and able to see, as Sidney Cohen titled his contemporary account of the impact of LSD on Anglo-American culture, 'the beyond within' (Cohen 1966).

---

1 Originally an exchange between Aldous Huxley and Humphrey Osmond. Huxley's original account is in Horowitz and Palmer 1977, p. 107. Quoted in Stevens 1987, p. 57.
2 Sheff 2000, p. 158.

Musically, psychedelia generated great interest in matters of the intellect, the spirit, ecstatic merging, hallucinatory clarity and meditative innerness, even the fate of the species. Instead of songs about stolen kisses, surfing great waves and souped-up hot rods, we get songs about death and rebirth, the nature of time and dreamlike visions of mountains disappearing and surreal journeys under the sea. We will consider several themes common to psychedelic culture and particular, if not original, to *Sgt. Pepper*. First, like many psychedelic musicians, the Beatles register a sense of snapping out of a daze or a fog and tuning in to the spectacle of newness and life that was hovering just beyond their ordinary perceptions. Closely related to this theme of waking up, the Beatles mount a social critique of ordinary existence, one based on the belief in having passed over some magical threshold and having awakened to a new, unusually beautiful and profound reality. Finally, *Sgt. Pepper's Lonely Hearts Club Band* stresses the complete fluidity and total interpenetration of all life forms, expressed most powerfully in Harrison's 'Within You Without You', a song whose lyrics, timbres, rhythms and tonalities constitute almost a dictionary of psychedelic imagery.

The birth of *Sgt. Pepper*

We must remember that *Sgt. Pepper's Lonely Hearts Club Band* makes an almost belated appearance in the psychedelic revolution. Psychiatrists, doctors, dentists, CIA operatives, NASA, Pentagon defence strategists, Wall Street bankers, officials of the Roman Catholic Church, governmental officials (including many heads of state), and many other economic, political and social luminaries throughout the 1950s and early 1960s had studied and often championed LSD. Henry Luce, founder of such influential magazines as *Fortune, Sports Illustrated, Life* and *House and Home*, and his wife, Clare Boothe Luce, who later served on Ronald Reagan's Foreign Intelligence Advisory Board, regularly hosted high-class LSD parties for social and cultural elites. Mrs Luce remembered her LSD experiences fondly, remarking, 'Oh, sure, we all took acid', on the Dick Cavett Show in 1982 (Lee and Shlain 1985, p. 71). Bill Wilson, founder of Alcoholics Anonymous, valued his own redemptive LSD experiences so deeply that, 'as he approached his 70th birthday, he developed a plan to have LSD distributed at all AA meetings nationwide', but was dissuaded by his trusted inner circle of alcoholics.[3] Rand Corporation defence analyst and inspiration for Stanley Kubrick's diabolical Dr Strangelove, Herman Kahn, became a devotee of LSD and, during one particularly fertile trip under the direction of Dr Sidney Cohen, 'lay on the floor murmuring "wow" every few minutes'; the next day Kahn reported that, during that trip, he had been reviewing nuclear bombing strategies he had concocted against the People's Republic of China (Stevens 1987, p. 63). While the Beatles would later sing about 'fixing a hole', Kahn, evidently, was thinking about creating some very large ones! The Cathedral of the Holy Rosary

---

3   Rich English writes: 'The drug rocked Wilson's world. He thought of it as something of a miracle substance and continued taking it well into the '60s. As he approached his 70th birthday, he developed a plan to have LSD distributed at all AA meetings nationwide. The plan was eventually quashed by more rational voices, and a few years later the Federal government made the point moot by making the drug illegal' (English 2004).

in Vancouver issued a formal statement indicating that even the Roman Catholic Church was interested in the potential of LSD for spiritual awakenings:

> We ... approach the study of these psychodelics [*sic*] and their influence on the mind of man anxious to discover whatever attributes they possess respectfully evaluating their proper place in the Divine Economy. We humbly ask our Heavenly Mother the Virgin, help of all who call upon her to know and understand the true qualities of these psychodelics, the full capacities of man's noblest faculties and according to God's laws to use them for the benefit of mankind here and in eternity. (Ibid., p. 71 – from the private archives of Dr Oscar Janiger)

In retrospect, these and other such remarkable revelations make even the surreal imagery of 'Lucy in the Sky with Diamonds' seem tame by comparison.[4]

Both the Yardbirds ('Heart Full of Soul') and the Kinks ('See My Friends') experimented with the psychedelically rich and evocative sitars and sitar-like sounds in 1965, even prior to George Harrison's use of the instrument on 'Norwegian Wood'. Sheila Whiteley has noted that 'Lucy in the Sky with Diamonds' 'drew and enlarged on the hallucinogenic vocabulary of other songs of the period' (Whiteley 1992, p. 44). Many important psychedelic recordings predate *Sgt. Pepper*. The Byrds released 'Eight Miles High' in 1965, and songs such as Dylan's 'Visions of Johanna', the Count Five's 'Psychotic Reaction', Love's '7 and 7 Is', and the Beach Boys' 'Good Vibrations', as well as the groundbreaking album *The Psychedelic Sounds of the 13th Floor Elevators*, all appeared in 1966. The Doors' 'The Crystal Ship', Moby Grape's 'Omaha' and the Jefferson Airplane's *Surrealistic Pillow* beat *Sgt. Pepper* to the shelves in 1967. As Big Brother and the Holding Company guitarist Sam Andrew remarked in an interview, it was with the release of *Revolver* that he and other members of the San Francisco music scene 'realized that the Beatles had definitely come "on board". It was obvious from the songs and from the treatment of the songs that the four lads had grown up' (Reising 2002, p. 7). In other words, Sam and the other members of Big Brother along with many others from the San Francisco scene had to wait for the Beatles to catch up with the ways in which psychedelic experiences finally informed songwriting and album arrangements.[5] Moreover, West Coast psychedelia influenced the Beatles more than merely musically. As Ian MacDonald notes, 'During the Beatles' final US tour, McCartney had been struck by the fanciful names adopted by the new American groups and the Op Art graphical blend of psychedelia and vaudeville used in West Coast pop posters' (MacDonald 1994, p. 184). West Coast psychedelic fashion and culture, including the pioneering psychedelic group the Charlatans, who all dressed up like Victorian dandies, might even have inspired the Beatles' colourful and anachronistic *Sgt. Pepper* costumes. Furthermore, Walter Everett notes the Beatles' debt to the Jefferson Airplane in the cover's depiction of the Beatles holding a French horn, a trumpet, a cor anglais and a flute mimicking the cover of *Surrealistic Pillow* on which the Jefferson Airplane hold

---

4   For three of the best social and cultural histories of LSD's impact on Western culture, see Kleps 1975; Lee and Shlain 1985; Stevens 1987.

5   While *Revolver* must be acknowledged as the first realization of the Beatles' psychedelic experiences, most fans believe that *Sgt. Pepper's Lonely Hearts Club Band* represents the full flowering of the Beatles' psychedelia.

French horn, violin, saxophone and recorder (Everett 1999, p. 123). They may not have got on the psychedelic bus as early as others, and they may not collectively have stayed on it as long, but it would be difficult indeed to find a greater account of the flourishing of the imagination under the influence of psychedelic substances.

Their release of *Sgt. Pepper* in the midst of the Summer of Love impacted popular culture in a way that no other recording had ever done before. Partly due to the almost obsessive interest of Anglo-American culture in LSD and other hallucinogenic drugs, it was the psychedelic nature of *Sgt. Pepper* that immediately dominated people's attention. As one cataloguer of psychedelic music puts it:

> Everything about the album literally emanated drugs. From the cover art, inside record sleeve, the color cutout insert, the mind-expanding lyrics, to the complex and aurally stirring music. SERGEANT PEPPER was an acid trip wrapped up in one package. (Belmo 1999, p. 22)

MacDonald similarly assesses the album: '... it would be silly to pretend that SERGEANT PEPPER wasn't fundamentally shaped by LSD. The album's sound – in particular its use of various forms of echo and reverb – remains the most authentic aural simulation of the psychedelic experience ever created' (MacDonald 1994, p. 199). As the editors of *Q* magazine define *Sgt. Pepper*'s essence, '*Revolver* signalled Lennon's initial immersion in Timothy Leary's manual *The Psychedelic Experience*, but *Sgt. Pepper* represented the full flowering. McCartney had turned on too, and the trippy vibe was augmented by producer George Martin's studio experiments' ('Absolutely Tabulous' 2001, p. 64). Even Ringo remarked that 'for [him] those psychedelic years were the most exciting' (Benson 1992).

Jim DeRogatis maintains that 'psychedelic rock must transport the listener to a place that he or she has never been before, to transcend the everyday and experience the extraordinary' (DeRogatis 1996, p. xii). Specific to the LSD trip or psychedelic trance, in general, are the aural synesthaesia in which sounds seem to burst into vibrant colours, the buzz with which individual sounds seem to blend into pure sonic energy, the wash of sight and sound in which it is difficult to distinguish foreground from background and vice versa, and the elasticity of space and time that expand and contract seemingly to fit the mood or aura of the environment. These effects can be evoked musically with 'circular, mandala-like songs; sustained or droning melodies, altered and effected instrumental sounds; reverb, echoes, and tape delays that create a sense of space, and layered mixes that reward repeated listening by revealing new and mysterious elements' (Ibid., p.10). Whiteley, too, explores the way in which the different styles of progressive rock have common techniques that convey a musical equivalent of hallucinogenic experience, what she calls 'psychedelic coding'.

> These include the manipulation of timbre (blurred, bright, overlapping), upward movement (and its comparison with psychedelic flight), harmonies (lurching, oscillating), rhythms (regular, irregular), relationships (foreground, background) and collages which provide a point of comparison with more conventionalized, i.e., normal treatment. (Whiteley 1992, pp. 3–4)

As a final example, the surprisingly good *Wikipedia* entry for 'psychedelic music' refers to its sonic showcasing of 'a wildly colourful palette' and suggests a '"magic carpet" of sound' as an umbrella phrase for the genre ('Psychedelic Rock'). John Lennon himself told George Martin that he wished to 'smell the sawdust' and wanted the music to 'swirl' in 'Being for the Benefit of Mr. Kite!' (Emerick and Massey 2006, p. 167).

These formularies for musical psychedelia must be taken in context, of course. With today's recording techniques and the widespread, routine use of synthesized sounds, a great deal of twenty-first-century pop music could be construed in some way as psychedelic. This was not the case in 1967, however, in an era when four-track recording techniques and the association of 'flower power' and colourful imagery with LSD and other spiritual intoxicants were commonplace. In fact, a song like 'Lucy in the Sky with Diamonds' seems to offer a veritable primer of psychedelic rhetoric. Even the most conventional observer understands that the rich and colourful imagery of 'Lucy in the Sky with Diamonds' communicates something otherworldly, something psychedelic. MacDonald suggests, quite beautifully, that 'Lucy in the Sky with Diamonds' 'circles lazily on melodic eddies in an iridescent stream of sound' (MacDonald 1994, p. 190). And Lennon's lyrics seem almost as though they were inspired by some of the scholarly studies of LSD visions. Dr Albert Hofmann, the discoverer-synthesizer of LSD-25 and the first person actually to 'trip' on it, believes that

> The true importance of LSD and related hallucinogens lies in their capacity to shift the wavelength setting of the receiving 'self', and thereby to evoke alterations in reality consciousness. This ability to allow different, new pictures of reality to arise, this truly cosmogonic power, makes the cultish worship of hallucinogenic plants as sacred drugs understandable. (Hofmann 1983, p. 197)

In *The Little Book of Acid*, Cam Cloud offers the following complementary description:

> Acid amplifies all of the senses to create a sensory experience of extraordinary intensity, richness, subtlety, and depth. An endlessly fascinating world of new detail opens to the eye. Previously overlooked facets of light, shading, and texture become apparent. Everything seems to be in motion: trees breathe, walls ripple, and normally dull surfaces sparkle and vibrate. Often the environment appears to arrange itself into a perfectly harmonious composition like a great work of art. (Cloud 1999, p. 9)

Largely because of such bracing and innovative attempts to recreate the aural thrill of the LSD experience, psychedelic music enacted the most significant revolution within popular culture and produced some of its most brilliant and most influential musical artefacts, both in terms of their enduring appeal and of their influence on subsequent musical evolution.

'Within You Without You'

After having his first contribution to the new album, 'It's Only a Northern Song', rejected by his bandmates (it later appeared on the Beatles' *Yellow Submarine* soundtrack), George Harrison returned to the studio on 15 March 1967 with a work that was heavily influenced by his recent study of Indian music and Hinduism.

'Within You Without You' uses an Indian scale (one akin to the C-Mixolydian mode in which the song is normally transcribed) and a lazy metre that wanders into and out of 3/4, 4/4 and 5/4 throughout the piece. With the exception of the violins and cellos that strain to imitate the sounds of the dilruba, the instrumentation in 'Within You Without You' is entirely south Asian: tabla, tambura, dilruba, suvar mandal and Harrison's sitar. None of the other Beatles plays on this track.

Apart from some makeshift efforts to dampen the instrumental sound, the use of Automatic Double-Tracking (ADT) to enhance Harrison's voice, close-miking and adjustments to signal processing 'to make things a bit more exciting sonically', no special effects were used on the recording (Emerick and Massey 2006, pp. 179–80). Harrison's song is heavily psychedelic, however. The incorporation of Eastern instruments and musical motifs creates an immediate, otherworldly environment distant in both time and space and a transcendence of everyday experience – for the Western listener at least. The drone of the tambura depicts aurally the energy with which all things animate and inanimate seem to buzz during a psychedelic session. The bends and swerves of the dilruba suggest sound in the midst of transformation, melting from one note to another, and paint 'dark, swirling colors and images' during the instrumental breaks (Madow and Sobul 1992, p. 35). The shifting metres of the piece destabilize regular, everyday tempo and introduce a drifting timelessness into the composition.

'Within You Without You' has been both praised and attacked. While she clearly appreciates the track, Whiteley, quite oddly, situates it outside of the psychedelic tradition altogether, contrasting it with the psychedelic evocations of side one, and suggesting that it references a cannabis rather than a psychedelic high (Whiteley 1992, pp. 50–51). Tim Riley offers one of the harshest critiques of the song when he suggests that 'listening to "Within You Without You" some twenty years later, it's hard to believe that lines such as "Life flows on within you and without you" were taken seriously – it's now the most dated piece on the record' (Riley 1989, p. 220), going so far as to argue that 'Harrison's track could easily have been left off with little or no effect to the larger idea at work on the record' (Ibid., p. 221).[6] But for many other listeners, 'Within You Without You' *has* been appreciated as the core of *Sgt. Pepper*. Perhaps closest to our estimation is MacDonald's assessment that:

> WITHIN YOU WITHOUT YOU is the conscience of *Sergeant Pepper's Lonely Hearts Club Band*: the necessary sermon that comes with the community singing. Described by those with no grasp of the ethos of 1967 as a blot on a classic LP, WITHIN YOU WITHOUT YOU is central to the outlook that shaped *Sergeant Pepper* – a view justifiable then, as it is justifiable now. (MacDonald 1994, p. 194)

Walter Everett similarly elevates the song when he acknowledges its philosophical range, incorporating the key psychedelic (and Hindu) concepts of a deeper reality

---

6   Mark Ellen more recently comes to a similar, though more nuanced conclusion: 'When I discovered years later that there had been two singles but that George Martin ... had allowed them to be sliced off ... I began rather pathetically to fantasize a reworked running-order and the songs I would drop to include them – Rita obviously, and probably Within You Without You, which I listened to intently for only the second time this morning, though to lose it would detach a spiritual dimension that seems so central to the package' (Ellen 2002, pp. 103–4).

behind the illusion of ordinary existence, its affirmation of love and of the existence of a transcendent reality both within and without the individual. He concludes his discussion by remarking that 'The seriousness of musical purpose gives the track much more weight than the gospel-sermon "The Word"' (Everett 1999, pp. 111–12).

So, unnecessary and directionless bit of *naïveté* or philosophical crystallization of the entire album? That Harrison's composition draws heavily on Indian sounds exemplifies psychedelia's rejection of many things Western in favour of what it saw as the exoticism of Eastern spiritual traditions of psychic liberation and transcendence, literatures and soundscapes. In fact, Art Kleps, one of the most energetic and complex of the early psychedelic pioneers living with Timothy Leary at the famous Millbrook Estate, offers one of the best accounts of psychedelic music in the following passage:

> Indian music is perfect for stabilizing a high because it in no way encourages you to notice the passage of time – or better, to notice that time has stopped passing and instead is sort of loitering around shooting the shit with space. When seriality re-establishes itself, as it were, taste seems to depend entirely upon what kind of a trip you are on. (Kleps 1975, p. 26)

Opening up side two of the vinyl recording, 'Within You Without You' provides a stabilizing core, both musically and lyrically, for the rest of the album. As a whole, *Sgt. Pepper* looks both within and without, with introspective songs exploring the personal mind and its psychedelic evolution (*within*), while the more outward-looking songs critique the social world beyond the mind (*without*). Of course, the whole point of the album is to bridge these apparently 'alternative' worlds via psychedelic experience, the realization that 'life flows on within you *and* without you' [emphasis added]. The album is about fixing holes, to be sure, but it is also crucially about opening oneself up to one's world, perhaps even by creating holes that result in a permeable self capable of letting life flow on within and without.

The dynamic of within/without also characterizes the bracing juxtapositions the album makes between songs of hallucinogenic and surreality ('Lucy in the Sky with Diamonds', 'Being for the Benefit of Mr. Kite!', etc.) and those of incredible ordinariness ('She's Leaving Home', 'When I'm Sixty-Four', etc.), managing to synthesize both worlds into one magnificent unifying moment. Such juxtapositions also figure prominently in the sounds of the album, with the cultural and aural exoticism of 'Within You Without You' giving way to the homely and conventional vaudeville of a dance hall ensemble with prominent clarinet in 'When I'm Sixty-Four'. The same could be said of the album's chronological scope, reflecting the mid-1960s context of the Summer of Love, as well as visiting both the past (in the guise of the Victorian personae of the Beatles' Sgt. Pepper's Lonely Hearts Club Band, the anachronistic circus of Mr. Kite, and perhaps even the ancient India evoked by 'Within You Without You') and the future ('it's getting better', 'when I'm sixty-four'). The nods to live performance and a world outside Abbey Road Studios (without), indicated by audience sounds and even barnyard animals, coexist with soundscapes possible only inside the insulated world of the recording studio (within). The Beatles fuse all of these worlds – the ordinary, the extraordinary, the present, past and future, the old and the young, auditorium and recording studio, the enlightened and not-yet-enlightened – into a comprehensive musical examination of the human condition. Furthermore, the Beatles exacerbate all such distinctions when, on the album's opening track, they nearly invite the audience into their homes: 'You're such a lovely audience ... we'd love to take you home'.[7] *Revolver*, of course, opens with only a faint gesture of live performance; *Sgt. Pepper* maintains and plays with effects of live versus recorded music throughout the album, consolidating, perhaps, the work's overall teasing relationship (both both/and and either/or) with relationships previously imagined as dichotomous.

More importantly, perhaps, for the present discussion are Harrison's lyrics. The psychedelic heart of *Sgt. Pepper's Lonely Hearts Club Band* lies in its reports of introspective journeys, its looking within and resulting insistence on the fluidity and interrelationship of all things, probably the hallmark of psychedelic visionary experiences. Written in the form of a recollected conversation, Harrison sings of the 'space between us all' that arises because of ego games and the 'wall[s] of illusion' behind which we often seek to hide. The singer urges his interlocutor to break through these walls and eclipse this interpersonal space: 'it's all within yourself ... and life flows on within you and without you'. Timothy Leary and his associates, who based their psychedelic manual on the *Tibetan Book of the Dead*, intone similar concepts: 'The life flow is whirling through you. An endless parade of pure form and sounds, dazzling, brilliant, ever-changing ... Enjoy the feeling of complete one-ness with all life and all matter. The glowing radiance is a reflection of your own consciousness' (Leary, Metzner and Alpert 1964, pp. 127, 133). Dr Hofmann succinctly expresses the clinical explanation of this phenomenon:

> In the LSD state the boundaries between the experiencing self and the outer world more or less disappear, depending on the depth of inebriation ... In an auspicious case, the new ego feels blissfully united with the objects of the outer world and consequently also with its fellow beings. This experience of deep oneness with the exterior world can even intensify to a feeling of the self being one with the universe. (Hofmann 1983, pp. 197–8)

Cohen draws similar conclusions from patients' LSD experiences when he notes, 'We found that ego boundaries tended to dissolve and that the separation between the self and the external world became tenuous and sometimes nonexistent' (Cohen 1966, p. 42), and also when he summarizes: '... self-identity is completely lost, and the self and that which is outside the self fuse. The ordinary subject-object relationships disappear, along with the conventional separateness of the external object' (Ibid., p. 96). And John Coltrane, to cite one final example from jazz history, reported that during his first trip he 'perceived the interrelationships of all life forms' (Lee and Shlain 1985, p. 79). Within you and without you for sure.

---

7   Without straining at this theme, we might even include the fact that part of 'Fixing a Hole' was recorded at Regent Sound Studio, not at Abbey Road Studios – in other words, within and without Abbey Road.

'Within You'

Speaking optimistically about LSD's potential in psychotherapy, Dr Stanislav Grof, one of the leading pioneers in LSD psychotherapy, affirmed that 'it does not seem to be an exaggeration to say that psychedelics, used responsibly and with proper caution, would be for psychiatry what the microscope is for biology and medicine or the telescope is for astronomy' (Grof 1980, p. 12). Indeed, the Beatles might be said to perform a lyrical psychoanalysis of their own times, identifying problems while also proposing solutions to the era's dominant social crises. Throughout 'Within You Without You', Harrison distinguishes between those who 'find peace of mind' and those 'who hide themselves behind a wall of illusion [and] never glimpse the truth'. In so doing, he suggests that those who 'see' that 'we're all one, and [that] life flows on within you and without you' have achieved a more desirable level of consciousness. They have awakened to life's 'truth'. Leary, too, exhorts readers to 'Wake up! ... You'll see ... You'll be reborn!' in *High Priest* (Leary 1995, p. 285), and the Beatles anchor much of *Sgt. Pepper* as a whole in this psychedelic imperative through their experimental plumbings of non-awakened consciousness and their attempts to see the world anew, with a socially conscious vision born of psychedelic insight. Both before and since *Sgt. Pepper*, psychedelic rock has used alarm clocks, chimes, bells, effects of clocks ticking and other effects to signal such psychedelic awakenings. There are Donovan's 'Sunshine Superman' and 'Hurdy Gurdy Man', the Rolling Stones' 'Something Happened to Me Yesterday', the Chambers Brothers' 'Time Has Come Today', It's a Beautiful Day's 'Time Is', the Steve Miller Band's 'Fly Like an Eagle' and Pink Floyd's 'Time' and 'Echoes' – to name a few instances in which rock artists have used this device. And Jimi Hendrix replaces the 'tick tock' sound of a clock with his riffing reversal of 'tock tick', which kicks off 'Purple Haze', with its unforgettable lyric 'lately things just don't seem the same'.

The Beatles incorporate two such moments on *Sgt. Pepper*, one with the crowing cock that opens 'Good Morning, Good Morning' and, of course, the ringing alarm clock in the middle of 'A Day in the Life'. The latter track also contains a scene of awakening in McCartney's 'middle eight': 'Woke up, fell out of bed'. Moreover, 'She's Leaving Home' begins with an indirect allusion to 'waking up': 'Wednesday morning at five o'clock as the day begins'. Other songs on *Sgt. Pepper* refer to the end of the day. The title song encourages us to 'sit back and let the evening go'. 'With a Little Help from My Friends' contains the lines 'How do I feel by the end of the day' and 'What do you see when you turn out the light' (a subtle anticipation of the infamous 'I'd love to turn you on' in the album's concluding 'A Day in the Life'). 'When I'm Sixty-Four' continues this 'lights out' theme when McCartney sings that he could mend a fuse 'when your lights are gone'. Bringing light to the darkness is what 'waking up' is all about. The bizarre visions of 'Being for the Benefit of Mr. Kite!' occur at night, and conclude side one on what some have understood as nightmarish visions, perhaps the internal drama of the 'dark night of the soul'.

The album's most explicit injunction to 'wake up' is, of course, the heavily psychedelic 'Good Morning, Good Morning'. After the rooster's crying overture, the first thing the listener hears are the significantly altered sounds of brass instruments, which were beefed up with ADT, flanged, limited, and enhanced through placement of microphones in the very bells of the saxophones – all at the behest of Lennon who didn't want the horns to sound 'ordinary' (Emerick and Massey 2006, p. 174). Lots of ADT was used for the lead vocal, as well, and on McCartney's Indian-flavoured guitar solo (reminiscent of the lead guitar work he performed on Harrison's 'Taxman' in 1966). The shifting metres in the song (4/4, 5/4 and 3/4) once again disrupt normal time and the overdubbed animal noises from EMI's sound effects collection complete the track's list of psychedelic musical touches. Far from enacting 'the constriction and conformity that aggrieves "A Day in the Life"', as Riley claims, 'Good Morning, Good Morning' itself constitutes a drama, a dialogue between the enlightened Beatles and a hypothetical workaday wage slave (Riley 1989, p. 223). But, overall, the song surges out of the doldrums towards awakening and transcendence, and 'the shriek from the guitar after that last line' of the song is not by any means, as Riley maintains, 'a howl of neurotic pain' (Ibid., p. 224). Henry David Thoreau's strategies in *Walden* provide a model. Throughout his spiritual autobiography, Thoreau yearns to alert people to the various ways in which they are wasting their lives by becoming the 'tools of their tools' and conducting their lives at a breakneck pace. As he notes in a passage that could almost stand as the definitive gloss on 'Good Morning, Good Morning': 'I do not propose to write an ode to dejection, but to brag as lustily as chanticleer in the morning, standing on his roost, if only to wake my neighbors up' (Thoreau 1983, p. 128). Indeed, the Beatles juxtapose phrases characterizing what appears to be a nightmarish existence ('Nothing to do to save his life', 'Going to work, don't want to go, feeling low down', 'Everybody knows there's nothing doing, everything is closed it's like a ruin') with exhortations that 'it's up to you', 'you're on your own' and 'glad that I'm here'. In other words, the 'I' of the song eventually internalizes the optimistic view that, while 'everyone you see is half asleep', he, at least, has heard the cock crow and is rousing from an existential slumber. By the final lines of the song, the entire ethos has surged upward. Far from the slavish despair implied in the first lines, the speaker has replaced a vision of everybody half asleep with one in which 'everyone you see is full of life', an exclamation ('glad that I'm here'), a reassurance that he's now 'in gear' and a hope of meeting a woman. It may well be this person's vision that comments wearily on the despairing world of 'A Day in the Life', but one which still desires to wake you up from your own deathlike dream. Bragging, like Thoreau, but ultimately with the goal of awakening the world and turning it on.

    Other songs on *Sgt. Pepper* approach interpersonal issues with the confidence that things are indeed improving. Although it contains sparse psychedelic musical coding (apart from Harrison's tambura), 'Getting Better', like 'Fixing a Hole', relates another way in which insights gained from LSD use can repair 'holes'. The lines 'Me used to be angry young man' and 'I used to be cruel to my woman, I beat her and kept her apart from the things that she loved' both acknowledge the speaker's realization of an unenlightened and cruel facet of his (hopefully) former self. By April 1962, before the Beatles had even sung 'I Want to Hold Your Hand' on the *Ed Sullivan Show*, Hollywood heartthrob and sophisticate Cary Grant had already taken 72 LSD trips and testified that, of all therapeutic techniques he had sought, only LSD enabled him to exorcize his personal demons. As Grant said as he was being interviewed while sitting on the pink submarine that served as *Operation Petticoat*'s principal set:

I have been born again ... I was horrendous. I had to face things about myself which I never admitted, which I didn't know were there. Now I know that I hurt every woman I ever loved. I was an utter fake, a self-opinionated bore, a know-all who knew very little. I found I was hiding behind all kinds of defenses, hypocrisies and vanities. I had to get rid of them layer by layer. The moment when your conscious meets your subconscious is a hell of a wrench. With me there came a day when I saw the light. (Quoted in Stevens 1987, p. 65)

As extravagant as Grant's claims may seem, they mesh not only with other first-hand testimonies, but with British LSD researcher Karl Jansen, who equates LSD experiences with the theoretical goals of psychoanalysis, which generate healing by 'bringing deep contents of the unconscious into consciousness' (Eagles 1997). In such cases, the journey within results in a more honest and loving without.

While its primary drift is affirmative, with an emphasis on 'fixing' rather than 'counting' holes, and a recognition of the unifying spiritual force unifying all existence and offering a vision capable of unifying diverse people and ideas, 'Within You Without You' also diagnoses and castigates the perceptions and values of people who 'hide themselves behind a wall of illusion' and, as a result, 'never glimpse the truth'. Like those in 'Rain' who 'run and hide their heads', who 'might as well be dead', these souls wander in a realm of illusion, a diminution of life both dangerous and pathetic. Similarly, Harrison's lyrics also target the people who 'gain the world and lose their soul'. Just what can Tim Riley and others mean when they refer to the song as dated, unnecessary, foolish? To suggest such would be to maintain that such lessons, the foundations of the world's great spiritual traditions and texts as well as the core of the thinking of the Buddha, Jesus Christ, Henry David Thoreau, Mahatma Gandhi, Mother Teresa and probably the majority of Nobel Peace Prize laureates, to name only a few, are equally naïve and bankrupt. It would require not only an ignorance of the ethos of 1967, as MacDonald argues, but a disdain for the entire tradition of human striving and quests for transcendence, specifically realized at the centre of the psychedelic tradition. Such a perspective might even reveal the very mindset that LSD in all its psychotherapeutic manifestations was intended to redeem. As Hofmann puts it in his autobiography:

In LSD inebriation the accustomed world view undergoes a deep-seated transformation and disintegration. Connected with this is a loosening or even suspension of the I-you barrier. Patients who are bogged down in an egocentric problem cycle can thereby be helped to release themselves from their fixation and isolation. (Hofmann 1983, p. 48)

Of course, 'Within You Without You' weaves within its lyrics a series of more optimistic, affirmative positions, focused on love, transformation, cosmic oneness and the interrelationships of all existence. On love, the song reaffirms its communal spirit by stressing that love is something, not to give or receive, but to share, a perspective vaguely reminiscent of McCartney's romantic 'Here, There and Everywhere' from *Revolver*. And, as in 'With a Little Help from My Friends', this sharing involves a unified vision of the human community, as suggested by the phrases 'when we find it', 'To try our best to hold it' and 'With our love we could save the world'. While some critics may find this naïve and even sappy (kudos to Elvis Costello for recognizing there's nothing too funny about peace, love and understanding), such powerful optimism has frequently characterized famous moments in LSD history. During Allen Ginsberg's first LSD trip outside of the research institute in Palo Alto, he was so convinced that the psychedelic experience could save the world that he wanted to get US President John F. Kennedy, Soviet Premier Nikita Khrushchev and Chairman Mao Tse-Tung of The People's Republic of China on a telephone conference call, believing that, if they could only turn on, the world might be lovingly coaxed back from the brink of nuclear destruction (Lee and Shlain 1985, p. 78).[8] Some of the most influential advocates and theoreticians of psychedelic experiences have offered their own visions of a future psychedelic panacea, sometimes in the form of warnings. Terence McKenna, for example, believed that the 'Archaic Revival' (his umbrella term for the return, through psychedelic experiences, to a more profound relationship with our environment) 'is a clarion call to recover our birthright, however uncomfortable that may make us. It is a call to realize that life lived in the absence of the psychedelic experience upon which primordial shamanism is based is life trivialized, life denied', partly 'because encounters with psychedelic plants throw into question the entire worldview of the dominator culture' (McKenna 1992, pp. 252, xx). Cohen agrees with McKenna when he affirms that 'the experience called hallucinogenic will play a role in leading us into the future' (Cohen 1966, p. 60). Dr John Lilly, one of the most ambitious LSD researchers, and the first to study the intelligence of dolphins under the influence of the drug, endorses LSD voyaging in nearly apocalyptic terms. 'It is my firm belief', he asserts, 'that the experience of higher states of consciousness is necessary for survival of the human species. If we can each experience at least the lower levels of Satori, there is hope that we won't blow up the planet or otherwise eliminate life as we know it' (Lilly 1972, p. 3). We will conclude this list of testimonials with one final passage from Malden Bishop's account in which he echoes the more messianic as well as the more scientific passages above. According to him, his LSD experience taught him that:

> There is no problem love cannot solve ... Love is the only force which can save mankind from the inevitable destruction of hate. There can be no thermonuclear war where there is love. There can be no poverty where there is love. There can be no lines of color, of creed, of nationality where there is love. There can be no misery, filth, hate, pain where there is love. This is all so simple, so plain, that it seems incredible that man in this so-called modern age of the 20th Century does not understand it, and does not proceed to practice it. (Bishop 1963, p. 139)

'Without You'

'Within You Without You' also anchors the stream of social criticism common to psychedelic culture that pervades *Sgt. Pepper*. Significantly, the song opens on a note of communality, sharing and discussion: 'We were talking'. Harrison's lyrical overture

---

8   There is fairly strong evidence suggesting that John F. Kennedy actually did take LSD during his Presidency, perhaps resulting in his fierce struggles with military brass and, if any dimension of some conspiracy theories is true, his assassination. See Lee and Shlain 1985, pp. 85–6 for a more thorough discussion.

differs strikingly from others on the album, which begin with individualistic gestures: picturing oneself on a boat on a river, fixing a hole, a young woman standing alone at the top of a staircase, an advert for a circus, thoughts about retirement. Harrison's song captures a shared moment of exploration, of mutual investigation and togetherness. As MacDonald notes, 'the countercultural spirit of 1967–69 was essentially communal, and the Beatles were, for a while, convinced that the coming Arcadia would be tranquilly collective' (MacDonald 1994, pp. 196–7). Nick Bromell also catches this drift when he notes that 'with rich historical allusiveness, the album's music and its graphics required listeners to locate themselves in a flow of time, to experience themselves living in a drama shared by other generations' (Bromell 2000, p. 111). 'Within You Without You' reflects just such a spirit, with the exotic instrumentation, metre and tonality providing both a bracing and a soothing aural environment for such utopian speculation. Whatever world we might imagine, the song suggests, it must be one of openness, discussion and shared values. This vision is apparent elsewhere on *Sgt. Pepper*, in particular in 'With a Little Help from My Friends', in which the singer appreciates his friends' help in getting by and, responding to the Jefferson Airplane, both wants and needs 'Somebody to Love'.

Elaborating on ideas introduced in *Revolver*'s 'Taxman' and 'Eleanor Rigby', however, the Beatles also draw on their psychedelic experiences to reinvigorate rock culture's critique of the status quo, the people who, in 'Rain', 'run and hide their heads' and 'might as well be dead'. The openness and dialogue of 'Within You Without You' and 'With a Little Help from My Friends' stand in direct opposition to the communicational disaster presented most dramatically in 'She's Leaving Home'. With its polarized cast of characters and emphasis on a failure to communicate – 'Leaving the note that she hoped would say more', 'What did we do that was wrong' – 'She's Leaving Home' stages such a generational and communicational impasse that it seems to squash all chances of 'getting better'. The Beatles' attention to the bereft parents and the lives of self-denial they've led for their child might mute their culpability. And yet, their infantilization of the daughter, 'our baby's gone', while endearing, would not have been experienced as loving by the young woman. Moreover, their grief rather quickly turns to defensiveness and blaming, as they ask 'Why would she treat us so thoughtlessly' and 'How could she do this to me', suggesting that their own neediness prevents them from understanding their daughter's concerns. Since she's been 'living alone for so many years', the daughter's escape moves her in the direction of some kind of greater intimacy, whoever this 'man from the motor trade' may be! Her parents' belief that giving her 'everything money could buy' helps to generate the song's clever pun on 'buy' and 'bye', and, as the Beatles reminded their fans three years earlier, 'money can't buy [you] love'. This young woman, like the 'refugee from a wealthy family' in Joni Mitchell's 1970 tune 'Rainy Night House', needs to see 'who in the world [s]he might be'.

As Art Kleps notes, while one may need to 'leave home', literally or metaphorically, as a result of psychedelic insight, the rupture needs not be burdened with guilt and recriminations:

The major insights gained from psychedelic experience are utterly at odds with the myths and fantasies of institutional life, and it is most often not a matter of choice that 'turning on' and 'tuning in' are swiftly followed by 'dropping out'. It isn't a matter of carefree abandon … but simply psychic incompatibility with the old order, once certain illusions have been shattered. (Kleps 1975, p. 63)

Apart from the rich, Beach Boyish vocal harmonies that 'soar angelic' (last heard in *Revolver*'s hallucinogenically suggestive 'Doctor Robert'), there is little of psychedelic musical interest in 'She's Leaving Home'. Nonetheless, while we cannot be certain the young woman in the song has necessarily 'turned on' or 'tuned in', her departure resonates with the sense of displacement and the longing for 'something new' characteristic of the late 1960s. In fact, the Beatles' melodrama actually recounts a common occurrence, probably on both sides of the Atlantic. In their sensationalistic study *LSD on Campus* (published a year before the release of *Sgt. Pepper)*, Young and Hixson shed further light on 'leaving home':

> The files of psychiatrists, like those of federal authorities and local law officials everywhere, are beginning to bulge with such sad cases and others – like that of the Midwestern girl who was inspired by the revelations of LSD to quit school to tour the country with her boyfriend and seemed to her mother 'like a different person inside' – which seems most tragic to the parents who see their cherished hopes turn to fog. (Young and Hixson 1966, p. 118)

'Shes' and 'hes' were 'leaving home' in droves, seeking new communities of like-minded people who were 'turned on' by their own psychedelic insight before they ever heard *Sgt. Pepper*.

The Beatles refuse to allow this to become a shouting match or diatribe, however, and they instead visit the so-called 'generation gap' with a tenderness perhaps unique to this song. We might fault the parents believing that giving their daughter 'everything [that] money could buy' would guarantee her loyalty, but we also feel their confusion and grief when the mother cries out and breaks down, and especially when they ask 'what did we do that was wrong' and, later, when they say 'we didn't know it was wrong'. If, in Buffalo Springfield's psychedelic classic 'For What It's Worth', whatever is 'happening here … ain't exactly clear', even to the hip and young, the Beatles put themselves in the position of somebody outside the swirl of the counterculture. And yet, as was the case with *Revolver*'s 'Eleanor Rigby', no Beatles play instruments on 'She's Leaving Home'.[9] Both tunes address loneliness and alienation, but might indicate more about the relationship of the Beatles themselves to the thematics and dramatis personae of the songs, suggesting their distance from the pathos of these dreary domestic dramas.

Three other songs from *Sgt. Pepper*, 'With a Little Help from My Friends', 'When I'm Sixty-Four' and 'Lovely Rita', initiate dialogue with others by posing a series of nervous questions about acceptance ('Would you stand up and walk out on me?'), all the while fearing the answers they might receive. Like Sgt. Pepper's Lonely Hearts Club Band, the protagonists of these tunes would like to be loved by someone or get some assurance that others will not desert them. The singer in 'When I'm Sixty-Four', for instance, worries that his partner might leave him when he gets up

---

9 Just as a bit of trivia, there are four Beatles songs on which no member of the group plays an instrument, the other two being 'The Inner Light' and 'Good Night'.

in years. However, the track's perky vaudevillian atmosphere, McCartney's weirdly youthful lead vocal (artificially sped up during the recording process – Emerick and Massey 2006, p. 137) and the singer's idealized happy and comfortable future, replete with a summer cottage and grandchildren, point to fulfilling and harmonious golden years if the song's couple can maintain their intimacy. In the following track, even the vaguely uncomfortable moment of sitting with 'Lovely Rita' on a sofa with her sister(s) does not dampen the ardour of desire in the singer's mind. Far from mourning 'about the love that's gone so cold', these songs forge ahead towards love bonds, confident that in such encounters lies a possible key to happiness. As Whiteley notes, 'When I'm Sixty-Four' and 'Lovely Rita' 'take a more pragmatic approach to life. The solution to problems, as demonstrated in the songs, is not through drugs or meditation, but through a comically casual and good-natured acceptance of life' (Whiteley 1992, p. 53).

There is something else going on in this latter McCartney composition, however. It is only with 'Lovely Rita' (and his work on 'A Day in the Life') that McCartney plays extensively with psychedelic coding. Pianos heavy with echo, subtle sound effects nearly buried in the extensive instrumental and vocal layering (such as the famous popping cork that accompanies the words 'over dinner'), sped-up vocals, and the 33-second jam with which the song concludes, awash with psychedelic buzz, all contribute to the track's strong psychedelic musicality. Of special note from a technological point of view is the 'wobble' on George Martin's piano solo, created through the placement of some editing tape on the guide rollers of EMI's period tape machine causing the tape to 'wow and flutter' (Emerick and Massey 2006, p. 171). Coincidentally, it was during the recording of 'Lovely Rita' that a tripping Lennon took his infamous walk on the roof of the Abbey Road Studios after Martin suggested that the seemingly woozy Beatle get some air (Ibid., p. 172). We might conclude that the apparent merger of psychedelic musical rhetoric with the pragmatic 'comically casual and good-natured acceptance of life' of the singer's story suggests that, while neither drugs nor meditation are likely to solve mundane, everyday problems, the insights gained from psychedelic experiences often translate into the most domestic contexts, redeeming the simplest and most intimate ranges of human life. MacDonald comments on the song's ethos of generosity, noting:

> ... a silly song in many ways, but imbued with an exuberant interest in life that lifts the spirits, dispersing self-absorption. (Based on a friendly encounter with a traffic warden called Meta Davis in Garden Road, St John's Wood, the lyric began as a satire on authority with its heroine a hate-figure – until, in keeping with the warm mood of the time, McCartney decided 'it'd be better to love her'.) (MacDonald 1994, p. 190)

In 'Within You Without You', Harrison talks about love to be shared and trying our best 'to hold it there'. Throughout *Sgt. Pepper*, especially in 'With a Little Help from My Friends', 'She's Leaving Home' and 'When I'm Sixty-Four', the Beatles realize the difficulty of holding on to love, of staying in the kind of conversation that can heal discord and transcend differences. The key, as Harrison puts it, is finding peace of mind within yourself and then, necessarily, by seeing beyond yourself and maintaining vital contact with others. We might have to fix holes in order to discover ourselves, but we cannot remain holed up, alienated, like so many Eleanor Rigbys, from the vital flow of existence. *Sgt. Pepper*, then, pays special attention to the ways in which psychedelic insight can illuminate the most homey and ordinary facets of the human condition, maybe even making 'this trivial world sublime'.

Sublime, in a word, sums up 'A Day in the Life'. The album's concluding track opens with the sound of Lennon's acoustic guitar gradually taking shape out of the sonic mist of the fading audience applause for the reprise of 'Sgt. Pepper's Lonely Hearts Club Band'. The quiet strumming, soon joined by McCartney's emotionless piano chords, backs the singer's echo-laden, dark and affectless reflections on the first of three news stories dealing, respectively, with death in a car crash, war and mysterious holes in Blackburn, Lancashire. Lennon's voice is distant and alien, and the shift in tone from the preceding tracks on the LP is aurally palpable. Geoff Emerick, who engineered the album, recalls that when Lennon began his first take of the piece 'the raw emotion in his voice made the hairs on the back of my neck stand up' (Emerick and Massey 2006, p. 148). The instrumental layering commences in the second verse with the entry of Starr's active, but electronically thickened kit work. In order to achieve a distancing effect from the drums, Starr tuned his tom-toms down significantly, leaving the top skins slack. Emerick further highlighted and distorted the normal sound of the toms by removing the bottom heads and miking them from underneath. He also severely limited the sound in the drum premix, 'which made the cymbals sound huge' (Ibid., p. 149). These technical tricks, along with Lennon's and McCartney's encouragement to Starr to embellish his work more on this track, resulted in the prominent, spooky percussion that adds to the slightly unnerving ambiance of the finished piece. The two 24-bar orchestral interludes have been extensively treated. Suffice it to say here that the controlled cacophony of the aleatoric, rising glissandos transcends whatever theme or meaning the surrounding bars may imply. The second orchestral bridge, into which Mal Evans's counting from an earlier take bleeds, suggests a kind of blast off into madness. And Lennon's distorted, soaring 'ahs', which follow McCartney's lines about having 'a smoke' and going 'into a dream', not only evoke a light and airy nightmarish condition (not an oxymoron in a psychedelic state), but allow the musicians to float from the E-major tonality of McCartney's sequence back to the original key of G major. Finally, the stupendous, sustained E-major chord with which the song concludes provides a powerful exclamation point to the album's final track and to *Sgt. Pepper* as a whole, as well as a kind of morbid, psychedelic, musical punctuation to the 'bad trip' motifs that immediately precede it. The drug references in 'A Day in the Life' – 'He blew his mind out in a car', 'I'd love to turn you on' and the second narrator's smoke-induced 'dream' – obviously support a psychedelic reading of the song, though the last two phrases, both written by McCartney, ostensibly refer to marijuana rather than LSD (Everett 1999, p 117). Nonetheless, the intense personal reflections of the newspaper reader in Lennon's verse and the dream sequence introduced by McCartney's bridge transport the listener out of the ordinary world. The electronic echoing and distancing effects serve to expand the musical space of the piece, and the quickened and stumbling metre of McCartney's segment, with bars of 2/4 interspersed within the section to suggest the singer's haste in getting on his way, create a sense of both expanding and contracting time within the five-minute composition. Perhaps the most noteworthy psychedelic element in the piece, however, are the two orchestral crescendos in which the chaotic buzz of the aleatoric gestures threatens to break down all distinctions among musical forms and meaning – a sonic representation of Leary's description of the peak of a psychedelic session, when the subject 'experiences direct sensation. The raw "is-ness". He sees not objects, but patterns of light waves. He hears not "music" or "meaningful" sound, but acoustic waves. He is struck with the sudden revelation that all sensation and perception are based on wave vibrations' (Leary, Metzner and Alpert 1964, p. 61).

'A Day in the Life' views the world both from within and without, with two different sections dramatizing both a 'turned on' perspective (indeed, one that would also love to turn us on) and life driven by gaining the world and losing the soul. In this respect, 'A Day in the Life' resembles and refines the work done in 'Fixing a Hole' and 'Good Morning' and also revisits many of the dominant themes of 'Within You Without You'. We agree with MacDonald's assessment of 'A Day in the Life' as 'A song not of disillusionment with life itself but of disenchantment with the limits of mundane perception', which 'depicts the "real" world as an unenlightened construct that reduces, depresses, and ultimately destroys' (MacDonald 1994, p. 181). Everett makes much the same point in another important observation on 'A Day in the Life' in the context of the entire album. He asserts that, for the Beatles,

> ... a truly meaningful life can be had only when one is aware of one's self and one's surroundings and overcomes the status quo. 'A Day in the Life' represents the Beatles' wake-up call for whomever might be listening. The song is not merely a warning of an ashy apocalypse, as it has often been taken, but suggests that there is yet hope for the phoenix. (Everett 1999, p. 116)

Lennon's sighing expressions of 'oh boy' represent the weariness and sadness he experiences upon seeing daily scenes of tragedy, tabloid-addicted, mindless and sheepish behaviours, and simply absurd forms of life avoidance. Car crashes, counting holes, fighting wars and the whole panoply of life's dreary pageant, perhaps even like the lurid and, at times, horrific imagery of 'Being for the Benefit of Mr. Kite!', seem utterly pointless and unnecessary. Once one 'sees' properly, such lives of quiet desperation reveal a new dimension of pathetic spectacle. In other words, both 'Being for the Benefit of Mr. Kite!' and 'A Day in the Life', the two side-closing songs, represent visions of the mundane, unenlightened world from a psychedelically 'experienced' perspective. Thoreau, as well, claims to have seen his own times as similarly impossible and grotesque:

> What I have heard of Bramins sitting exposed to four fires and looking in the face of the sun; or hanging suspended, with their heads downward, over flames; or looking at the heavens over their shoulders 'until it becomes impossible for them to resume their natural position, while from the twist of the neck nothing but liquids can pass into the stomach'; or dwelling, chained for life, at the foot of a tree; or measuring with their bodies, like caterpillars, the breadth of vast empires; or standing on one leg on the tops of pillars – even these forms of conscious penance are hardly more incredible and astonishing than the scenes which I daily witness [in Concord]. (Thoreau 1983, pp. 46–7)

Once one has 'turned on', the world as previously accepted often becomes untenable and lurid, not unlike the swirling hoops of fire and somewhat menacing imagery of 'Mr. Kite'. As MacDonald maintains:

> Though clouded with sorrow and sarcasm, A DAY IN THE LIFE is as much an expression of mystic-psychedelic optimism as the rest of *Sergeant Pepper's Lonely Hearts Club Band*. The fact that it achieves its transcendent goal via a potentially disillusioning confrontation with the 'real' world is precisely what makes it so moving. (MacDonald 1994, p. 182)

The same could be said of 'Mr. Kite'.

We'd love to turn you on

Clearly, Paul McCartney, John Lennon and George Harrison all brought different levels of psychedelic insight and input to *Sgt. Pepper*. McCartney's creative stamp is dominant on the album and his musical sense is the broadest and the most flexible of the three. He seems equally comfortable writing and playing hard rock, introspective progressive pieces, beautifully harmonized ballads and vaudevillian throwbacks, all the while dabbling in psychedelic sounds and counterculture. Psychedelic musical rhetoric seems to have been a thematic tool for him, like other devices in his creative inventory, for constructing the Beatles' continually evolving brand of popular music. On the other hand, psychedelia had become an increasingly significant part of Lennon's musical and personal life. Synthetic intoxicants (like LSD) and television (including shows like *Meet the Wife*) played a large role in his everyday existence at Weybridge in 1966 and 1967 (Coleman 2000, pp. 433–6). Lennon was constantly looking for new sounds and ways to distort existing ones – like his own voice. His lyrics became more inward looking and surreal. His work on *Sgt. Pepper* is evidence of his interest in bringing insights gleaned from his drug experiences into the music he was writing and playing. Harrison's newly developed interest in India, south-Asian music and Hinduism shows as well. Like Lennon, Harrison sought to bring insights from his changing lifestyle into his music, and the single George Harrison composition that survives on the album is completely psychedelic in a spiritual sense, with the composer having graduated from LSD to Eastern religion and meditation. With Harrison's 'Within You Without You' at its core, *Sgt. Pepper* surges beyond all varieties of parochialism to consolidate its own vision of 'the interpenetration of all life forms'.

We considered titling this essay 'Never could see any way', a long-standing mishearing (by one of us!) of the record's famous run-out groove. The mishearing may be instructive, however, for this tape loop, often unheard on the vinyl recording, might represent the album's final testament to new ways of both seeing *and* being in tune with the forces of life flowing within and without us. Such 'seeing' and 'being' also constitute the only way of adapting to the consistently fluid nature of reality grasped during psychedelic experience and never forgotten, whether recollected from 20 years ago, 40 years ago, or sometime in the future.

Chapter 9

The whatchamucallit in the garden: *Sgt. Pepper* and fables of interference

John Kimsey

'The Beatles as nature intended': so reads the headline of a 1969 Apple Corps press release for the Beatles' then-new single, 'Get Back'. The song, we are assured, is 'a pure spring-time rock number' recorded 'as live as can be, in this electronic age'. Just in case someone might miss the point, the ad copy goes on to aver that 'Get Back' features a 'fab live guitar solo' and a flip side – 'Don't Let Me Down' – that is equally 'live'. Above all, we are told, the record involves 'no electronic whatchamucallit' (Beatles 2000, p. 319).

'Why the insistent tone?', one might ask; why should the Beatles, of all late-1960s pop groups, need to convince the public that their music is pure, rocking and, well, live? And yet such a question will seem naïve to anyone familiar with the standard-issue Beatles story arc, for that story sees the Beatles as desperately needing to 'get back' on the right track by this late point in their career. The rhetoric of the press release suggests much is indeed at stake. On one side, we have nature, purity and springtime; on the other, a nameless, apparently incomprehensible technology – the enemy, it would appear, of all things 'live'. Our heroes seem to have strayed far from the path of virtue. Where did things go so frightfully wrong?

Ian Shoales can tell you where. In his 1985 essay, 'Rock Music Today', he explains:

> Rock music used to be about dancing and parties, stolen kisses and fast cars. Then, in the late '60s, the Beatles pretended to be Sergeant Peppers' Lonely Hearts Club Band. The producer overorchestrated every track, the critics dubbed it a *concept* album and the beginning of the end had begun. (Shoales 1985, p. 126)

According to Shoales, the Beatles have a lot to answer for: 'All the Bad Boys are gone, and all the slow-talking platter pushers in the dead of night. The ghosts of rock and roll used to haunt us as we drove. But that's rock-and-roll history and it's over. The Beatles killed it' (Ibid., p. 125).

Now granted, Ian Shoales is not a real rock critic, he just plays one on television ('Ian Shoales' being the arch-pundit alter ego of satirist Merle Kessler).[1] Nonetheless, on this topic Shoales can be said to represent what Robert Christgau in 1981 called a growing 'constituency' – a core of real-life rock critics who have argued much the

---

same thing. Consider, for instance, the remarks of Lester Bangs, 'godfather of punk journalism' (Heylin 1992, p. 103): '*Sgt. Pepper*: first rock opera – Richard Goldstein was right, in his much-vilified review in the *New York Times* when it first came out, predicting that this record had the power to almost singlehandedly destroy rock 'n' roll' (Bangs 1981, p. 46).

For critics and fans such as these, *Sgt. Pepper* represents not so much a break*through* as a break *with* all that's good, true and rocking. It marks a fall from primal grace into pretence, production and self-consciousness. What is at stake of course is authenticity, that value seen, by wide consensus, as being key to rock – this, despite the fact that various camps disagree sharply over just what authenticity consists in. The unstable quality of the category is crystallized in Keir Keightley's image of the 'fault line':

> Emerging as it does out of the confluence of a number of distinct musical cultures, rock culture is seldom univocal in its beliefs, agendas or practices. Rock's complex genealogy means that there are a number of fault lines running through the center of rock, and these are perhaps most visible in the competing definitions of authenticity … Although all rock genres emphasize authenticity as their core value, not all understand and express authenticity in an identical fashion. (Keightley 2001, p. 136)

Sgt. Pepper can be seen as sitting precariously atop this fault line; hence the rhetoric of danger and destruction from critics like Bangs and Shoales.

According to Keightley, the concern with authenticity 'underlines a general anxiety about the status of the modern self' (Ibid., p. 134). This concern arose in the historical context of industrial capitalism among those who saw forces of mechanization, mass production and rapid social change posing a threat to 'community, tradition and meaning' (Ibid., p. 120). Over time, it developed into a vision and critique of 'mass society' centred on 'questions of mediation and alienation, authenticity and community, conformity and complicity', a set of questions which were eventually taken up by 'rock culture' itself (Ibid., p. 128). Rock also reproduced 'the critique's overarching emphasis on distinctive individualism as the key defence against … alienation' (Ibid.). 'In the twentieth century', Keightley contends, 'the alienation of music and musicians … has largely been understood in terms of mediation, of those things which interfere with an ideal of direct communication between artist and audience' (Ibid., p. 133).

It may seem ironic that such concerns lie at the centre of rock, the paradigm case of a mass-mediated popular music form. But rock lore holds that it is possible to consume the products of mass culture while remaining distinct from the mass. Other modern popular musics – for example urban folk – had held out the prospect (or fantasy) of an unalienated musical experience. The difference, says Keightley, is that where folk was a relatively uncommercial music, marginal to the sales charts, rock was founded on stars and millionsellers (Ibid., pp. 120–21). Nonetheless, rock lore frames the music, its makers and its fans as dedicated opponents of the commercial system. An aura of seriousness is said to attend the production and consumption of rock, such that, unlike pop, it stands uncompromised by commercialism and commodification (Ibid., p. 127). According to Keightley, 'negotiating the relationship between the "mass" and the "art" in mass art has been the distinguishing ideological project of rock culture since the 1960s' (Ibid., p. 109).

Paraphrasing Keightley, we might say that at the centre of this profoundly mass-mediated music lies a great anxiety about mediation itself – about the possibility that mediation will 'interfere' with 'the ideal of direct communication' and 'render musical expression of the self compromised or distorted' (Ibid., p. 134). Keightley adds that 'different segments of rock culture will define "interference" in very dissimilar ways' (Ibid.). I propose to survey a range of commentators – rock critics, academics, the Beatles themselves – each of whom invokes some pattern of interference as a frame for assessing *Sgt. Pepper*. In some accounts, the interference derives from recording technology; in others from division of labour; in others from the music's perceived audience, mode of expression or relation to regimes of taste and power. I suggest that a given commentator's evaluation of *Sgt. Pepper* will track closely with his/her definition of 'interference' in this sense. Beyond the accounts themselves, I am interested in what they suggest about rock ideology and its dominant modes of inscription. Such accounts mix 'aesthetic' with 'ethical' considerations (Ibid., p. 133), so I call them fables of interference.

People and machines

Often rock writers frame the interference problem as a man-versus-machine scenario in which the rocker fights to preserve his humanity in the oppressive environment of the recording studio. Charlie Gillett's well-known discussion of Elvis Presley in *The Sound of the City* is a case in point. Gillett paints Presley's 1954 Sun sessions as a triumph of genuine feeling and small-group interplay, in stark contrast to the RCA sessions which commenced in 1956:

> At Victor, under the supervision of Chet Atkins, Presley's records featured vocal groups, heavily electrified guitars, and drums, all of which were considered alien by both country and western audiences and by the audience for country rock music. Responding to these unfamiliar intrusions in his accompaniment, Presley's voice became much more theatrical and self-conscious as he sought to contrive excitement and emotion which he had seemed to achieve on his Sun records without any evident forethought. (Gillett 1996, p. 29)

Supervision, self-consciousness, busy arrangements, phoney excitement: such constructions have become familiar in rock lore, where they typically signify the sorry state into which authentic rock seems always in danger of sinking. Ian MacDonald, arguably the Beatles' most thoughtful popular chronicler, invokes this narrative frame in his account of the ten-hour 'marathon' recording session of 11 February 1963, at which the band recorded most of its first LP. His entry on the recording of 'There's a Place' concludes as follows:

> Taking into account the taming effects of compression and the then-standard UK studio practice of damping the bass to stop the stylus jumping on domestic record decks, this is the authentic contemporary sound of the Beatles live – the singers miked in front of their 'backline' of amps, unsegregated by baffles. With the studio clock ticking implacably and a near-impossible schedule to keep, the immediacy of the take was everything and no concession to tidiness could be afforded. Pitches wobble, microphones 'pop', drums stumble, larynxes tear: 1:47 of the real thing. (MacDonald 1998, p. 58)

Sounding a bit like he's covering the last scrimmage of the Superbowl, MacDonald paints the Beatles as an underdog team, bravely facing down a domineering opponent. With its 'taming effects', standardized practices and merciless schedule, the studio threatens to squeeze the life out of the group's 'authentic ... sound'. But despite missteps and injuries, the team pulls through and, in the end, even the numbers bear witness: 'There's a Place' consists of one minute 47 seconds – of what? Not just magnetic tape, or even simply music, but 'the real thing'.

Rock writers who are favourably disposed towards *Pepper* often emphasize the band's early live performance history as way of establishing the Beatles' rock bona fides. The implication is that the band banked so much street cred in Hamburg and Liverpool that it could afford to risk its integrity on the artistic ventures of 1966–67. In addition to MacDonald, Mark Hertsgaard uses this strategy, as does Greil Marcus in the *Rolling Stone Illustrated History of Rock & Roll*. Writing in 1976, Marcus sees himself confronting a critical 'consensus' that assesses the Beatles as 'imitative, lightweights, yea-sayers, softies, ordinary musicians, vaguely unhip, unimaginative lyrically and, above all, "clever" – that is, merely clever. You know – the Beatles just wanted to hold your hand, while the Stones wanted to pillage your town, etc.' (Marcus 1980, p. 184). In response, Marcus frames the Beatles as rooted in 'the forms of rock and roll', as opposed to, say, Dylan or the Stones, who had folk and blues, respectively, as their 'fallback position' (Ibid.). Though rootedness in older vernacular forms like folk or blues is often seen as a sign of authenticity in rock, Marcus turns this seeming asset into a deficit. Dylan and the Stones, he suggests, never fully committed to rock per se. By contrast, the Beatles' relationship to rock was direct – 'they were rock and roll or they were nothing' (Ibid., p. 185). Moreover, they were so steeped in rock history that they became that history:

> When the Beatles signed with EMI they were not merely in touch with their roots; in a significant and probably unique sense, they were their roots. They were not only a product of the pre-Beatles era of rock, they were a version of it ... The Beatles had absorbed that history because – year by year, playing and listening and writing, in Liverpool and on the bottoms of British tours and in Hamburg – they had, albeit invisibly, made it. (Ibid.)

Noting that the word 'authentic' derives from a Greek root meaning 'self-made', Keightley argues that 'the ideal of the rock band as self-sufficient ... self-contained unit' encourages 'a sense of freedom from mediation, a feeling of autonomy ... This "self-direction" of the ideal rock band signifies an independence from external interference and control, and, therefore, a greater authenticity' (Keightley 2001, pp. 134, 138).[2]

This notion of the band as autonomous entity informs John Gabree's unfavourable review of *Pepper*, published in *Downbeat* in late 1967. Given that *Pepper* draws on resources far in excess of those provided by a four-piece beat combo, Gabree speculates as to where proper credit lies:

---

2   While the Beatles certainly came to embody this ideal, it would be wrong to say they invented it. For example, they – along with many of their British invasion cohorts – were fans not just of Presley, but of his original, 'downhome' backing band, the trio of Scotty Moore, Bill Black and D.J. Fontana, considering them to be integral to Presley's early 'authentic' sound (see Burke and Griffin 2006).

The question ... becomes whether we are to credit the group, the producer or the engineer. I have heard – and whether it is apocryphal or true, it is true enough – that *A Day in the Life* was born when the Beatles' producer, engineer, and musical midwife, George Martin, soldered together the strands of two separate compositions. Shouldn't we laud Martin instead of the quartet? (Gabree 1991, p. 135)

The story recounted by Gabree appears to conflate the making of 'Strawberry Fields Forever' (where Martin and Geoff Emerick spliced together two radically different takes) with that of 'A Day in the Life' (where the group segued between two compositional fragments, one by Lennon and one by McCartney). But, says Gabree, such nitpicking is beside the point. Though it may be 'apocryphal', the story is 'true enough', presumably because it raises the question so dramatically. And the question is really an ethical one.

Keightley observes that rock conceptions of authenticity mix judgements about aesthetics ('Is this music beautiful?') with judgements about ethics ('Is this music compromised?') (Keightley 2001, p. 133). In this light, Gabree can be read as suggesting that interventions by a behind-the-scenes Svengali pose a threat to the integrity of 'the quartet'. In other words, by emphasizing production, the Beatles have surrendered to hierarchy and mechanization – the technocratic system that rock is supposed to oppose. Quoted in the *Time* cover story of 22 September 1967, McCartney appears to have considered this set of objections. In claiming that 'we haven't pushed George Martin out of the engineers' booth ... but we've become equals' (quoted in Porterfield 2006, p. 113), he effectively asserts that the band has expanded its sphere of integrity to include the producer's chair and the recording desk. He then quickly moves to the question of whether it is ethical for a rock band to traffic with technology: 'The music has more to do with electronics now than ever before. To do those things a few years ago was a bit immoral. But electronics is no longer immoral' (Ibid.).

Writing in the 1990s, MacDonald is unperturbed by *Pepper*'s ethos of high production. Yet he agrees with Gabree in that he does not celebrate production per se. Like a good rocker, he sees 'the pulse of the machine' as invidious to quality and authenticity. It's just that he locates the fall from grace in the 1980s, with the rise of MIDI sequencer, drum machines and pitch correction technology, rather than in the late 1960s with, say, multitrack tape, overdubbing and ADT (MacDonald 2003, pp. 148–52; MacDonald 1998, pp. 338–42).[3]

For MacDonald, initial victories over studio interference like 'There's a Place' effectively inoculate the group against domination by machines and foreshadow more victories to come. In the period from 1963 to 1966 the Beatles will, in his account, move from being overawed by the studio to 'defeating the desk' to mastering and transforming the possibilities of modern recording. Unlike Gillett's Presley, the Beatles will not be undone by the modern studio. Rather, they will make the wasteland bloom: 'Devouring an unprecedented fifty-five hours of studio-time, STRAWBERRY FIELDS FOREVER extended the range of studio techniques ...

---

3   At the close of *Revolution in the Head*, MacDonald pointedly credits the Beatles with 'coining almost every trend that succeeded them *apart* from musical mechanisation' (MacDonald 1998, p. 335) [emphasis added].

opening up possibilities of pop' and generating 'unprecedented sound-images' (MacDonald 1998, p. 194). In this formulation, the studio clock still ticks, but now the Beatles dominate it rather than vice versa. By 1966 and the recording of 'Tomorrow Never Knows', the studio itself has changed, in MacDonald's view, from intimidating mechanism to nurturing womb: 'Abbey Road', he writes, 'mothered the most dazzling aural invention to emerge from any studio in Britain or America during the late sixties' (Ibid., p. 168).

A strange dialectic has emerged, though; for whereas the studio had once posed a threat to the integrity of 'the Beatles live', by 1966 the source of interference has become live performance itself: 'In summer 1966, the Beatles' career was in a state of acute self-contradiction. Having evolved a new musical identity in the studio, they were obliged by touring commitments to step back into their earlier pop style and trudge around the world churning out under-rehearsed sets to audiences screaming too loudly to notice how bad they were' (Ibid., p. 188).

Artist and audience

In this scenario, the audience has become the source of unwanted interference, such that the Beatles feel dehumanized by live performance. As Lennon put it in 1966, 'I reckon we could send out four waxwork dummies of ourselves and that would satisfy the crowds. Beatles concerts are nothing to do with music any more. They're just bloody tribal rites' (quoted in Lewisohn 1992, p. 210). 'Tribal rites', indeed: Ehrenreich, Hess and Jacobs have argued that Beatlemania amounted to a proto-feminist expression of girl power (Ehrenreich, Hess and Jacobs 1997). The screaming, fainting, frenzied female fans were indeed communicating something, if only half-wittingly – namely, their collective capacity for ecstatic abandon. If this appalled parents and paralyzed security guards, so much the better: Beatles concerts became for them a unique public space where it was permissible to act out of control. MacDonald's reference to 'acute self-contradiction' is apt, for we sense here a tremor along Keightley's fault line.

The 'direct communication' prized by rock is typically one-way – from artist to audience, not the reverse. Moreover, this transaction is gendered to the extent that the artist in question is typically assumed to be male. When audiences behave less passively or predictably than the rules of rock or gender permit, there is trouble. And of course in response to such behaviour, the Beatles ceased performing live. Yet this gesture, which might itself be seen as undermining the possibility of direct communication, was and still is widely read in terms of the quest for authenticity. The question became: can a band communicate more profoundly by turning away from its audience?

The answer depends. Keightley speaks of rock's 'two families of authenticity', labelling them 'Romantic' and 'Modernist', respectively (Keightley 2001, p. 136). Noting that authenticity is a value central to both Romantic and Modernist aesthetics, he delineates the divide as follows:

> While Romanticism locates authenticity principally in the direct communication between artist and audience, Modernism manifests its concern with authenticity more indirectly, at

the aesthetic level, so that the authentic artist is one who is true to the Modernist credos of experimentation, innovation, development, change. Where Romantics see sincere, unmediated expression as essential, Modernists believe their first commitment is less to reaching an audience than to being true to their own artistic integrity. (Ibid.)

One might add that the Romantic version of authenticity is rooted in folk revival conceptions of community and tradition, while the Modernist version invokes the existentialist notion of 'authentic existence', that project of self-realization wherein 'we create our own comprehensive life-meanings' despite pressures to retreat from 'growth choices' into 'bad faith' (Park 2004). If the Romantic rocker is descended from Wordsworth's 'man speaking to men' (Wordsworth 1973, p. 601), then the Modernist echoes Blake: 'I must invent my own system or be enslaved by another man's' (Blake 1987, p. 91). MacDonald and many other writers depict the Beatles' move from stage to studio in terms of Modernist self-realization. Framed thusly, *Sgt. Pepper* marks the moment when the Beatles' pursuit of authenticity required them to reconsider previously accepted ideas of artist, audience and community. This in a sense mandated that electronics no longer be seen as 'immoral'.

Such concerns are central to Richard Goldstein's famous panning of *Pepper*, published in the 18 June 1967 edition of the *New York Times*. After praising 'A Day in the Life' as 'a historic Pop event' (reprinted in Skinner Sawyers 2006, p. 99) and applauding the ascent of 'electronic-rock' (Ibid., p. 100), he concludes as follows:

> What a shame that 'A Day in the Life' is only a coda to an otherwise undistinguished collection of work. We need the Beatles, not as cloistered composers, but as companions. And they need us. In substituting the studio conservatory for an audience, they have ceased being folk artists, and the change is what makes their new album a monologue. (Ibid., p. 101)

The Beatles as 'folk artists': such a categorization sounds quaint today, when one can open *Variety* and find the group ranked as the number one entertainment icon of the twentieth century or join the boulevardiers on the Vegas strip and be wowed by the pricey spectacle *Beatles: Love*.[4] But, as Frith has pointed out, the notion that rock music was a kind of folk music was a cornerstone of rock ideology in the 1960s (Frith 1981, p. 159). Jon Landau, the influential rock critic who edited the *Rolling Stone* record reviews section in the early 1970s (before moving on to manage Bruce Springsteen's career), formulated the point as follows in his 1972 collection, *It's Too Late to Stop Now*:

> And yet both [rock & roll of the 1950s and rock of the 1960s] were essentially folk musics. The best music in both idioms came from men who recorded their own material, or worked very closely with a collaborator on it. While producers have been important in both fields, the music was essentially controlled by the performing artist – unlike the music

---

4   *Beatles: Love* is the Cirque du Soleil show permanently installed at the Mirage Hotel on the Las Vegas strip. Having grown out of conversations between Cirque founder Guy Laliberté and Cirque fan George Harrison, *Love* opened in summer 2006 with the official blessing of McCartney, Starr, Yoko Ono and Olivia Harrison. It is the only theatrical production ever permitted to use original Beatles recordings as a soundtrack.

from 1959–63. And in both situations there existed a strong bond between performer and audience, a natural kinship, a sense that the stars weren't being imposed from above but had sprung up from out of our own ranks. We could identify with them without hesitation. (Reprinted in Heylin 1992, p. 161)

In his 1981 essay, Frith pointed out that, from a sociological perspective, this claim tended to fold under scrutiny. The 'rock-folk argument', he suggested, rested on two premises: 1) that rock music was an authentic 'reflection of experience'; and 2) that it 'represented the experience of a community' (Frith 1981, p. 159). The problem, according to Frith, was that there was 'no independent, non-musical description of the "rock community"' and no account 'of how such a community came to make music for itself' (Ibid., p. 160). Rather, the existence of such a community was inferred from a given piece of music. If a 'song or record or performance exhibited the necessary signs of authenticity', then it was taken as the sign 'of a real community' (Ibid.). And the 'signs of authenticity' in question derived not from sociological information, but from a set of 'musical conventions' (Ibid.).

According to Frith:

> ... the rock-folk argument focused on aesthetics: folk songs worked differently than pop songs; the folk experience was 'authentic', rooted in the experience of creation; the pop experience was unauthentic, involved only in the act of consumption. In terms of musical practice (rather than scholarship or politics), the task, then, was not to develop the community that would create the right sort of music, but to use the right sort of music to create the lost sense of community. The emphasis (and this was obvious even in the radical aspects of the American folk revival) was on developing the appropriate conventions of performance. The use of these conventions enabled students and bohemians in their campuses and clubs to have a 'folk' experience of music without having to have a 'folk' experience of life. 'Community' was something that was created by the music, that described the musical experience. This was the argument that became central to the ideology of rock. (Ibid., pp. 166–7)

This description suggests that in rock, authenticity is less a state of being than a species of rhetoric – a set of gestures and conventions deployed by performers and audiences to produce certain effects. As Frith insists, this doesn't mean that authenticity is a trivial category or meaningless notion (people do, after all, believe in it and use it to map their experiential worlds), but it does mean that rock ideology's 'authentic experience' is a myth in Barthes's sense of the term – that is, a discursive construct whose rhetorical origins have been forgotten, such that it can masquerade as natural fact (Barthes 1957, pp. 142–3).

If, following Frith, we denaturalize the notion of rock as folk music, we can read Goldstein's complaint in a different light. In this sense, to say that with the release of *Sgt. Pepper* the Beatles had 'ceased to be folk artists' is not to say they had turned their backs on community. Rather it is to say they had discarded, or at least disturbed, a particular set of musical conventions – namely, those associated with the Romantic mode of authenticity.

But this action on the Beatles' part proved to be no problem for the 'folk' whom writers like Landau and Goldstein saw as making up the 'rock community'. Unbothered by what Goldstein saw as the Beatles' withdrawal into ivory-tower isolation, the hippy subculture embraced *Sgt. Pepper* as one of its own. According to Stephen Gaskin, leader of the Farm commune, '... we always felt we were talking about Sgt. Pepper as if he were really some sort of mythical leader for *all* hippies. We were really talking about worldwide transformation – and we weren't just talking about music but about everything' (quoted in Taylor 1987, pp. 47–8).

The Beatles' answer to the problem of audience interference was to 'let [the record] do the touring' (George Martin in Beatles 2000, p. 241). And so *Sgt. Pepper* did, at the fortuitous moment when the record industry, free-form underground radio and the rising hippy counterculture came together to make the 33-rpm LP the format of choice in rock. In this setting, the Beatles' personal absence from the stage was counterbalanced by what seemed to many an ubiquitous electronic presence. Recalling the experience of hearing the record for the first time as a young teenager, musician Eric Goulden reports, 'The room spun round in glorious double vision as *Sgt. Pepper* played endlessly on – side one followed by side two followed by side one in endless rotation. It was the most fabulous thing I'd ever heard in my life ... I never had my own copy of *Sgt. Pepper* because everybody else had it – you could hear it anywhere so I didn't need one' (quoted in 'Sgt. Pepper's Lonely Hearts Club Band').

This image, of *Sgt. Pepper* as world-navel, axis pole of the swinging sixties, is highlighted in accounts such as Taylor's *It Was Twenty Years Ago Today* (1987) and Hertsgaard's *A Day in the Life* (1995). Making the case for *Pepper*'s greatness, such writers typically place strong emphasis on the text in relation to its sociohistorical context. Indeed, argues Moore, the album was not just a reflection of its time, but the chosen representative of its audience: 'From the numbers of people immediately enraptured by *Sgt. Pepper* – whether ordinary listeners, engaged critics or working musicians – the album seems to have spoken (in a way no other has) for its generation, by the direct wish of that generation, through their appropriation of it, rather than through any imposition of it on them' (Moore 1997, p. 68).[5]

Pepper came to be seen as offering just 'the right sort of music' for restoring the lost sense of community key to the myth of rock as folk. Far from interfering with communication, electronic media and the music industry were seen as making such a transaction possible. In the oft-quoted words of *Rolling Stone*'s Langdon Winner:

At the time [*Sgt. Pepper* was released] I happened to be driving across country on Interstate 80. In each city where I stopped for gas or food – Laramie, Ogallala, Moline, South Bend – the melodies wafted in from some far-off transistor radio or portable hi-fi. It was the most amazing thing I've ever heard. For a brief while, the irreparably

---

5   Writers working to slam *Pepper* often invoke the 1960s context too, typically framing the period in terms of 'wretched excess' (Bangs 1981, p. 46) rather than renaissance. In *Kill Your Idols: A New Generation of Rock Writers Reconsiders the Classics*, Bangs biographer Jim DeRogatis, exasperated at what he sees as special pleading on behalf of the album as well as the decade, refuses to consider context at all. 'Great art', he proclaims, 'stands on its own even if it's removed from the specific context of when and how it was made' (DeRogatis 2004). Stripping history away, he finds an album that 'sucks dogs royally' (Ibid.). Thus, to counter the hoary myth of *Pepper* as zeitgeist, we get the even hoarier myth of the text as autonomous artwork. Having begun with Lester Bangs's attitude, DeRogatis ends with T.S. Eliot's aesthetic.

fragmented consciousness of the West was unified, at least in the minds of the young. (Quoted in Marcus 1980, p. 183)

But for critics less favourably disposed towards *Pepper*, the sounds wafting into Winner's ken seem siren-like – comely on the surface, empty underneath.

Substance and style

Another way rock writers frame the interference problem is to speak of style overwhelming substance. Indeed, the basic theme reiterated throughout Goldstein's 1967 review is that in *Sgt. Pepper*, 'tone overtakes meaning' (reprinted in Skinner Sawyers 2006, p. 99). To convey this point, metaphors of staging, spicing and ornamentation are invoked repeatedly. In each instance, the lower term in a normative hierarchy gets uppity and abandons its proper station. Thus, we hear of 'elaborate musical propwork' (Ibid., p. 98); a 'melodramatic' saga with 'saucy accompaniment' (Ibid.); a voice that 'oozes over the melody like melted cheese' (Ibid.); 'an honest vision ruined by the background which seeks to enhance it' (Ibid., p. 99); 'an engaging curio ... drenched in reverb, echo and other studio distortions' (Ibid.); and, in the slightly revised 1970 version of the review, a bag of 'slicks and tricks' amounting to 'Beatles baroque – an elaboration without improvement' (reprinted in Heylin 1992, p. 542).[6]

This great inversion results in an 'album of special effects, dazzling but ultimately fraudulent' (reprinted in Skinner Sawyers 2006, p. 99). The Beatles' penchant for 'posturing and put-on' makes *Sgt. Pepper* into 'a game' (reprinted in Heylin 1992, p. 545). Gleeful assertions that the album 'has no meaning' simply won't do, because 'even from fantasy, I expect authenticity' (Ibid., p. 547). Quoting the Lovin' Spoonful, Frith had argued that the myth of rock community amounted to a belief in rock as 'the magic that can set you free' (Frith 1981, p. 159). For Goldstein, that sort of 'real' magic is being displaced in *Sgt. Pepper* by the bad, 'surrogate magic of production' (reprinted in Heylin 1992, p. 543).

In the 1970 *Rolling Stone* interview 'Lennon Remembers', Yoko Ono advanced a similar view of late-1960s-era pop/rock music:

> The thing is, the psychedelic age brought this thing about music with lots of decorative sounds, *so* decorative ... John's stuff is like – instead of medium is the message, which was the psychedelic age ... *He*'s like the *message* is the medium. And it's really the message. Because it was so important, he didn't need any decorative sound, or decorativeness about it. (Wenner 2000, p. 117)

Ono is here contrasting the 'overdressed' music of psychedelia with the stripped-down minimalism of her partner's then-new release, *Plastic Ono Band*. As the interview made abundantly clear, Lennon's agenda at this early post-Beatles moment

---

6   This view is echoed by Riley: '... even though *Pepper* is a model of psychedelic design ... too much ... winds up as texture for the sake of texture, surface sliding around on light substance instead of enriching it' (Riley 1989, p. 230).

was a radical divestment – a shedding of clothes, hair, finery, production and, above all, repression and inhibition – in the name of personal liberation.

Remarks made by Ono elsewhere in the interview suggest that 'decorative' is for her a loaded term. The downfall of 'classical music', she asserts, is that 'it went further and further away from the heartbeat' (Ibid., p. 76).

> Yoko: Heartbeat is 4/4, and it goes [*demonstrates*] you know? And then they started 1–2–3, all that. And then...
> John: Perversion.
> Yoko: ... rhythm became very decorative and then you know like Schoenberg, Webern, all their rhythm is like – [*demonstrates*] – like that. It's highly complicated and interesting, and our minds are very much like that, but they lost the heartbeat. (Ibid., pp. 76–7)

The assumption that 'heartbeat' is the ground of all musical possibilities places the entire discussion under the sign of animal nature. Rhythm that is 'decorative' can then quickly be characterized as (overly) complicated and (merely) cerebral – a betrayal of the body and a 'perversion' of proper order. Summing up what MacDonald calls this 'puritan' aesthetic (MacDonald 1998, p. 211), Lennon remarks: 'If it's real, it's simple usually. And if it's simple, it's true' (Wenner 2000, p. 76).

Seriosus and rhetoricus

The binaries sketched above – style/substance, medium/message, complicated/ simple, decorative/plain – represent variations on a theme. For a literary theorist such as Stanley Fish that theme is recognizable as the age-old debate about the nature of rhetoric – those design elements in discourse which, according to Plato (among others), empower communicators who harbour dubious designs on you and me (Dillon 1994, p. 616).

> The quarrel between philosophy and rhetoric survives every sea change in the history of Western thought, continually presenting us with the (skewed) choice between the plain unvarnished truth straightforwardly presented and the powerful but insidious appeal of 'fine language', language that has transgressed the limits of representation and substituted its own forms for the forms of reality. (Fish 1995, p. 206)

When they speak of 'the surrogate magic of production' and the '*so* decorative' sounds of psychedelia, Goldstein and Ono may be discussing music, but they echo philosophy's long-held suspicion of rhetoric. That view sees rhetoric – in particular, the rhetorical canon of style – as the 'dress' of thought, not as its 'incarnation' (Covino and Jolliffe 1995, p. 87). In this realist view, rhetoric/style is the dangerous supplement to direct, truthful communication.

Quoting the rhetorician Richard Lanham, Fish contrasts two fundamental 'species' – *homo seriosus*, or serious man, and *homo rhetoricus*, or rhetorical man. *Homo seriosus* 'possesses a central self, an irreducible identity' (Fish 1995, p. 208) and, together with others like himself, inhabits 'a homogeneously real society which constitutes a referent reality for the men living in it. This referent society is in turn contained in a physical nature itself referential, standing "out there" independent of man' (Ibid.). By contrast, *homo rhetoricus*

> is an actor; his reality public, dramatic. His sense of identity depends on the reassurance of daily histrionic reenactment … The lowest common denominator of his life is a social situation … He is thus committed to no single construction of the world; much rather, to prevailing in the game at hand. (Ibid.)

Fish adds, 'What serious man fears – the invasion of the fortress of essence by the contingent, the protean and the unpredictable – is what rhetorical man celebrates and incarnates' (Ibid.).

In many ways, *Sgt. Pepper* sides with rhetorical man. In 'Strawberry Fields Forever', the song with which the *Pepper* sessions began, Lennon had proclaimed, 'Nothing is real'. Goldstein quotes this line disapprovingly in his review, but restated as 'No *one* thing is real' it is a fair summation of rhetorical man's position. From early on, *Pepper*'s 'reality' was construed as 'dramatic'. As McCartney put it, 'We would be Sgt. Pepper's band, and for the whole of the album we'd pretend to be someone else' (Beatles 2000, p. 241). Beyond the members of Sgt. Pepper's band, the album featured a cast of additional characters depicted in what Lennon later called 'third-person songs' (Wenner 2000, p. 9). In its shuffling of genres and pursuit of sonic surprise, the album might well be said to celebrate 'the protean and the unpredictable'.

Fish notes the affinity between the rhetorical orientation and that of postmodernism. Both decentre the subject and dethrone meta-narratives. Perhaps this is the abyss Goldstein glimpses when he complains about excessive 'posturing and put-on' and the LP being a mere 'game' while insisting that 'even from fantasy, I expect authenticity' (reprinted in Heylin 1992, pp. 545, 547). Postmodernism's endless play of signifiers – its vision of turtles all the way down – was implicit in psychotropic drug-taking as experienced by many counterculturalists. Indeed, psychedelic theorists such as Timothy Leary and Richard Alpert imported frameworks such as the spiritual quest (and texts such as the *Tibetan Book of the Dead*) in order to contain and give shape to the metamorphic flow of mental states induced by LSD.

Similarly, *Sgt. Pepper*'s carnivalesque play is yoked to serious purpose. According to McCartney, pretending 'to be someone else … liberated you – you could do anything when you got to the mike or on your guitar, because it wasn't *you*' (Beatles 2000, p. 241). From a late-1990s perspective, Barry Miles sees *Pepper* as 'a Post-Modernist shopping trip which passed effortlessly from genre to genre' (Miles 1997, p. 330). But McCartney's remark points to play not as bourgeois escapism, but as a means of escaping prescribed roles, a way of unleashing the authentic self. At least one key Western meta-narrative – that of the individual's progress towards greater and greater freedom – remains firmly in place here. In this sense, *Sgt. Pepper* is better termed a modernist, rather than postmodernist, text.

This fits with readings provided by several critics of 'A Day in the Life', the album's 'encore to end all encores' (Hertsgaard 1995, p. 220). Though such writers hear in the song's aleatoric orchestral crescendos a hint of ultimate chaos, they see the song itself as providing a note of sober, even transcendent closure. According to Tim Riley, though the song

... dismantles the illusory world the Beatles entered as Sgt. Pepper's Band ... the *Sgt. Pepper* journey isn't futile; its despair is ultimately hopeful. 'I'd love to turn you on' is a motto of enlightenment, of Lennon's desire to wake the world up to its own potential for rejuvenation, not self-annihilation ... The final blow doesn't summon the fate of modern man; it decries the tragedy of the fullness available and denied in our culture. (Riley 1989, p. 229)

According to Keightley,

> it is never the artificial alone that is the point of rock artifice. Instead, rock artifice involves a deliberate rejection of the Romantic mode of authenticity, in favor of a complex and nuanced Modernist strategy of authenticity in which the performers' ability to shape imaginary worlds – rather than being shaped by this world – is foregrounded. (Keightley 2001, p. 138)

In the modernist mode then, the rocker can be authentically artificial.

Artifice and artiness

In the 1970 interview, Lennon and Ono cast psychedelia in the role of a frivolous *homo rhetoricus* while aligning themselves with *homo seriosus*. This is itself a highly (though unacknowledged) rhetorical move, a version of Fish's 'skewed choice'. Walter Everett has recently provided a rejoinder to the 'tone overtakes meaning' claim, suggesting that it rests on a false dichotomy. In 'Painting their room in a colorful way: the Beatles' exploration of timbre', he argues that in the Beatles' late work – and on *Pepper* in particular – musical values often considered secondary become central and substantive.

> [The Beatles'] call to the imagination was placed by musical elements just as much as it was by words. But whereas values such as melody, counterpoint, harmony, rhythm, and formal construction are sometimes crucial in such expression the Beatles most directly paralleled the acutely detailed sensory world of their lyrics in the realm of tone color – timbre. (Everett 2006, p. 69)

Everett is not just claiming that the Beatles excelled at the ornamental art of 'text-painting' (Ibid., p. 85). He is arguing that this seemingly supplemental register carried their message – their 'call to the imagination': 'Lucy in the Sky with Diamonds', he writes, represents the 'quintessential psychedelic recording, *with its timbres just as essential* as are its innovative harmonic structure, rhythmic relationships, and formal design in transporting the listener from this world into another' (Ibid., p. 88) [emphasis added].

In numerous aspects, *Sgt. Pepper* draws attention to itself as an artefact that has been shaped by human hands. The key gestures include the highlighting of the recording process per se through the emphasis on overdubbing; the deletion of rills between tracks; the manipulation of tape speed and direction; the use of editing to achieve startling juxtapositions; the layering of sounds to create exotic textures; the conspicuous deployment of signal processors like compressors, limiters and reverb units; the furthering of studio techniques such as close-miking, phasing and ADT;

the imposition of the 'show' frame (along with the periodic breaking of that frame); and the sustained orchestration of these elements across 39 minutes. In recounting the first time he heard 'Strawberry Fields Forever', Pete Townshend recalls being struck by the 'worked' quality of the artefact:

I remember being taken aback at the complexity of the sound. It was obvious that the master had been partly cut into shape physically, like electronic music ... It was full of images and colour, textures – almost like the brilliantly indulgent film we had just watched, but of course this was just music, just a pop song. (Townshend 2000, p. 146)

Producer George Martin has also noted the analogy to filmmaking, with its emphasis on cutting, editing and assemblage:

I think there was a gradual development by the boys, as they tried to make life a bit more interesting on record. They felt: 'We don't have to go up onstage to do this; we can do it just for ourselves, and just for the studio.' So it became a different kind of art form – like making a film rather than a live performance. That affected their thinking and their writing and it affected the way I put [Sgt. Pepper] together, too. (Beatles 2000, p. 252)

But from his 1972 vantage point, Landau saw this trend as another offence against nature:

Producers and engineers, increasingly the equivalent of movie director and editor (or cameraman), have greatly increased their roles in the recording process. The negative result is a potential reduction in spontaneity and feeling. Over-dubbing as a recording technique has virtually eliminated the need for musicians to play together at all. Mixing, in turn, offers vast opportunities to affect the sound of the record after the actual recording has been done. Together they make it possible to formalize and standardize the sound to a higher degree than before. (Reprinted in Heylin 1992, p. 167)

In other words, beware: electronic whatchamucallit ahead. According to Michael Jarrett, such 'negative' results are a built-in component of rock ideology, part of the spurious 'common sense' in which consumers are trained by the music industry.

We must ... remember that the music industry organizes itself around naturalized oppositions. It has a discourse. It speaks. Industrialization, through institutions such as radio, music publishing and licensing, and recording, sanctioned the antithesis that holds that 'authentic' music is something distinct from 'commercial' music. We consumers, in turn, inherit – organize our thinking by means of – this and other antitheses ... The assumption that bad ... things happen to 'authentic' music is sufficient to generate the real/fake distinction that has become musical common sense. It creates a consumer who understands the history of rock as a series of authentic moments that deteriorated into conventionalized moments. (Jarrett)

Jarrett notes that such a history imposes a tragic plot – 'a deviation from the Good' – on the process of music's popularization. Heylin describes it in more mythic terms, as a 'fall from grace', an expulsion from the garden (Heylin 1992, p. ix). In his critique of *Pepper*, Riley invokes loss of innocence and separation from the primal source:

Sgt. Pepper, he claims, 'has a degree of self-consciousness throughout that primitive rock 'n' roll snubs in favor of urgency and raw energy' (Riley 1989, p. 203).

'Primitive' is another shibboleth of rock – and especially punk rock – ideology. In the words of Bangs, punk rock 'is rock in its most basic, primitive form' (reprinted in Heylin 1992, p. 103). This supposedly primordial form is profoundly unselfconscious.

> The point is that rock & roll, as I see it, is the ultimate populist art form, democracy in action, because it's true: anybody can do it. Learn three chords on a guitar and you've got it. Don't worry whether you can 'sing' or not ... For performing rock & roll, or punk rock, or call it any damn thing you please, there's only one thing you need: NERVE. Rock & roll is an attitude, and if you've got the attitude you can do it, no matter what anybody says. Believing that is one of the things that punk rock is about. Rock is for everybody, it should be so implicitly anti-elitist that the question of whether somebody's qualified to perform it should never arise. But it did. In the sixties, of course. And maybe this was one reason why the sixties may not have been so all-fired great as we give them credit for. Because in the sixties rock & roll began to think of itself as an 'art-form'. Rock & roll is not an 'art-form'; rock & roll is a raw wail from the bottom of the guts. (Ibid., p. 104)

Here, the spectre of compromise is raised by rock that is upwardly mobile – upward being downward for Bangs, who inverts Plato like a proper Romantic. Thus, rock is the music of the people and the people are blissfully simple, in touch with the nerves and the guts. Meanwhile, art, with its qualifications, is snootily undemocratic. Of course, it is with that icon of the 1960s, *Sgt. Pepper*, that rock began to be called most emphatically an art form. And indeed, this was partly due to a shift in the attention of bourgeois tastemakers. For example, William Rees-Mogg, editor of *The Times* in 1967 and (then as now) a pillar of the British Establishment, was duly impressed:

> It was a period of great change. It was a time when the so-called generation gap suddenly seemed to become much wider; it was of course before the 1968 riots in the universities and all of that. I was very conscious that something was happening and that people were just coming out with new ideas, a new vision of the world. The Beatles were at the beginning of it, and *Sgt. Pepper* was a great recording which everybody enjoyed. It went right across the age groups, right across society, and it was perfectly apparent that this was music of real quality. It was the first Beatles record I bought. It summed up the Beatles' coming into the consciousness of non-pop-music people. (Quoted in Taylor 1987, p. 44)

'Music of real quality': for a purist like Bangs, rock music that could be blessed by someone like this was a problem – 'this record had the power to almost single-handedly destroy rock 'n' roll' (Bangs 1981, p. 46). But the rock music in question could not be briskly dismissed as inauthentic; *Pepper* had, after all, helped legitimize experimental artifice as a mode of rock authenticity. To counter this Modernist trend, punk ideologues like Bangs replayed rock Romanticism in a new, more Rousseauian key. Bangs's attitude-driven everyman, uncorrupted by skill or self-consciousness, is a rock version of Rousseau's noble savage. In this sense, *Pepper* can be said to have called forth, in dialectical fashion, the discourse of punk.

As for raw wails from the lowly people: to a sober eye, punk's populist credentials look thin. In the United States, for example, it has always been a coterie taste, with none of the broad appeal of, say, heavy metal. Moreover, when one considers its founders – figures such as conceptual artist Malcolm McLaren, fashion designer Vivienne Westwood, neo-beat poet Lou Reed, avant-garde actor David Johansen – it becomes clear that punk has its own art-world pedigree. Riley writes that primitive rockers *snub* the self-consciousness of *Pepper*. Well, it takes a snob to snub.

Pepper's artiness arguably does reflect a 1960s version of upward mobility – the high-culture aspirations of working-class Liverpudlians. McCartney did not feel oppressed by the upper-middle class Asher family, with its concert- and theatre-world connections. He saw them, much as he saw London avantists like Barry Miles, as useful guides to more refined taste. Like many working-class people, he associated art with 'classy' sophistication. With the loosening of social barriers in 1960s Britain, he felt comfortable moving in such circles; so much so that a figure such as Stockhausen could become an influence, with a place of honour on the *Pepper* cover (MacDonald 1998, pp. 168, 198; Miles 1997, pp. 232–43). Appalled by such assimilation, Bangs and company eschewed 'art-rock' for punk. But punk was simply the latest in a long line of art movements opposed to artiness – a fantasy of 'raw' proletarian 'nerve' promoted by urban sophisticates.

Of course the rhetoric of noble savagery is often the last refuge of scoundrels. In *Tropics of Discourse*, historian Hayden White demonstrated that the eighteenth-century European revolutionaries who deployed the figure in service of their cause showed little concern for the condition of actual 'savages' (White 1978). Rather, the noble savage provided a handy club with which the rising bourgeoisie could bludgeon its rival for hegemony, the landed aristocracy. The point was not the anti-elitist one – that is lowly savages can be noble – but that, if savages can be noble, then what is a class of noblemen worth? Similarly mythical, rock noble savagery has served similar parochial purposes.[7] As Bangs himself confides, punk rock, as a concept, did not exist before the early 1970s. It arose at that time in response to the discourse of art-rock with its privileging of musical skill. It proposed to supplant skill with 'attitude' – or, as Bangs quickly notes, the *belief* in attitude. Bangs knows a myth when he sees one.[8]

The same cannot be said of John Lennon, at least not the figure speaking in *Lennon Remembers*. Asked why rock 'means so much to people' (Wenner 2000, p. 76), Lennon responds by reciting what Pattison calls the 'myth of rock's black origins' (Pattison 1987, p. 30):

---

7   For an earlier and more elaborate discussion of these themes, see Kimsey 2002. The text transcribes a presentation given by the author to the 1994 Conference on Rock 'n' Theory, held at the University of Illinois, Urbana.

8   In the words of Moore: 'A great deal of critical commentary has always promoted music that seems full of "feel", is largely improvised, and is by players who are unlikely to be able to expound with any verbal precision the techniques they use. The reason for such critical valorization was, in large part, to demonstrate that the aesthetic criteria of the Central European canon do not have universal validity, but the result was to assume (in ignorance of the operation of musical technique and skill in practising musicians of all kinds) that such music was a vehicle for the direct expression of raw, sub- (or super-) literate, unmediated experience. I believe all such critical attempts to be wishful thinking ...' (Moore 1997, p. 76).

Because it's primitive enough and it has no bullshit – the best stuff. And it gets *through* to you. It's beat. Go to the jungle and they have … the rhythm going, everybody gets into it. I read that Malcolm X or Eldridge Cleaver or somebody said that, with rock, the blacks gave the middle-class whites back their bodies … It's something like that. It gets through. (Wenner 2000, p. 76)

Pattison labels this scenario 'the canonical version of the birth of rock', going on to assert that 'acceptance of the myth is the irreducible dogmatic minimum that defines rock orthodoxy' (Pattison 1987, p. 33).[9] The myth celebrates 'beat' that 'gets *through*' – a rhythm that defies interference. Of course it also naturalizes racial stereotypes and exploitative hierarchies in classically colonialist fashion, something Lennon's bullshit detector failed to help him see. But given his investment in the myth, it is interesting to note that when the Beatles decided, post-*Pepper*, to try and get back to their roots, they sought the help of Billy Preston. According to George Harrison, Preston's presence put the band on its 'best behaviour' and defused the hostility that had stymied the initial *Get Back* sessions. As an old friend from the Hamburg days and a superb ensemble player and soloist, Preston was well suited to becoming the sessions' fifth Beatle (Beatles 2000, pp. 318–19). As a black man ministering to uptight whites, he also fit the mythic bill.

I shall close with yet another fable:

The impotence of being honest

The truth is rarely pure and never simple.[10]
Oscar Wilde

By January 1969, a mere 18 months after the release of *Pepper*, the Beatles were by all accounts in crisis. Some of the difficulties were business related and some were interpersonal, but a number concerned the band's sense of musical integrity. They now felt compromised by the technology they had previously mastered. George Martin recalls that 'John … actually said to me', in reference to the upcoming recording project, '"I don't want any of your production shit. We want this to be an honest album." I said, "What do you mean by an honest album?" He said, "I don't want any editing. I don't want any over-dubbing. It's got be like it is. We just record the song and that's it"' (Beatles 2000, p. 317). In effect, electronics had again become immoral.

They also felt their aptitude as an ensemble slipping away. According to Lennon,

We stopped touring and we'd only get together for recordings … we'd be off for months and we'd suddenly come into the studio and be expected to be spot on again … Although we'd learnt a lot of technique where we could produce good records, musically we weren't as together as some of the earlier years and that's what we all missed. (Ibid., p. 322)

---

9   Pattison 1987 is the indispensable text on Romantic ideology in rock.
10 Wilde 1965, p. 35.

McCartney thought the solution would be a concert performance of new material, since 'for all our success, the Beatles were always a great little band, nothing more, nothing less' (Ibid.) and rehearsals would be restorative. However, no suitable setting could be agreed upon and issues of scale, expense and commitment made a one-off live show by the world's most sought-after musicians daunting (Ibid., p. 315). Almost as an afterthought, they appeared on the rooftop of Apple headquarters, 'playing', in McCartney's words, 'virtually to nothing – to the sky, which was quite nice' (Ibid., p. 321).

Material-wise, the Beatles were pursuing a 'return to simplicity' by reacquainting themselves with good old rock 'n' roll (Everett 1999, p. 215). This move may have been inspired by Harrison's late-1968 sojourn in Woodstock with Bob Dylan and the Band. According to Christgau, the Dylan/Band basement tapes of this period 'were the original laid-back rock, early investigations of a mode that would … eventually … pervade the whole music' (Christgau 1975) much as the Band itself would go on to model a roots-oriented, Romantic authenticity. However, in 1967–68 'an inspired artificiality was the rule' (Ibid.) and though they personified this Modernist aesthetic, the Beatles were now determined to be less 'pretentious' and 'more natural' (John Lennon, quoted in Everett 1999, p. 215). With this goal in mind, they moved out of Abbey Road, decamping first to Twickenham Film Studios and then to the basement of Apple.

In rejecting studio production, the group was also attempting to reject the Modernist identity it had fashioned with its *Pepper*-era recordings. Much as in 1966, the iconic entity known as the Beatles was seen as generating interference, only now it wasn't the four moptops blocking the signal, it was Sgt. Pepper's band. Lennon, for one, was pleased to see *Get Back* turn into the debacle of *Let It Be*. He thought it would show the Beatles with their 'trousers off' and so 'break' psychedelia's messianic 'myth' (Wenner 2000, p. 102).

But the attempt to be more natural itself proved alienating: 'With cameras rolling on a brightly lit movie set, the Beatles' best efforts to undo the shackles of their mythology were bound to fail' (Womack and Davis 2006, pp. 106–7). Having made *Get Back* the subject of a documentary film, the Beatles subjected themselves to relentless audiovisual surveillance. This generated an atmosphere of decidedly uninspired self-consciousness and 29 hours of what Lennon called 'badly recorded shit' (Wenner 2000, p. 101). Striving to play out one myth – the return to the primal garden – the Beatles ended up enacting another: the revenge of the electronic whatchamucallit.

Following this disastrous lapse into honesty, the Beatles made their next album an emphatic 'return to *production*' (Kehew and Ryan 2006, p. 510). In George Martin's words, *Abbey Road* was a conscious attempt by the Beatles 'to get back into the old *Pepper* way' and its aesthetic of inspired artifice (Beatles 2000, p. 338); to get back, one might say, where they once belonged.

Chapter 10

The act you've known for all these years: a re-encounter with *Sgt. Pepper*

Allan Moore

How robust should an interpretation be? As we change, grow, mature, should our interpretation of something which remains unchanging itself remain unchanged? Should it solidify, perhaps, as we reach adulthood? I first came to know *Sgt. Pepper* in the early 1970s as a heterogeneous, contingent collection of vibrant songs, some of which I knew well ('Lucy in the Sky with Diamonds', 'She's Leaving Home'), others of which I barely recognized ('Within You Without You', 'Fixing a Hole'). At the time, somehow, I had gone to sleep between *A Hard Day's Night* and the White Album. Not for me, then, the wonder of this new notion of a unified album, made particularly manifest by its packaging, since during this interval I became inducted into the world of the piano sonata (and of sets like Schumann's *Kinderszenen*), and by the time I came to *Sgt. Pepper*, then *Tarkus*, *In the Court of the Crimson King* and *Thick as a Brick* constituted a far more substantial part of my world. I came upon the historical significance of *Sgt. Pepper*, then, from the outside.

By the still later time I came to see it as a precursor of progressive rock's infatuation with unified concepts (see Moore 2002, pp. 94–6), I had been sufficiently persuaded of its importance but this was, still, to perceive it in terms of historical, rather than necessarily aesthetic, success. And it was this recognition, I think, which led to my proposing it as a worthy subject for the *Cambridge Handbooks* series, as what became the book I published in 1997. By means of this intervention I think I have been seen, entirely reasonably, as implying that, as a work, it stands alongside other great monuments to European musical thinking. However, that was not an argument I attempted to make in the book, with the exception of a rather half-hearted attempt in the final chapter, and it is still not an argument I would make with any conviction today.[1] Rather, I saw it as representative of a way of making music which, as a practice, was of equivalent importance to the practices traced in the works which were the subjects of other volumes in that series. But of course, I have no more right to insist that this was what the book 'meant' than did John Lennon to insist that 'Lucy in the Sky with Diamonds' was not a drug song. In my view, the album was a token of its type, rather than necessarily of stature in its own right. But then I am suspicious of the notion of genius, and of the products of genius, of those artistic statements which, because they 'stand the test of time', are perceived to have

---

1   In contrast, perhaps, to the position enabled by the 'language and conceptual approach of postmodernism' referenced by Paul Gleed, and about which I remain sceptical (see Gleed 2006, p. 166).

transcended their time and place and to have acquired an extra-cultural universality of reference. I really don't want to say that this transcendence was achieved by *Sgt. Pepper*, but in insisting on this position, I do not intend to diminish its value. Its great strength, it seems to me, is that it manages to capture, more vividly than almost anything contemporaneous, its own time and place. And I also suspect that one reason why the late 1960s appears so prominently in the imagination of so many people, whether they experienced the period first hand or not, is that it has artefacts as vibrant as *Sgt. Pepper* so to represent it (see Moore 2000).

So, other than being provided with the opportunity to do so, why should I return to music I have previously dealt with rather exhaustively? Well, one reason is precisely to address the question of whether interpretations change. I suspect I am not alone in finding the sort of detailed work required of effective analysis psychologically very difficult to begin. Having begun, the process of working tends to have a momentum all of its own, but the first actual steps are something I put off again and again (as, of course, do so many of my students, with the exception perhaps that some of them never convincingly do get started). The more work that can be done at one remove, without grappling with note-to-note details, the happier (and yet unsatisfied) I am. Maybe this is simply an aspect of white-paper syndrome. A result of this prevarication, though, is that the closer I get to the point where the analytical work becomes possible, the larger the music has loomed in my imagination and has begun to take over, almost in the same way that composing music takes over. I am not particularly aware of any fundamental difference in preparation between these two activities, which is one key reason why I maintain that analysis is necessarily a form of interpretation, which is in itself a creative act. Interpretation is not simply, or even mostly, the decoding of a musical artefact but, as David Sless's critique of semiotics maintains (Sless 1986), it is marked initially by a quality called 'letness' – one begins from the creative act of allowing something, in one's own experience, to stand for something else. Anyhow, having taken over, that music (as experienced) has of course changed in some way – it is more vivid, more enveloping, I move closer to it (or it to me). This again I think is a reason why students often complain at having to do analysis – it changes their perception of what it is they are analyzing. And frequently, of course, they complain that it 'ruins' what it is they are analyzing. My answer to them is always that the analytical process represents a brick wall through which it is worth going: having reached the other side, their pleasure in the music will be restored and, indeed, I always say (and find), enhanced. Now, of course, the time I spent with *Sgt. Pepper* in 1995–96 was far more intense than what I would expect of a student, but I am not convinced that it represents a qualitative difference, rather than a quantitative one. So, what happened to my pleasure with *Sgt. Pepper*? The first thing to say is that it had not previously been particularly intense. This was certainly not my favourite music. I respected it, and very much liked a couple of tracks, but my affection for it was no stronger than that. My experience of working on it, then, certainly changed my perception of those tracks. Indeed, up to the point of writing the book, I was barely conscious of making an interpretation of any of them, with the exception of my frustration at seeing them always uncritically referred to the drug experience. As a result, with a rather wilful operation of Sless's 'letness', I entertained a desire to see if they could be made sense of in any other way, a way that resonated with my own experiences, and come to an interpretation I indeed did (even if many of the subtleties I have forgotten in the meantime). The sense of 'A Day in the Life' as being external to the album, as turning experience on its head, was perhaps the only concrete reading I brought in to that intensive period of work, and that interpretation did not change, although I can hardly say that it deepened either – perhaps I found a way to express it, and I shall come back to this issue later. With the other tracks, though, my understanding certainly did change as the result of my analysis, my experience of them was enriched and I am indeed glad of that change. But that was a decade ago. Since then, I have barely listened to the music (except 'A Day in the Life', which I have explored further in other contexts), and so I returned to it in late September 2006 rather fresh.

I think a number of interpretive strategies come through the book. The first, of course, is the drug-related one, which I tie to understandings of the album as presenting a fantasy, and the dangers of mistaking that fantasy for a reality (Moore 1997, pp. 60–62). The second concerns its level of sophistication, and whether this should be read as maturity or as pretension (Ibid., pp. 62–3). A third concerns its provinciality – its subject matter being peculiarly English, and largely northern (Ibid., p. 63) – and, hence, its equivocation over the sort of transcendence I referred to earlier. The fourth is the whole question of its unity and the status of its underpinning concept (Ibid., pp. 64–5). A final one questions the difference between judgements of its musical and cultural importance (Ibid., p. 68), on which I have already trespassed in suggesting I had previously perceived only its historical, not its aesthetic, value. I remain pleased with the emphasis I made on the comparative sparseness of the album's textures (Ibid., p. 50), and also by the emphasis I put on the interpretations implied by cover versions – I am still convinced that this is a fruitful line of enquiry, although its results are hard to verbalize. And it is that difficulty, concerning the verbalization of an interpretation which, I think, troubles me most in returning to my earlier effort.

I have, however, noticed things that I didn't notice before. My ears are now much more attuned to the implied spaces present in recordings. The opening track, for instance, now seems to me to emphasize excessive space, represented by the dramatic cut-off of the snare throughout the first verse and of the crash cymbal during the central section. That this latter fails to ring out suggests a large performance space. Having noticed this, when listening back to the empty texture of the first verse, somehow it no longer sounds empty. It is as if I have carried across in my memory the presence of both the audience and an orchestra, made manifest in the album's introduction, even though they are not present in the song. After all, a large physical space is actually required to accommodate so many people. Thus the cymbal, although it sounds somewhat tinny, also conveys that larger impression. In the second track, I remark for the first time the strange pacing of the shuffle rhythm of the tambourine. Because of the speed at which one needs to move a tambourine to get a decent rattle of the jingles, the particular speed of this tambourine sounds just too slow (particularly in the chorus preceding the final bridge). It seems to me this helps to portray Ringo Starr's awkwardness, perhaps reluctance to admit his dependence in that final bridge, in a way I had missed before. So, there are a number of such little moments, thrown away at the time (or at least, instinctively rendered), which perhaps remain to be uncovered explicitly (although it would surprise me were there not countless listeners who had already intuited the links I am making here). I think I gave far too little attention to the closing portions of both 'Being for the Benefit of Mr. Kite!' and 'Lovely Rita', particularly, with the latter, to the way the outro is signalled ahead, the way it is sewn into the final reprise of the opening vocal (especially notable in the piano and bass from 2'01"). Perhaps the best way of describing this is to observe that the 'sister or two' appear to have left the sofa vacant for the singer's heavily amorous encounter with Rita during that coda. I wonder, now, whether the casual mention of walking 'by the old school' in 'Good Morning, Good Morning' could have been tied into attempts to revivify the concept of revisiting childhood locations (which, even with that, I am not inclined to do), and also whether something should be made of the way the opening of 'A Day in the Life' seems to echo in David Bowie's early 'The Bewlay Brothers'.[2] Finally, with hindsight, I also think I should have made something of the observation that seven of the 13 songs have running times of within 11 seconds of each other. So, on that score at least, perception can grow richer, even if the overall effect of these little details on my own interpretation of the album is nil. However, at this distance, I must reinterrogate the key aspect of my own initial reading.

At the end of Chapter 4 of my study, I argued that 'Resistance to exegesis is the only valid option' (Ibid., p. 56). The context for this statement is formed by other writers who aim to summarize, to reduce the meaning of either the final track, or the album, to a particular form of words. I argued there that the attempt to do so was misguided. But there is a still larger context for this concern, which impacts the very status of musical enquiry, and to address this I must digress somewhat. Over the past decade, it has become necessary in the United Kingdom to construe both compositional and performance activity within higher education as forms of 'research', parallel to musicology. The simple reason for this is that research activities are funded from the national science purse, but cultural activities are not centrally funded, unless they are either populist or serve the ideologies of the funders, which tend to be at odds with the aesthetic of very many university musicians (and, even then, they are not funded to the same level). Research, in this way, is defined as 'original investigation undertaken in order to gain knowledge and understanding',[3] with the necessary assumption that the knowledge or understanding gained is made public, or at least is communicated. In order to fund quality practical activities in higher education departments, it has been necessary to construe those activities as research, to make them susceptible to – and subject to – evaluation by that and subsidiary criteria. That means that music itself (arguments about whether there is any objective 'music itself' being clearly ignored) is to be taken as embodying knowledge. This means that the translation of – or mediation of – that knowledge by means of words becomes not only unnecessary, but also dangerous, since it undermines the construction of music as embodying knowledge. Now, mathematical symbols and their manipulations are held to embody knowledge without being translated into other symbolic languages, but they represent objective, not (inter-)subjective, knowledge. And knowledge, to be usable, has to be transferable,

---

2   The track closes *Hunky Dory* (1971).

3   This definition refers to work assessed by the United Kingdom's Research Assessment Exercise, 2007.

from one situation to another, from one realm to another. If we insist on construing music as embodying knowledge on a par with language, if we insist on construing the composition of music, the activity itself, as a research activity, then we are bound by the definition of research, the foremost term of which definition is that the work be original. And yet this is a historically and geographically bounded aesthetic position, not a universal one. It is only under (Western-industrial) modernism that originality is a supremely valued concept (presumably ensured by genius). It is therefore only modernist music which can acceptably be construed as research. But having signed up to this position (that university practical work shall only be funded from the higher education science pot), we rule all other aesthetic positions out of court. And, by holding that knowledge is embodied in the musical object, this knowledge becomes inaccessible to those who do not use that particular symbolic language as a means of communication (most people, after all, unfortunately do not produce music). On the contrary, it seems to me an imperative that the music be interpreted verbally, in order to make communication possible: as I say elsewhere, 'simply identifying that something matters, and then what it is, is insufficient. We must endeavour to identify why it matters, for communicating our understanding, rather than allowing ourselves to inhabit an hermetic aestheticized space, carries a morally imperative charge' (Moore 2008). I have recently criticized Albin Zak's interpretation of the Beatles' 'I'm Only Sleeping'. Referring to the distorted acoustic guitar sound, a typical Beatles sound, he notes 'that this is not your average acoustic guitar sound ... and [I] take my delight from its unusual sonic texture ... By its raw, harsh tone it has gotten my attention, and even if I cannot put it into words, I know that it is saying *something*' (Zak 2001, pp. 191–2). But it is precisely this 'putting it into words' that is so crucial. And yet, by putting it into words, even by putting into words the interpretation we make, by moving from one symbolic language to another, we inevitably change that interpretation. How can we do the one without the other? Perhaps we cannot, but I think (hope) that what I offered on 'A Day in the Life', that the album's structure translates its normality into our unreality, and its unreality (that final track) into our reality, is acceptably close. Refusing to put anything into words, allowing the music simply to 'speak for itself', is insufficient. Not only may we not be listening, but from an interpretive point of view, if we accept that knowledge is embedded in the music, there can be no interpretation to be made (as the meaning seems to be for us individually – 'second nature'), but neither is there any communication to be had, unless we all become musicians. No less insufficient, I think, are the views which insist on *Sgt. Pepper*'s coherence. I should like to address two here, that of Sheila Whiteley, and the more recent interpretation of Walter Everett.

Whiteley's argument is that the entire album can be understood as encoding the psychedelic experience – indeed, that is presumably the best interpretation to make. In arguing, thus, not only does she call to her defence 'realist' devices (double entendres, timbral manipulation), but she interprets anything which seems to evade the normative (such as the metric irregularity of 'Good Morning, Good Morning') as necessarily 'psychedelic coding' without at any point investigating alternative possibilities. It is not the grounds of the interpretation I question here (we are, after all, individually entitled to observe how our different experiences make sense of each other), but her fundamental begging of the basic question: the necessity of a relationship between 'With a Little Help from My Friends' and 'Lucy in the Sky with Diamonds', which she proposes is explained because *Sgt. Pepper* is a concept album (Whiteley 1992, p. 42). And why? The import of her opening pages appears to be because people want it to be (following McCartney's own lead, of course). Once again we are prey to the intentional fallacy. Everett's argument is quite different – the book appeared too late for me to address it in mine. In terms of the entire album, he argues (briefly) that 'its musical unity results ... from motivic relationships between key areas, particularly involving C, E, and G' (Everett 1999, p. 122). He expends little space on this (about as much as commenting on the value of the packaging for the album's identity as a concept), and even less than he spends on individual songs, but the desire to find the same means of addressing all the songs seems to be that of Whiteley. And I discover that I, too, am prey to this slightly woolly thinking. In *Rock: The Primary Text*, in a passage originally conceived nearly 20 years ago, I argue that the conceptual unity of the album is ensured by, among other things, the use of common harmonic patterns and falling melodies (Moore 2002, p. 95). I can no longer accept either this, or Everett's motivic relationships, as ensuring 'unity'. This term implies an experience in which everything belongs, in which the order of events is necessarily fixed – I take it as a form of narrative unity. I think that what I find in the album, and what I find in Everett's interpretation, too, is more a family resemblance, a sharing of merely one facet, and not conclusively the most important one. William Northcutt's recent study argues that a variety of factors 'made [the album] all seem more cohesive than is obviously true' (Northcutt 2006, p. 134), and I take 'cohesive' and 'unified' to be co-extensive here. These are not, however, innocent comments to my mind: I prefer my slightly qualified 'resistance to exegesis' since modernist musicology appears to have been in thrall, not (quite) to the notion that everything was susceptible of explanation, but certainly to the view that the function of all parts of a work (in this case, an album) could be figuratively laid out in relation to each other – that fundamentally everything belonged (this is nowhere more visible than in serial and set theoretic analyses) as part of the 'work', that nothing was extraneous. And it seems to me this thrust, this particular pernicious hermeneutic imperative, is apparent in both Whiteley's and Everett's (and my) otherwise very different interpretations. I consequently prefer now a looser explanation, to the effect that all that is actually necessary to the quintessential experience of *Sgt. Pepper* are tracks 1, 12 and 13, separated by various things which approximate to what we actually have on the album (although they should presumably conform to the same contemporaneous production practices and instrumental and vocal techniques). It seems to me that all desires to see the album as a unity are modernist in orientation, and I cannot see any objective criteria for agreeing or disagreeing with this ideology.

Indeed, the drive for unity is not restricted to this Beatles album. Let me digress once more to view a parallel approach to the album *Revolver*. The aim of Russell Reising's chapter (Reising 2006) in the recent collection I have already minded here appears to be to demonstrate unity beneath the surface diversity of *Revolver*: his demonstration is organized around couplets from the final track, 'Tomorrow Never Knows', from which he draws themes, and he then finds these themes echoed in the remaining songs on the album. To make these connections, of course, he needs to make assumptions about how songs work, that is, that they are always 'about' something (that themes can be abstracted from isolated couplets), that they can be reduced[4] to another form of words. I am sceptical of such an assumption, particularly when (for example) he claims that by incorporating the line 'It is not dying, it is not dying', the song embodies a 'wilful transcendence of death' (Ibid., p. 115). 'Transcendence' in what sense? (And 'wilful' in what sense?) The song is no less ephemeral than any other recorded song (in itself) and would not live longer in cultural memory (if, indeed, it does) by virtue of its inclusion of those words. I think the song is made to do far too much work here. Reising quotes lines out of context (and ignores how they are delivered – the irony apparent in how Lennon's persona delivers the initial word 'relax', for instance, the implied excessive tightness of the vocal cords and narrowing of the nasal passage which enact the word's very opposite appear entirely to pass him by), and offers interpretation effectively masquerading as the analysis of intention ('The Beatles' are frequently the subject of his sentences). And, were *Revolver* indeed aesthetically 'unified' despite each song being sonically unrelated to every other (Ibid., p. 112), then we are given no guidance (other than through taking lines out of context and reading themes into isolated phrases) as to why any similar assertion, with any other eclectic album, would not be equally valid. To search for underlying unity (even if it is a human trait) does not mean to find it, even were such seeking possible to demonstrate on the part of the originators.

So, the search for unity is problematic, and putting into words, interpreting, is not the same as reducing the song to a form of unsung words, as declaring what it is about. If nothing else, reflection on my attempt at accounting for the musical experience of *Sgt. Pepper* all those years ago has taught me that, and perhaps given me a programme for my next interpretive foray.

---

4   I have now twice criticized the notion of 'reducing' meaning to another form of words, rather than the more interrogative hermeneutic I try to engage in. The difference may appear subtle, but I believe it to be substantial.

Chapter 11

'A lucky man who made the grade': Sgt. *Pepper* and the rise of a phonographic tradition in twentieth-century popular music

Olivier Julien

In this final chapter, I intend to put *Sgt. Pepper's Lonely Hearts Club Band* in perspective with regard to the rise of a 'phonographic tradition'[1] in twentieth-century popular music. If the term 'phonography' is universally understood as synonymous with 'sound recording' (I shall come back to its origins later), the term 'tradition' may require some preliminary explanation: it refers here to the centricity of a culture on a medium that determines its mode of preservation, its modes of dissemination and transmission, and eventually the nature of what is regarded as the 'creative act' within the scope of that same culture. Such a conception is based on the 1954 International Folk Council definition of folk music:

> Folk music is the product of a musical tradition that has evolved through the process of oral transmission. The factors that shape the tradition are: (i) continuity which links the present with the past; (ii) variation which springs from the creative impulse of the individual or the group; (iii) selection by the community which determines the form or forms in which music survives. (Quoted in Middleton 1990, pp. 132–3)

It also draws on the following description of the written tradition in Western art music by Jean-Jacques Nattiez:

> In Western tradition, what results from the composer's creative act is clearly the score; it is the score that makes the work performable and recognizable as an entity; and it is also the score that enables the work to travel down the centuries.[2]

As I shall argue, the specificity of popular music as we know it today lies in its dependence upon the third medium that has been available since the late nineteenth century for preserving, disseminating and transmitting music: phonography. This

---

1 '*Tradition phonographique*' (Julien 1998, pp. 27, 342–5; Julien 2006, p. 69).

2 '*Ce qui résulte du geste créateur du compositeur, c'est bien, dans la tradition occidentale, la partition; ce qui rend l'oeuvre exécutable et reconnaissable comme entité, c'est la partition; ce qui lui permet de traverser les siècles, c'est encore elle*' (Nattiez 1987, p. 98).

music certainly has roots in orality;[3] it was also first associated with mass production through printed sheet music (which was, not so long ago, the only medium suited to a song aiming at a wide diffusion);[4] but since the late 1920s and the rise of the recording industry, it is phonography that has been the vector of the musical syntheses that determined the course of its history:

> For the first time, white guitar players from Kentucky were able to listen carefully to the music of black bluesmen from Texas, and rural medicine-show entertainers could hear the latest cabaret hits from New York. Early recordings documented musical changes rather than determining them, but by the mid-thirties records were the primary source of inspiration for many musicians. (Palmer 1992, p. 7)

To put it differently: as popular musicians began to rely on phonography to preserve their songs and spread them beyond geographical, social, cultural and even chronological boundaries that might have seemed impossible to cross a few decades earlier, popular music entered the era of phonographic transmission.

Furthermore, it appears that the centricity of a musical culture on a medium is bound to have a profound influence on the nature of what Jean-Jacques Nattiez calls the 'creative act' (or the so-called 'creative impulse of the individual or the group' in the 1954 International Folk Council definition of folk music). Among such examples, orality did shape folk music in the sense that it is the very nature of oral composition that explains why '"folk songs" often draw on a pool of collectively owned, pre-existing schemes and materials' (Middleton 1990, p. 137). And it is quite certain too that the developments that took place in post-Renaissance Western art music would have never been possible without musical notation. As Jean-Claude Risset observes:

> If musical notation first served as an aid to memory, it subsequently influenced composition by encouraging music *writing* ... Symmetries with the coordinates axes of the score, apparent in the graphic representation, suggested the melodic transformations of counterpoint – inversion of intervals, retrograde melodies – while those very transformations are hardly ever used in oral-tradition music.[5]

---

3   According to Richard Middleton: '... under the impact of Romanticism, "popular songs" could in the nineteenth century ... be thought of as synonymous with "peasant", "national" and "traditional songs". Later in the century, "folk" took over these usages from "popular", which was transferred to the products of the music hall and then to those of the mass market song publishers of Tin Pan Alley and its British equivalent' (Middleton 1990, pp. 3–4).

4   As an example, Ian Whitcomb begins his remarkable history of popular music with the publication of 'After the Ball' by Chas K. Harris in 1892, arguing that this song, which sold ten million sheet music copies within 20 years, was 'the first million seller to be conceived as a million seller, and marketed as a million seller' (Whitcomb 1994, p. 4).

5   '*Si la notation musicale a servi d'abord à aider la mémoire, elle a par la suite influencé la façon de composer en permettant un travail d'écriture ... Les symétries selon les axes de coordonnées de la partition, évidentes sur la représentation graphique, ont suggéré les transformations mélodiques du contrepoint – le renversement des intervalles, la rétrogradation des mélodies – alors que ces transformations ne sont guère utilisées dans les musiques de tradition orale*' (Risset 1998, p. 99).

It is, in a way, the connections of *Sgt. Pepper* with a similar shift in the rise of a phonographic tradition that will be examined throughout the following pages: the shift from phonographic preservation, dissemination and transmission to phonographic composition.

The origins of popular music as a phonographic tradition

Looking back at the early days of sound recording, it is somehow surprising that the preservation and reproduction of music became the main purpose of that technology. As his personal notes reveal, when Thomas Edison began working on the phonograph in July 1877,[6] he was actually looking for a way to 'store & reproduce automatically … the human voice perfectly' (quoted in Millard 1995, p. 25). This original focus on speech is also attested by the crowds of people who arrived at his Menlo Park laboratory to hear 'the sounds of their own voices' (Ibid., p. 26) during the weeks that followed the demonstration of the first working phonograph, five months later, and by an 1878 article for the *North American Review* in which Edison himself suggested the following uses for his invention:

1. Letter writing and all kinds of dictation without the aid of a stenographer.
2. Phonographic books, which will speak to blind people without effort on their part.
3. The teaching of elocution.
4. Reproduction of music.
5. The 'Family Record' – a registry of sayings, reminiscences, etc., by members of a family in their own voices, and of the last words of dying persons.
6. Music-boxes and toys.
7. Clocks that should announce in articulate speech the time for going home, going to meals, etc.
8. The preservation of languages by exact reproduction of the manner of pronouncing.
9. Educational purposes; such as preserving the explanations made by a teacher, so that the pupil can refer to them at any moment, and spelling or other lessons placed upon the phonograph for convenience in committing to memory.
10. Connection with the telephone, so as to make that instrument an auxiliary in the transmission of permanent and invaluable records, instead of being the recipient of momentary and fleeting communications. (Quoted in Gelatt 1977, p. 29)

It was only during the late 1880s and early 1890s, with the commercial failure of the phonograph as a business machine, that the companies involved in the early developments of sound recording began to consider refocusing their activities on music. The first significant move of the so-called 'talking machine' towards its legitimization as a musical device occurred in March 1902, when an employee of the British Gramophone Company named Fred Gaisberg heard Enrico Caruso at La Scala opera house and asked him to record ten songs. At that time, Caruso was already a tenor on the rise, but he was far from being an international star. When

---

6   Demonstrated at the office of *Scientific American* on 6 December 1877, the phonograph was the first machine that could practically store and reproduce sound. Drawing its name from the Greek terms *phone* ('sound', 'voice') and *graphein* ('to write'), it was, in Edison's mind, a 'sound-writing machine'.

those recordings that he made with Gaisberg in Milan were released in the United States on Victor Red Seal records, they generated so much interest that he was offered a contract to appear at the Metropolitan Opera House – as Andre Millard remarks, it was 'probably the first time a singer received an invitation to perform solely on the basis of a recording' (Millard 1995, p. 60). Five years later, another of Caruso's recordings ('On with the Motley' from Leoncavallo's *Pagliacci*) became the first recording to sell a million copies.

Caruso, whose tenor voice was perfectly suited to the talking machine, owed much of his fame to recording, and this encouraged other stars of the concert hall like Adelina Patti and Nellie Melba to follow his example. Yet those names, however prestigious, belonged to a tradition of written musical expression; this tradition had been shaped by centuries of musicians relying on notation for the transmission of sound-making possibilities and it had evolved up to the point where musicologists regarded 'printed music [as] the primary manifestation of music' (Bennett 1983, p. 221). Caruso's, Patti's or Melba's recordings were, at best, historic performances of works that had been embodied in the latter fashion.

On the other hand, it was fairly predictable that the invention of sound recording would have a more profound impact on musicians whose repertoire had been shaped by centuries of oral transmission. Among those musicians were white folk musicians, of course, but also Afro-American musicians, who may be regarded as the first non-literate musicians who adopted the record as 'a means, frequently the only means through which music is propagated' (Chanan 1995, p. 52). Several reasons have been advanced to explain their predisposition to switch from orality to phonography. According to Richard Middleton, it has to do with the fact that 'Black music *was* different in many respects from almost all other Western music of the time. In some of these respects (such as improvisation, or blue tonality or pitch inflection) it was more suited to transmission in recording than in notation' (Middleton 1990, p. 72). Michael Chanan also argues that such a predisposition harks back to the place and forms of music making in Africa, where performance and creation are one and the same process:

> This is … completely different from the European tradition of written music which has allowed what the composer-conductor Lukas Foss once called the very unmusical idea of dividing what is essentially indivisible – music – into two separate processes: composition, the making of music, and performance, which is also the making of music. In the African and Afro-American traditions, composition and performance are part of a single act. (Chanan 1995, p. 52)

Whatever the reason (or the *reasons*, Middleton's and Chanan's analyses being, in no way, antinomic), the contribution of recording to the preservation, dissemination and transmission of early forms of Afro-American music has been widely documented. One only needs to consider the formative years and the legacy of such an influential figure as Robert Johnson: born in Mississippi in the 1910s, he learned from musicians like Kokomo Arnold, Leroy Carr, Skip James and Lonnie Johnson on phonograph records; during the 1940s, it would be by copying what they heard on his records that Chicago bluesmen like Muddy Waters would assimilate the Delta blues, before their own records would finally bring the guitar playing techniques that Johnson had learnt and perfected to British guitarists like Eric Clapton and Keith Richards (see LaVere

1990; Rothenbuhler 2007). In other words, Johnson's key position in the history of blues and popular music clearly appears as the result of his being at the heart of a web of phonographic filiations that gave birth to Chicago blues and then to British rock.

More importantly, as its rapid and wide diffusion intensified the impact it had on other musicians, the record proved to be the means to shape Afro-American music. Here too, the history of blues offers significant examples. Like jazz, this music was originally an improvised music that was inconsistent with the time limitations of the 78-rpm disc record. As Andre Millard points out:

> [It] had to fit within the 3-minute boundary of sound recording, although the original blues, as sung in the rural South, was not constrained by time or the technical limitations of the recording studio. It appeared in many forms and had many functions: work music, personal expression, and dance music for entertaining a crowd. Putting it on record shaped its structure ... (Millard 1995, pp. 101–2)

Michael Chanan corroborates this view when he asserts that 'the ten-inch, 78 rpm disc', as a recording and distribution format, 'gave home to the genre called the "classic blues"' (Chanan 1995, p. 47). And those early forms of shaping were not even confined to formal aspects such as the number of stanzas included in a song; as reported in the following anecdote, they might also concern the very sound of the music that was being recorded:

> Alan Lomax, the Library of Congress musicologist who documented [Robert] Johnson and many others with his field recordings, recalls that the sessions [during which Don Law recorded Johnson] took place in his hotel room and that Johnson was so shy that he faced the wall. Ry Cooder, in a 1982 BBC radio interview, believes that this was not due to timidity at all, but was Johnson utilizing a technique called 'corner loading' which entails playing towards hard surfaces, which are at right angles to each other in order to increase ambiance and bass response. (Backer 2002, pp. 119–20)

As explained here by Ry Cooder, Johnson's use of 'corner loading' is quite likely to have represented one of the earliest occurrences of the sound of a music being thought and shaped by its performer 'with attention to a kind of for-the-record aesthetic' (Rothenbuhler 2007, p. 78). For this reason, it should be regarded as a decisive moment in the process that would soon lead songwriters to claim: 'We didn't write songs, we wrote records' (Jerry Leiber and Mike Stoller, quoted in Zak 2001, p. 21).

A new form of publication

Commenting on the changes that were occurring in the music publishing business since the late 1940s, Robert Burton declared in 1957: 'What we are now enjoying in the United States is a new form of publication. It is an *acoustical* publication' (quoted in Whitcomb 1994, p. 211). By coining such an expression as 'acoustical publication', Burton (who was then a vice-president of BMI) was obviously referring to the fact that the technological improvements in the making of phonograph records and sound reproduction had finally led the record to become the dominant vehicle of the music industry. It has often been emphasized that this revolution in the mass distribution of music coincided with the advent of rock 'n' roll, that is, a music which itself drew on traditions whose history had been determined by the early developments of the recording industry:

> Recordings brought the sounds of black music to rock 'n' rollers like Elvis Presley and Buddy Holly. Scotty Moore (who played guitar behind Elvis Presley) had learned a lot from the playing of Muddy Waters and Howlin' Wolf on record. Records also brought country and western to singers such as Chuck Berry, whose first Top Ten hit 'Maybellene' (initially called 'Ida Red') had an unmistakably country sound. (Millard 1995, p. 252)

Indeed, by the early 1950s, the musical traditions whose synthesis gave birth to rock 'n' roll had been relying on phonographic transmission for quite some time. But what clearly distinguished rock 'n' roll from its predecessors was that it was also the first music to have literally grown out of phonographic transmission:

> Rock and roll emerged as an eclectic, unruly mixture of various musical styles and idioms – blues, R&B, gospel, country, jazz. And in all of these, records were conceived not as works but as snapshots of live performances.
>   Even if rock and roll had its roots in live performance traditions, it was nevertheless, and unlike any of its precursors, first and foremost a recorded music. (Zak 2001, p. 12)

Its unusual focus on sound was probably the most obvious sign of rock 'n' roll's phonographic origins. To quote the words of Steve Jones: 'As popular music has evolved from the early twentieth century and Tin Pan Alley days to rock music, it has become sound – and not music – that is of prime importance … the primary impact of recording technology has been to make the sound of a recording its identifying characteristic' (Jones 1992, pp. 11–12). Jones's reference to recording technology is of particular interest here since rock 'n' roll's focus on sound was not only the consequence of its synthesizing musical traditions that had been shaped by decades of phonographic transmission: it was also the result of its appearing at a time when the evolution of recording technology made it possible for that very technology to become more than a means to preserve, to disseminate and to transmit music. To put it clearly: it was with the advent of rock 'n' roll and the arrival of the tape machine that the sound-shaping techniques whose prototype may be regarded as Johnson's 'corner loading' somehow became the norm in popular music.

It must be added, though, that with respect to what I have elsewhere called 'the diverting of musical technology' (Julien 1999), the first major breakthrough occurred a few years prior to the arrival of Elvis Presley, with the release of 'How High the Moon' by Les Paul and Mary Ford. By occupying the number one position in the American chart for nine weeks during the spring of 1951, this single was the recording that actually brought the sonorities of tape echo, multitracked voices and close-miking to the wide American audience. As a matter of fact, it heralded such a change in terms of studio practice that Bruce Swedien would still remember his first hearing the song years after becoming a renowned sound engineer and producer:

> The first time I really got excited about popular music was when I discovered that it was possible to use my imagination. That had come with a record which I myself didn't work on; Les Paul and Mary Ford's 'How High the Moon' in 1951. Up to that point the goal of music recording had been to capture an unaltered acoustic event, reproducing the music of

big bands as if you were in the best seat in the house. It left no room for imagination, but when I heard 'How High the Moon', which did not have one natural sound in it, I thought, 'Damn, there's hope!' (Buskin 1999, p. 274)

Nevertheless, it was almost inevitable that Les Paul's pioneering achievements would be overshadowed by those of early rock 'n' roll producers, whose success turned out to be beyond compare. Among those producers, Sam Phillips, for example, would soon go down in history as such a fervent adept of tape echo that over 50 years after his first recording session with Elvis Presley, many people believe it was he who introduced the technique in popular music. As for Norman Petty and Buddy Holly, they would not only experiment with tape echo, but with overdubbing and close-miking too, which would become essential ingredients in the shaping of Holly's sound from late 1956 to his death, on 3 February 1959. And it would finally be the latter producers' records that would bring the sonorities associated with Paul's techniques to a whole new generation of British musicians during the late 1950s.

This new instance of phonographic transmission brings me back to my initial question regarding the position of *Sgt. Pepper's Lonely Hearts Club Band* in the shift from phonographic transmission to phonographic composition. Following on from what I have discussed previously, it appears that by the time rock 'n' roll first reached the United Kingdom, several generations of musicians relying on phonography to preserve, to disseminate and to transmit their work had already established popular music as the art of 'acoustical publication' in the same way that art music was (or might be regarded as) the art of written publication. Furthermore, this acoustical mode of publication had begun to influence music making in such a way that the shaping of one's sound with a view to putting it on record was on its way to becoming a well-established feature in popular music when John Lennon and Paul McCartney first met, on 6 July 1957.

The Beatles' relationship with the phonographic medium

Long before the Beatles even knew what a recording studio was, their musical practice was characterized by the trends described above. To begin, numerous accounts indicate that they learned, like so many popular musicians, to sing and play their respective instruments by copying what they heard on their favourite records (see, for example, Davies 1992, pp. 99, 128; Norman 1981, pp. 28–9). According to Philip Norman, their tendency to rely on the phonographic medium for its educational and mnemonic potential survived throughout the days of the Cavern Club:

It seemed to Bob Wooler [the Cavern's disc jockey] that they took a perverse delight in playing what no rival group would dare to do. 'They had to let you know they were different. If everyone else was playing the A-side of a record, they'd be playing the B-side ...' Wooler himself possessed a number of rare American singles which he would play as surprise items over the Cavern loudspeakers. One of these, Chan Romero's 'Hippy Hippy Shake', besotted Paul McCartney, who begged to be allowed to borrow it and copy down the words. 'Hippy Hippy Shake' became the climax of their catalogue of sheer stage-stamping Rock. (Norman 1981, p. 102)

As McCartney puts it: '… records were the main objective. That was what we bought, that was what we dealt in. That was the currency of music: records. That's where we got our repertoire from …' (Lewisohn 1988a, p. 6). And quite naturally, when the Beatles came to Abbey Road for their first recording session, on 4 September 1962, they brought those same records with them. Folk musicians would have come to the studio solely with their instruments; art musicians would have certainly turned up with scores; as for them, the Beatles 'brought in loads and loads of records from Liverpool to show [the engineers] what sounds they wanted' (Norman Smith, quoted in Southall, Vince and Rouse 1997, p. 68). This anecdote alone reveals what the dissemination and transmission of their musical culture already owed to phonography.

What is more, the fact that the Beatles relied on records to show the EMI engineers 'what sounds they wanted' is a plain hint of what was really being transmitted through the latter records; to quote the words of Steve Jones again: 'Recording … did more than liberate music from the constraints of space and time … it enabled music to be organized around sound and timbre instead of notes' (Jones 1992, p. 48). More concretely, the mark of those records that the Beatles brought to Abbey Road was to be found not only in their songwriting and performing styles but also in the sound, that is, in the production of their own records. Their cover of Buddy Holly's 'Words of Love' clearly illustrates this point:

> … the only Beatles recording of a Buddy Holly song, 'Words of Love', bears a striking sonic likeness to the original. The chiming guitar and the tone of Holly's voice, both of which the Beatles emulate, were clearly as important to them as the song itself. Further, the pat-a-cake effect of the eighth-note handclaps is a reference to another Holly track, 'Everyday' (1958). (Zak 2001, p. 27)

This recording was included on *Beatles for Sale* (1964), but it should be noted that the type of transmission described by Albin Zak continued throughout the Beatles' recording career – among such examples, one might also mention Lennon asking his voice to be treated with tape echo on 'A Day in the Life' as he wanted to 'sound like Elvis Presley on "Heartbreak Hotel"' (Martin with Pearson 1994, p. 53) or McCartney stating that the Beatles 'Phil Spector'd' the coda of 'Hello Goodbye' by asking Geoff Emerick to '*really* whack up the echo on the tom-toms' (Lewisohn 1988a, p. 15).

It should also be noted that before the Beatles got 'better technically' and 'finally took over the studio' (John Lennon in Wenner 2000, p. 58), George Martin's role as a producer made him the very catalyst of such occurrences of 'sonic transmission' on their records:

> By then I had been a record producer for so long that whenever I listened to anything new I was not listening only to the music: I was listening to the way the recording had been made, technically. What amazed me about the … music that the Beatles played me … was the sheer technical ferocity of the stuff. The US studios managed to pack so much volume on to a disc, much more than we could over here in the UK. I could pick up the newly imported piece of 45-rpm vinyl, look at it, and actually see the ear-splitting loudness of the record before I had even put it on. It was, as they say, in the groove. (Martin with Pearson 1994, p. 45)

To carry the parallel between popular music as a phonographic tradition and art music as a literate tradition further, it might be deduced from the latter words that his producing skills allowed Martin to 'decipher' the records that the Fab Four played him in the same way that a conductor would have deciphered a score.

Of course, indications of the Beatles' musical practice being centred on phonography would become more apparent after they would have officially entered their 'studio years', in late 1966; but such indications are nonetheless to be found in the most early days of their recording career too. As an example, the legend has it that their first album, *Please Please Me*, 'reproduce[d] the Cavern performance in the comparative calm of the studio' (Martin with Hornsby 1979, p. 131); and yet that same album featured several types of 'studio tricks' that were absolutely incompatible with the idea of a recorded live performance – namely the overdubbing of a piano track at half-speed on 'Misery', that of celesta on 'Baby It's You', that of handclaps on 'I Saw Her Standing There', that of harmonica on 'There's a Place' and 'Please Please Me', and that of backing vocals and drum sticks tapped together on 'Do You Want to Know a Secret', the double-tracking of Paul McCartney's lead vocals on 'A Taste of Honey', and the fading out of 'Love Me Do', 'Misery', 'Chains', 'Boys', 'Baby It's You', 'Do You Want to Know a Secret' and 'There's a Place'. Despite Martin's desire to 'give the fans on record what they [could] hear on stage' (Martin with Pearson 1994, p. 77), the recording of this album had actually consisted in shaping the Beatles' performance – even in the most rudimentary way – with a view to putting it on record. With regard to the Beatles' relationship with phonography, it may thus be stated that it contained the seeds of what would determine their sound throughout the first phase of their recording career.

This phase would see them gradually moving away from the idea of capturing the sound of a live act and it would culminate with the recording of 'Tomorrow Never Knows', which Virgil Moorefield calls 'a total departure from anything the Beatles had attempted before' (Moorefield 2005, p. 30). There is little doubt, indeed, that the average pop music fan had ever heard anything like it in 1966. And there is little doubt too that, to most listeners, the most intriguing sounds on the recording were those of the tape loops that the Beatles had created at home on their Brennell tape recorders.[7] Listening back to the four-track master tape in 1995, George Martin recalled the 7 April session during which five of the latter loops were overdubbed to the pre-recorded backing track of the song, some 29 years ago:

> When we made that record, we could never reproduce it again; it would be impossible to reproduce it again because the way we made it was the actual mix. And all over this building, in different rooms, were tapes, tape machines with loops on them and people holding the loops at the right distance with a bit of pencil, going all the time, being fed to faders on our control

---

7   Geoff Emerick describes the origins of those loops as follows: 'Paul [McCartney], already developing a taste for avant-garde music, had discovered that the erase head [of his open-reel tape recorder] could be removed, which allowed new sounds to be added to the existing ones each time the tape passed over the record head. Because of the primitive technology of the time, the tape quickly became saturated with sound and distorted, but it was an effect that appealed to the four of them as they conducted sonic experiments in their respective homes' (Emerick and Massey 2006, p. 111).

panel on which we could bring up the sound like an organ, at any time. So the mix we did then was a random thing at that time. It could never be done again. (Beatles 2003d)

For quite obvious reasons, this session – which was the second recording session in the making of *Revolver* – represented a major breakthrough in the Beatles' approach to the act of recording. It also signalled a turning point in their relationship with the phonographic medium in the sense that it inaugurated a two-and-a-half-month period during which they would experiment endlessly with tape manipulation techniques such as retrograding and speed changing. But as far as the determination of the 'creative act' by that same medium was concerned, it consisted nonetheless of capturing a live performance; it was, in Martin's words, 'a live mix of tape loops' (quoted in Lewisohn 1988b, p. 72). George Harrison somehow shares this view when he notes: 'In those days ... if we did stuff in the studio with the aid of recording tricks, then we couldn't just reproduce them on stage ... Nowadays you could: you could do "Tomorrow Never Knows", have all the loops up there, on a keyboard' (Beatles 2003a). In short, if *Revolver* saw the intrusion of the phonographic medium in the Beatles' creative process, their use of that medium was still shaped, some way or another, by the idea of performability; while clearly on its way, the separation of recording and performance had not occurred yet. And this is precisely what makes this album 'the vital plateau between the Beatles' touring activities and what was to become known as their "studio years"' (Lewisohn 1988b, p. 84).

Sgt. Pepper and the transformation of the recording industry

As I have already argued in the introduction to this book, 'Strawberry Fields Forever' should not only be regarded as the starting point of the Beatles' 'studio years' for its status as the first song that they recorded after they had decided to stop performing live: it was also, and above all, the track whose production made the separation between recording and performance complete in their musical practice. Before examining the signs that confirmed the latter tendency throughout the series of recording sessions that followed, I would like, however, to address another important aspect of *Sgt. Pepper*'s determination by phonography by emphasizing the fact that this very work was aimed at a very specific phonographic format: the 33-1/3-rpm vinyl album.

In 1966–67, the 45-rpm vinyl single and the 33-1/3-rpm vinyl album were almost 20 years old (the formats had been invented in 1949 and 1948 respectively); but since they had overtaken the old 12- and ten-inch 78-rpm shellac discs as the dominant music industry vehicles during the mid-1950s, popular music had been literally dominated by the 45-rpm vinyl single, whose many advantages made it the Trojan Horse of independent record companies willing to enter the national US market and compete with the established national distribution systems of the major labels.[8] It

---

8   The 12-inch 33-1/3-rpm vinyl long-playing record (LP) was launched by Columbia in the United States in 1948 and the seven-inch 45-rpm vinyl single a year later by RCA-Victor, but the major record companies only began to send 45-rpm singles to radio stations instead of the heavier and more delicate 78-rpm shellac discs in 1954. Concurrently, the vinyl album, with its 20 minutes per side, was an immediate success in the classical market.

was not until the middle of the following decade that the long-playing record began to emerge as a popular format of its own. The growth of overall album sales from the late 1950s through the early 1980s exemplifies this shift from single to album while bringing to light the Beatles' contribution to the latter:

> Overall LP sales rose steadily from 1959, grew alongside the advent of prerecorded cassettes in 1966, pulled ahead of singles sales in 1967, and peaked in the late 1970s and early 1980s. This growth was represented increasingly by the youth market, largely created by the Beatles. The only albums prior to 1970 that sold 7 million or more copies in the United States through 1992 are the Beatles' *Abbey Road* (9), *Sgt. Pepper's Lonely Hearts Club Band* (8), and *The Beatles* (7). (Everett 1999, p. 91)

As with so many trends that characterized the recording industry during the 1960s, the Beatles were, indeed, driving forces in this major evolution of the popular music market. Yet the first and most significant step towards the transformation of the album from a distribution format into a creation format was not taken by the Fab Four; it was taken by Phil Spector with his late-1963 release, *A Christmas Gift for You*, whose overall concept was explained as follows in the liner notes of the record:

> ... Twelve Great Christmas Songs ... treated with the same excitement as is the original pop material of today; sung by four of the greatest pop artists in the country; produced with the same feeling and sound that is found on the hit singles of these artists, without losing for a moment the feeling of Christmas, and without destroying or invading the sensitivity and the beauty that surrounds all the great Christmas music. (Spector 1963a)

In addition to those 12 Christmas songs, the so-called Christmas Album also featured a very special thirteenth and final track on which Spector came in and reinforced the cohesion of the whole recording by concluding it with the following reading, over a choral and orchestral arrangement of 'Silent Night':

> Hello, this is Phil Spector. It is so difficult at this time to say words that would express my feelings about the album to which you have just listened – an album that has been in the planning for many, many months. First, let me thank all the people who worked so hard with me in the production of this album, and in my endeavour and desire to bring something new and different to the music of Christmas, and to the record industry which is so much a part of my life. Of course, the biggest thanks goes to you, for giving me the opportunity to relate my feelings of Christmas through the music that I love. At this moment, I am very proud of all the artists and, on behalf of all of them (the Crystals, the Ronettes, Darlene Love, Bob B. Soxx and the Blue Jeans, and myself), may we wish you the very merriest of Christmases and the happiest of New Years ... And thank you so very much for letting us spend this Christmas with you. (Spector 1963b)

Unfortunately, on 22 November, just as *A Christmas Gift for You* was being released, the news came that John F. Kennedy had been assassinated in Dallas. As Spector's biographer Richard Williams remarks: 'Phil Spector's magnum was dead in the water. It would take ten years and the patronage of the Beatles before the album emerged from the status of collectors' item to claim a permanent place as a seasonal favourite' (Williams 2003, p. 80).

Less than three years later, in August 1966, Frank Zappa and his Mothers of Invention went one step further with their debut two-record set *Freak Out!* Judging by Zappa's own liner notes, the thematic unity, this time, relied upon a much looser concept:

> On a personal level, *Freaking Out* is a process whereby an individual casts off outmoded and restricting standards of thinking, dress, and social etiquette in order to express CREATIVELY his relationship to his immediate environment and the social structure as a whole. Less perceptive individuals have referred to us who have chosen this way of thinking and FEELING as '*Freaks*', hence the term: *Freaking Out*. On a collective level, when any number of '*Freaks*' gather and express themselves creatively through music or dance, for example, it is generally referred to as a *FREAK OUT*. The participants, already emancipated from our national *social slavery*, dressed in their most inspired apparel, realize as a group whatever potential they possess for *free expression*. We would like to encourage everyone who HEARS this music to join us ... become a member of *The United Mutations ... FREAK OUT!* (Zappa 1966)

With regard to album unity, though, sides three and four inaugurated a trick that was to become quite popular in years to come: the deletion of the customary empty groove spaces between tracks. Were those two sides of segued songs, movements and tape pieces an inspiration for the Beatles when they put sides one and two of *Sgt. Pepper* together? It is actually difficult to answer such a question since neither they nor any of their close collaborators ever really addressed that issue. On the one hand, Mark Lewisohn asserts that the prototype master tape of the album was assembled 'utilising George Martin's specification unique for a pop music album – it was to have no "rills" or gaps between songs' (Lewisohn 1988b, p. 107). On the other hand, it has been reported that 'Throughout the *Sgt. Pepper* sessions, Paul McCartney kept saying, "This is our *Freak Out*"' (Philip Norman, quoted in Dowlding 1989, p. 160); according to Walter Everett, Chet Flippo also 'has it that [Paul] McCartney was inspired to make a "concept" album upon hearing the Mothers' ... *Freak Out*' (Everett 1999, p. 332); as for Barry Miles, he simply observes how much the 13-minute-and-48-second sound effects tape that McCartney produced in the midst of the recording sessions of 'Penny Lane' for the *Carnival of Light* 'resembles "The Return of the Son of Monster Magnet", the twelve-minute final track on Frank Zappa's *Freak Out!* album' (Miles 1997, p. 309).[9]

If Zappa's *Freak Out!* therefore appears to be no more than a possible influence on *Sgt. Pepper*, the same cannot be said of the Beach Boys' *Pet Sounds*. Interviewed by David Leaf in 1990, McCartney went so far as to confess: 'I played it to John so much that it would be difficult for him to escape the influence. If records have a director within a band, I sort of directed *Sgt. Pepper*. And my influence was basically the *Pet Sounds* album' (quoted in Leaf 1996, p. 126). Released a mere three months before *Freak Out!*, this record, which showed none of the thematic unity of Spector's Christmas Album and featured no innovative mastering tricks that might have helped reinforce its musical cohesion, is today considered by many as one of the most

---

9   The *Carnival of Light* was an avant-garde psychedelic event that took place at the Roundhouse, London, in January 1967.

serious pretenders to having been the first concept album. Tony Asher, who wrote most of its lyrics, explains:

> I don't know if Brian [Wilson] had a sense – and I suspect he may have – of sort of – the overarching kind of concept of the album. I don't mean in terms of what subjects would be covered; that I know didn't exist because we truly spontaneously generated a lot of those songs. Let me say as far as I know, there wasn't a premeditated concept. But I've read that Brian had a goal in the sense that he really wanted this to be a particular kind of album, and I think 'personal' is a good word because I think that was one of the things he really was after. And there's no doubt that he guided what I did – in some ways, we guided each other – but certainly if he had a sense that he wanted it to be a personal, more intimate and sensitive kind of project, he had the capacity in the course of working on songs to choose those things that satisfied those criteria and reject those things that didn't. (Ibid., p. 39)

In other words, if *Pet Sounds* had a sense of concept about it, it was, first and foremost, the result of its being conceived as a whole. Having decided to quit live performance in 1965, Brian Wilson had actually spent late 1965 and early 1966 arranging, producing and recording a good number of the album's backing tracks while the rest of the Beach Boys were on tour. What is more, in most cases, he had dealt with the writing work inside the studio, in close collaboration with the sound technicians and session musicians whom he had hired for the occasion. Chuck Britz, who was then a sound engineer at Western Recorders Studio Three, remembers:

> When Brian would come in, there were usually no sheets, no music. Everything was going on inside his head. A lot of times, he didn't even have a title for the song. He would play it for [bass player] Ray Pohlman; Ray would take what Brian was telling him and write it out. That was the chord structure. (Ibid., p. 53)

Notoriously inspired by Phil Spector's approach to recording, Wilson experimented for months with different instrumental combinations, different arrangement and production ideas, searching for the right balance, manipulating the mixing desk and watching over the overall sound from the control booth. As Virgil Moorefield accurately observes in the last lines of the few pages he wrote on the album:

> Already in 1966, then, the composer, arranger, and producer are melded into one person, prefiguring a practice which has become increasingly common in the contemporary recording studio. Brian Wilson was at the controls himself, making on-the-spot decisions about notes, articulation, timbre, and so on. He was effectively composing at the mixing board and using the studio as a musical instrument. (Moorefield 2005, p. 19)

The release of such albums as *A Christmas Gift for You*, *Freak Out!* and *Pet Sounds* between late 1963 and mid-1966 indicates a clear trend towards the transformation of the long-playing record from a distribution format into a creation format during the mid-1960s; each of those three albums introduced a trick that was aimed at reinforcing the thematic, the musical and the sonic cohesion of the latter format, and it might be stated, in a way, that the Beatles succeeded in combining those three cohesive aspects on *Sgt. Pepper*, which is why, while other albums have 'claims as the first "concept" album ... *Sgt. Pepper* was the record that made the idea convincing to most ears' (Riley 1989,

p. 11). Yet this brief survey of the gradual shift of popular musicians' focus from single to album would not be complete without stressing the fact that it had also begun to take root in the Beatles' own pre-*Pepper* records due to George Martin's idea of the music business. To him, there were basically ethical reasons to the long-playing format being more than a mere compilation of actual or potential singles:

> From the outset, Brian [Epstein] and I had been determined to give the buying public good value for their money. We had agreed that if a song had been released as a hit single, we should try not to use it as a cynical sales-getter on a subsequent album. To our way of thinking, this was asking people to pay twice for the same material. (Martin with Pearson 1994, p. 27)

This unwritten rule had quite logically led the producer to develop a more thoughtful ordering of album content than was the norm in the early 1960s: 'My old precept in the recording business was always "Make side one strong", for obvious commercial reasons ... Another principle of mine when assembling an album was always to go out on a side strongly, placing the weaker material towards the end but then going out with a bang' (Ibid., pp. 148–9).[10] Such strategies were certainly less radical than those used on Spector's, the Beach Boys' or Zappa's seminal albums, but they nonetheless pointed in a similar direction: the aforementioned transformation of the long-playing record into a creation format.

As far as the Beatles are concerned, it is widely admitted that this direction first became apparent with *Rubber Soul*, in late 1965. According to Martin, 'It was the first album to present a new, growing Beatles to the world. For the first time, we began to think of albums as art on their own, as complete entities' (quoted in Lewisohn 1988b, p. 69). The creative leap that this album represented in terms of formal design left few people unaffected indeed. Tim Riley, for example, observes: 'On *Rubber Soul*, the formal mastery that informed *A Hard Day's Night* ripens into something that eluded both *Beatles for Sale* and *Help!*' (Riley 1989, p. 171). As for him, Brian Wilson simply describes *Rubber Soul* as the main inspiration for his own contender for the title of the first concept album: 'When I first heard it, I flipped. I said, "I wanna make an album like that, where all the songs seem to be like a collection of folk songs" ... And we did *Pet Sounds* after that' (Beach Boys 2006). But whether it was the Beatles, the Beach Boys, Phil Spector or Frank Zappa who first indicated that direction does not really matter here. What matters is that through the work of those visionary artists, the determination of popular music by the phonographic medium went one decisive step further during the mid-1960s; by 1966–67, this music was no longer shaped with a view to putting it on record: it was being created for the record. In other words, it had reached a point in its evolution where the determination of the creative process by phonography was on the eve of inducing the decisive and permanent separation of recording and performance. All that popular music needed now was the record that would epitomize this key moment in its history. As Timothy

---

10 Considering the position of the encore-like 'Twist and Shout' on *Please Please Me* (a record that was itself supposed to recreate the atmosphere of a live show at the Cavern), it may reasonably be assumed that such strategies were used when assembling the Beatles' albums as early as 1963.

Leary observed, referring to other types of cultural transformation, *Sgt. Pepper* did '[come] along at the right time in that summer' (quoted in Taylor 1987, p. 49).

'Never could be any other way'

It is noteworthy that the bands and artists whose work exemplifies the transformation of the album into a creation format were all associated with the other key aspect of the determination of popular musicians' creative process by phonography during the mid-1960s, that is, the transformation of the recording studio into what Steve Jones calls a 'compositional tool' (Jones 1992, p. 130). Phil Spector, for example, was known for '[building] his instrumental accompaniments by experimenting with mixes and balances of sonorities as the ... musicians played their parts over and over again in an hours-long process' (Zak 2001, p. 58), and this experimental approach was precisely the reason why his Christmas Album took months to record; in a similar vein, much has been written about Zappa's '[obsession] with the activity of recording' (Moorefield 2005, p. 35) and his being 'present at every stage of the creation of his sonic artifacts' (Ibid., p. 40), while the Beach Boys' *Pet Sounds* was most appropriately described by Charlie Gillett as the album that 'inspired several British groups to make more experimental use of recording studio techniques' (Gillett 1996, p. 329).

As for the Beatles, they were given a first insight into the potentially experimental nature of the recording process in October 1963, when it was finally decided that Abbey Road would 'join the world of modern recording' (Martin with Hornsby 1979, p. 147) and go to four-track. In his autobiography, George Martin describes this change in format as 'a huge leap forward' (Ibid.):

> ... most important of all, if we weren't satisfied with one track, we could replace it without having to do the whole performance again ... Nowadays, the various components of the rhythm will be split into different tracks, but in the days of four-track the first one took the drum and the bass. To that you would add, on a second track, the harmonies, which might be played by guitars, piano or something else. The lead voice would go on a third. The fourth track would be for extra little bits – what today we call the 'sweetening'. (Ibid., p. 149)

Until then, the Fab Four's approach to recording had been severely limited by their use of twin-track. They could certainly record overdubs, but each of those overdubs implied bouncing from one stereo tape machine to another with the loss of one generation of sound quality. Besides, once two tracks had been mixed down to one track and a new track added, there was no turning back – for example, they could not afford the luxury of changing their minds afterwards regarding the level of the bass guitar within the rhythm section or the amount of compression on the drums.

By comparison, four-track clearly encouraged the separation of recording and performance in the sense that it made it possible for the band to build its arrangements layer by layer, through successive experiments:

> ... the rhythm track would usually be taped first and then they would overdub or 'drop in' extra sounds onto the tape at will. In this way, they might superimpose onto an existing take a good many unnumbered overdubs, which in previous years would each have been allotted a new number. (Lewisohn 1988b, p. 54)

This gradual integration of arranging and recording into one and the same process is what I shall call the vertical determination of the creative process by phonography. Introduced in the Beatles' work in late 1963 and intensifying throughout the recording of *Rubber Soul*, it went one decisive step further with *Revolver* and ultimately blossomed during the making of *Sgt. Pepper*; by the time of the album's release, George Harrison confessed to Hunter Davies:

> Now that we only play in the studios, and not anywhere else … we haven't got a clue about what we're going to do. We have to start from scratch, trashing it out in the studio, doing it the hard way. If Paul has written a song, he comes into the studio with it in his head. It's very hard for him to give it to us and for us to get it. When we suggest something, it might not be what he wants because he hasn't got it in his head. So it takes a long time. Nobody knows what the tunes sound like till we've recorded them then listened to them afterwards. (Quoted in Davies 1992, p. 345)

At first sight, Ringo Starr's own recollection of the *Sgt. Pepper* sessions may seem a little more prosaic, but it nonetheless confirms a major evolution in terms of studio practice while outlining the true nature of the latter evolution: 'We were really spending a long time in the studio, and we were still doing the basic tracks like we always did. And then, it would take weeks for the overdubs' (Beatles 2003c). In sum, if the Beatles becoming a studio band provided them with the freedom and the time to experiment, it was four-track that provided them with the means. A clear indication of this increasing determination of their creative process by multitrack technology may be found in the unprecedented number of tape-to-tape reductions that were made during the recording of the album. In four-track, such an operation consists in mixing down the four tracks of a first tape down to one or two tracks on another tape so as to vacate two or three tracks for additional overdubs (hence additional 'layers' in the recording). With the exception of the reprise of the title track (which the Beatles intended as a straightforward rock recording), every song that ended up on *Sgt. Pepper* required at least one tape-to-tape reduction; on certain songs ('Lovely Rita', 'Good Morning, Good Morning', 'A Day in the Life'), the number of tape-to-tape reductions went up to two; and on 'Getting Better', it even went up to three (see Lewisohn 1988b, pp. 89–107). It is quite common to interpret such recording strategies as signs of Martin 'trying to reconcile an infinity of new ideas with … antiquated and inhibiting four-track recording machine[s]' (Norman 1981, p. 283). But considering the limitations of the stereo tape machines that the Fab Four had to cope with in the earliest days of their recording career, it may also be concluded that 'By the time they could create *Pepper*, the technology was in place to help them do it. If they had tried to make *Pepper* earlier, maybe it wouldn't have been quite the same album' (Dave Harries, quoted in Cunningham 1996, p. 139).

To this vertical dimension in the determination of the Beatles' creative process by phonography, 'Strawberry Fields Forever' added a horizontal dimension that made the separation of performance and recording complete in December 1966. This new dimension was most obvious in the way *Sgt. Pepper* was assembled, its 13 tracks being either crossfaded or edited so as to run directly into one another, 'as if the listener were present at a live performance of the esteemed Lonely Hearts Club Band' (Emerick and Massey 2006, pp. 183–4). And it was also apparent at the level of individual songs, as one may judge from examining the formal development of 'A Day in the Life' as its recording progressed. When John Lennon first played this tune to Paul McCartney, he already had the lyrics and the music for four verses. McCartney suggested a one-line refrain ('I'd love to turn you on...') and then offered to contribute a bridge:

> There was a great deal of discussion about what to do, but no real resolution. Paul thought he might have something that would fit, but for the moment everyone was keen to start recording, so it was decided to leave twenty-four empty bars in the middle as a kind of placeholder. This in itself was unique in Beatles recording: the song was clearly unfinished, but it was so good nonetheless that it was decided to plow ahead and get it down on tape and then finish it later. In essence, the composition was going to be structured during the recording stage. (Ibid., p. 146)

The day after, McCartney arrived at Abbey Road with a snippet from an unfinished vaudeville-like song of his. This snippet, he thought, might fit in the 24 empty bars. Unfortunately, it turned out to be so different in tone with the verses that it was finally taped separately and edited into the four-track master tape before Lennon's fourth verse. In other words, at that point, it was still left to the 24 bars to do the transition between the third verse and what was now the song's bridge.

As history has it, it took the Beatles two weeks before they finally agreed on filling in those 24 bars with the now-famous aleatoric orchestral crescendo. They were so excited with the idea of using an orchestra that a copy of the 24-bar count used in the gap was edited into the multitrack tape after the final verse so that the build-up effect could be recorded one more time and serve as a conclusion to the song. But what interests me here is less what the Beatles did put in those 24 bars than how those 24 bars were originally inserted into the recording. Indeed, when reading Geoff Emerick's description of the first recording session of 'A Day in the Life', it is difficult to resist the temptation to compare Lennon and McCartney with composers leaving blank bars in the score they are working on or filling in the bars of that same score as their work progresses. As a matter of fact, neither they nor George Martin and the other Beatles even knew how the song would end until they heard the effect of what was supposed to be their last addition to it: 'Having done all the orchestral bit, we wanted something to finish off the song. When you reached that high note at the close of the orchestral sequence you were left hanging there; the song needed bringing sharply back to earth' (Martin with Pearson 1994, p. 60). It was only then that the decision to conclude it with a 'gigantic piano chord' (Ibid., p. 61) was made.

To carry the parallel between popular music as a phonographic tradition and art music as a literate tradition an additional step further, the 19 January, 20 January, 10 February and 22 February 1967 sessions that I just evoked may be seen as encapsulating the transformation of the phonographic medium into popular music's score – a score on which the composer's thought progresses in two directions, vertical and horizontal. But what of the creative act itself? To what extent was the Beatles' musical thought shaped by sound recording? It is obviously quite a delicate question to answer without giving in to the 'rush to interpretation' (Middleton 1990, p. 220) for which popular music scholars have often been reproached. I shall therefore try and approach it starting with a very concrete and personal experience: my first encounter with the album.

Like many people who were born in the late 1960s and early 1970s, I bought my first copy of *Sgt. Pepper* in 1987, when it was being reissued on CD. I already knew some of the songs, I was vaguely aware of the record's reputation of being the first concept album, but I had never heard about those strange few seconds of speech played backwards that concluded it and whose *raison d'être* was explained as follows in Mark Lewisohn's liner notes:

> Then, as the *coup de grâce*, there is a few seconds of nonsense Beatle chatter, taped, cut into several pieces and stuck back together at random so that, as George Martin says, purchasers of the vinyl album who did not have an auto return on their record player would say 'What the hell is that?' and find the curious noise going on *ad infinitum* in the concentric run-out groove. (Lewisohn 1987)

The curious noise was no longer looped *ad infinitum* on CD (it lasted for 16 seconds or so before fading out); but since my first childhood record player did not feature auto return, I could easily figure out what Lewisohn meant when he mentioned it potentially going on forever.

Another intriguing detail regarding this mysterious loop was that the more I listened to it, the more I was convinced that it was saying something that resembled what has since been described by Walter Everett as 'Lennon saying "been so high", answered by McCartney's "never could be any other way"' (Everett 1999, p. 122). Far was I, indeed, from imagining the true nature of the words whose meaning had been obscured by tape manipulation. As Paul McCartney revealed in a 1974 interview with Paul Gambaccini:

> The piece at the end of *Sgt. Pepper*, that backward thing. It was some piece of conversation that we recorded and turned backwards. After I'd been told by some fans what it was supposed to say I went inside and played it studiously, turned it backwards with my thumb against the motor and did it backwards. And there it was, sure as anything: 'We'll f... you like Superman'. (Quoted in Southall, Vince and Rouse 1997, pp. 96–8)[11]

20 years have now passed since I first heard those few seconds of edited tape; and in addition to discovering the actual words from which they originated, after having spent over 15 years working on popular musicians' relationship with phonography, I have finally come to consider them as an equivalent of a piece like the *Canon a 2 'cancrizans'* of Johann Sebastian Bach's *Musical Offering* in terms of their epitomizing the musical tradition that gave birth to them. I am definitely not arguing here that getting high on drugs, 'chattering' and manipulating the resulting recording requires skills that might be compared to those involved in Bach's virtuoso contrapuntal work: I am rather referring to the significance of both artefacts when examined from the angle of the determination of the creative act by a specific medium.

---

11 Careful manipulation of the corresponding sound file in a digital sound editor indicates that the piece of conversation was actually sped up, heavily compressed and reversed. By putting it back forward, expanding it and playing it at lower speed, one can easily identify McCartney yelling 'I will fuck you like a superman!' while two other persons (probably Ringo Starr and George Harrison) are giggling in the background.

Like the two ricercari, the trio sonata and the nine other canons of the *Musical Offering*, the *Canon a 2 'cancrizans'* is based on the contrapuntal manipulation of the musical theme attributed to Frederick the Great (the so-called 'Royal Theme'). In this particular case, the manipulation consists of a retrograde canon (also known as 'crab' canon), which means that while the eight-and-a-half-bar theme and the following nine and a half bars of counterpoint are being stated, the canonic voice states those same theme and nine and a half bars simultaneously backwards. Needless to say, no human ear could ever appreciate such a compositional *tour de force*: one has to see a graphic representation of the piece to discover the technical prowess that lies behind it. Besides, Bach insisted on the visual dimension of his creative work by presenting the ten canons of the *Musical Offering* as a set of short snippets of music with enigmatic Latin titles to be solved by the performers before they could develop them into full-fledged pieces, which is why the *Canon a 2 'cancrizans'* appears in the original manuscript as an 18-bar monodic melody noted on a single staff with a reversed clef and key signature placed at the end of the latter staff (the clue to the riddle). As intended by its composer, it should thus be deciphered not once, but twice before it may even come to life and then reveal its true nature, such a clear emphasis on the graphic representation of music making it the most perfect illustration of how musical notation 'influenced composition by encouraging', in Jean-Claude Risset's words, 'music *writing*'.[12]

Similarly, the true nature of the vocal gibberish that concludes *Sgt. Pepper* does not become fully apparent until one examines it from the perspective of its relationship with the phonographic medium. First, it was basically inspired by that medium:

> How does an artist know when – or how – to apply the final brush stroke to a masterpiece? With 'A Day in the Life', *Sgt. Pepper's Lonely Hearts Club Band* was already set to end with the tremendous, crashing piano chord lasting more than 40 seconds. But as no silence had been left between each song, it would be a pity, the Beatles thought, if there was a silence *after* the final chord. Why not put something in the concentric run-out groove? (Lewisohn 1988b, p. 109)

Second, it was also shaped by that same medium in the sense that the Beatles conceived it as a loop, that is, by transposing to tape the principle of a closed groove. Third, the duration of the latter loop was the exact duration of a round on a 33-1/3-rpm record: 1.8 seconds. Finally, and maybe more importantly, to come out as intended by the Beatles, those 1.8 seconds of backward speech literally needed to be played *by* the turntable, as if, when reaching this part of the record, the player symbolically turned itself into the performer of a score that had been cut into vinyl.

> Their reasoning was that the automatic record players of the day would play it for a few seconds before lifting the needle off, while those people who still owned manual players would hear it drone on indefinitely until they got fed up and raised the needle themselves. (Emerick and Massey 2006, p. 189)

---

12 '... *influencé la façon de composer en permettant un travail d'*écriture ...' (Risset 1998, p. 99).

It would naturally be absurd to assume that the Beatles intended this final addition as the climax of *Sgt. Pepper*. It would be even more pointless to argue that such an addition was carefully thought out and planned (all accounts confirm the impromptu nature of their decision to 'put something in the concentric run-out groove'). In fact, I believe it should rather be interpreted as the result of a last-minute impulse of theirs to drive the logic underlying the recording of the album to its full conclusion after they heard the final version of the master tape and just before the overall creative process was completed by transferring the latter tape to disc. It was, *au fond*, the most obvious and the most perfect postscript to *Sgt. Pepper* as a whole: the sound of popular music entering the era of phonographic composition.

The Beatles' relationship with the phonographic medium (reprise)

Most contributors to this book insisted on how *Sgt. Pepper* embodied the social, the musical and, more generally, the cultural changes of the 1960s. As I have tried to show throughout the previous pages, putting the album in perspective with regard to the rise of a phonographic tradition in twentieth-century popular music somehow leads to a similar conclusion: it was, as Allan Moore puts it, 'the high point of a cumulative process which changed the nature of the game that was Anglophone popular music' (Moore 1997, p. 70). Why, one might ask, *Sgt. Pepper* more than *A Christmas Gift for You*, *Freak Out!* or *Pet Sounds*? Why the Beatles and not Phil Spector, Frank Zappa or Brian Wilson? After all, as Walter Everett pointedly remarks:

> Compositional factors aside, one of Wilson's greatest influences on the Beatles might have been his decision to not tour with the Beach Boys ... This approach may have made it thinkable for the Beatles to quit touring in 1966 while continuing their career of composing and recording. Certainly, the ingenuity of the LP *Pet Sounds* (released May 1966) and the reports that the Beach Boys required over ninety hours in four different studios to record 'Good Vibrations' to Wilson's satisfaction must have seemed great challenges to the Beatles, who themselves began exploring the great creative possibilities of the recording studio. (Everett 2001, p. 276)

What is it, then, that makes *Sgt. Pepper* the epitome of the transformation of the recording studio into a compositional tool during the mid-1960s? To answer such a question, one needs, precisely, to take compositional factors into account and examine them in the light of the aforementioned artists' and producers' relationship with the phonographic medium.

Strictly speaking, Wilson's experimental approach to recording did not consist in experimenting with tape: it consisted in experimenting with the recording process through microphone placement, balance and equalization, having Phil Spector's musicians (the famous Wrecking Crew) playing their parts over and over again until he was satisfied with the overall sound. As for the arrangements and the songs themselves, their coming to life inside the studio did not rely on Gold Star's, Sunset Sound's or Western Recorders Studio Three's three- and four-track facilities: it relied on Wilson's experimenting with live musicians throughout hours-long sessions – that is, on his extending Spector's production methods to arrangements and songwriting. Zappa certainly went further down the road to phonographic composition with his extensive use of tape editing on *Freak Out!*, but his considering the tape as the 'definitive document' (see Moorefield 2005, p. 36) finally showed more through the horizontal than through the vertical determination of the creative process by phonography (the entire album was recorded in a mere four days, which, compared with *Sgt. Pepper*'s four and a half months, did not leave much time for experimenting with overdubs). Besides, it must be added that *Freak Out!* definitely lacked the social and cultural resonance of such albums as *Pet Sounds* and *Sgt. Pepper* (initial sales amounted a poor 30,000 copies).

In contrast, at a distance of 40 years, *Sgt. Pepper* appears as the record that made popular musicians' shift to phonographic composition complete insofar as it was, in essence, the product of tape recording and multitrack technology. By way of illustration, most parts on the songs were performed by a virtual band whose line-up was increased at will by means of overdubbing and tape-to-tape reduction. This virtual band conceived what might be called 'virtual head arrangements' as the recording progressed (even though 'multitrack tape arrangements' might be more appropriate), and it often played instruments and sang with voices whose tones resulted of their being affected during the recording process.[13] Such an approach to arrangements and songwriting explains why, in Steve Jones's words, 'Comments that the recording studio is a "compositional tool" are generally first associated with the Beatles' (Jones 1992, p. 170). And it probably also accounts for *Sgt. Pepper* being 'often seen as the album in which the rock *auteur* was invented' (Moore 1997, p. 71).

Interestingly, many professionals of the recording industry whose career was associated with Abbey Road during the 1960s pointed out the seminal nature of this evolution in the Beatles' approach to the studio. Helen Shapiro, for example, reported that they were 'the first artists to go in the studio and say, "I've not quite finished yet", and then rehearse a song and add things to it' before adding that 'This effectively put an end to the old concept of three-hour sessions' (quoted in Southall, Vince and Rouse 1997, p. 81); Bruce Welch (the Shadows' rhythm guitarist) noted that 'they wrote in the studios which was unheard of and … worked all through the night which was something people had never done before' (Ibid.); Sir Joseph Lockwood, Chairman of EMI from 1954 to 1974, conceded that 'The Beatles were the big drivers in the development of four, eight and 16-track' (Ibid., p. 93), while Alan Parsons maintained that the origins of what he sees as a 'revolution' in the recording studio (Ibid., p. 101) should be traced back to the making of *Sgt. Pepper*:

> … people then started thinking that you could spend a year making an album and they began to consider an album as a sound composition and not just a musical composition. The idea was gradually forming of a record being a performance in its own right and not just a reproduction of a live performance. (Ibid.)

Parsons's reference to an album being considered as a 'sound composition' naturally echoes the other key aspect of popular musicians' shift to phonographic composition during the mid-1960s, that is, the transformation of the long-playing record into a creation format. From that angle too, *Sgt. Pepper* is widely regarded as the record

---

13 Sound treatment techniques like speed changing, ADT, tape echo or retrograding all depended on tape recording.

that made the shift complete. As early as 1973, Wilfrid Mellers commented in the first lines of his analysis of the album: '… the long-playing record is a more radical innovation than we once realised' (Mellers 1973, p. 86). Ten years later, Terence O'Grady concluded his own study of the Beatles' discography by writing:

> There is no question that, by the late 1960s, the old rock concept of a string of unrelated songs had begun to give way in many cases to a more thoughtful formulation and ordering of album content. An example of this can be seen in the production of the *Rubber Soul* album as early as 1965 … Nevertheless, there seems to have been no achievement comparable to *Sergeant Pepper's Lonely Hearts Club Band* prior to its release in June 1967. (O'Grady 1983, p. 182)

Finally, another 24 years later, John Harris observed in *MOJO*'s *Sgt. Pepper* anniversary edition:

> Soon enough, music appeared thoroughly transformed by The *Pepper* Effect. In its immediate wake came albums that were built on a new level of ambition: Cream's *Disraeli Gears* [1967], the Hollies' *Butterfly* [1967] … the Moody Blues' cod-symphonic *Days of Future Passed* [1967] – and perhaps best of all, *The Who Sell Out* [1968], the album whose central idea was not some earnest attempt to inflate pop into art, but rather a conceptual celebration of the primary-coloured garishness that made the form what it was. (Harris 2007, p. 88)

Not mentioning the 1970s-lengthy progressive rock pieces that form what Allan Moore calls the 'second strand of what followed *Sgt. Pepper*' (Moore 1997, p. 73), one should obviously add to this list of early victims of 'The *Pepper* Effect' records like the Moody Blues' *In Search of the Lost Chord* (1968), *On the Threshold of a Dream* and *To Our Children's Children's Children* (both released in 1969), the Rolling Stones' *Their Satanic Majesties Request* (1967), Zappa's self-proclaimed parody *We're Only in It for the Money* (1968), the Who's *Tommy* (1969), the Kinks' *Arthur (Or the Decline and Fall of the British Empire)* (1969), David Bowie's *The Rise and Fall of Ziggy Stardust* (1972) and, on the other side of the Channel, Gainsbourg's *Histoire de Melody Nelson* (1971). Even the Beatles' own post-*Pepper* releases confirmed, each in their own different way, what seemed to be the permanent transformation of the 33-1/3-rpm vinyl record into a creation format.[14] Yet, as George Martin comments, 'none of these other albums … ever attained the status of *Pepper*' (Martin with Pearson 1994, p. 159). And neither did any

---

14 Notwithstanding Martin's complaint that the White Album (1968) was 'not as unified as any of the other [Beatles' post-*Help!*] albums in terms of overall sound' (Martin with Pearson 1994, p. 159), it extended the idea of linking each successive song with either a crossfade or a straight edit to the four sides of what would be the Beatles' one and only double LP. *Let It Be* (1970), which was originally intended as 'an album shorn of all studio artifice' (Norman 1981, p. 355), ended up featuring snatches of chatter and jokes that were inserted into the master tape so as to emphasize the overall live feel of the album. Finally, the second side of *Abbey Road* (1969) saw the Beatles getting back to the idea of a 'continuous work, in the style of *Pepper*' (Martin with Pearson 1994, p. 139) while featuring the first instance of a concluding 'hidden track' ('Her Majesty', which ends the album abruptly after the 14 seconds of silence following 'The End', did not appear in the back-sleeve track listing until the 1983 reissue).

of the records whose formal unity resulted from their being aimed at the newly introduced compact disc during the 1980s and 1990s.[15]

Be it in terms of popular musicians' relationship with the recording studio or with the long-playing format, *Sgt. Pepper* did mark a genuine turning point in the sense that it represented the outcome of a several-year process while paving the way for years, even decades to come. It must be added, though, that at the time of writing, the era that was inaugurated with this milestone record is most probably coming to an end. Not that the determination of popular musicians' creative process by phonography is beginning to wane – on the contrary, from hip hop to turntablism through house music, techno music or jungle, many of the genres that this musical tradition engendered from the late 1970s to the present days have made popular musicians' shift to phonographic composition even more apparent by drawing on disc manipulation techniques.[16] I am, in fact, referring here to the growing popularity of MP3 as a way to distribute and access music, and to its indicating an inevitable new shift back to single from album. It may, of course, eventually give rise to an entirely new type of creation format (which is actually quite likely to happen too); but whatever the future holds, it is very difficult to believe that the album will survive this technological and cultural revolution as such. On that account, commemorating *Sgt. Pepper*'s fortieth anniversary also had a nostalgic edge to it: it was finally a way to pay tribute to the phonographic format that was the vector of popular music coming of age as a phonographic tradition just when that same format, as we thought of it for the past 40 years, is on the point of disappearing. To use the words of a songwriter whose lyrics have often been quoted and examined in the previous chapters: 'All things must pass, all things must pass away' (Harrison 1970)…

---

15 Introduced at the turn of 1982–83, the compact disc offered a 74-minute playing time (the latter playing time has since been extended to a maximum duration of 80 minutes). Besides, as Prince's *Lovesexy* demonstrated in 1988, it also solved the problem of the side break when putting an album together – on early CD copies, the whole album was sequenced as a single track.

16 Even the now-widespread use of sampling may be seen as a consequence of popular musicians relying on compositional techniques that are being increasingly determined by the phonographic medium – the way this technology is used today in most recording studios actually aims at recreating the effects of the quick-mixing technique pioneered by influential hip hop DJs Kool Herc and Grandmaster Flash (see Brewster and Broughton 1999, pp. 226–36, 266–7, 277).

References

'Absolutely Tabulous'. 2001. *Q* 173, 62–4.

Assayas, Michka and Claude Meunier. 1996. *The Beatles and the Sixties*. New York: Henry Holt.

Backer, Matt. 2002. 'The guitar', in Allan Moore (ed.), *The Cambridge Companion to Blues and Gospel Music*, pp.116–29. Cambridge: Cambridge University Press.

Bangs, Lester. 1981. 'Musical innovations: how the Beatles broke the rules and made new ones', in Milton Okun (ed.), *The Compleat Beatles*, pp. 44–6. Greenwich (Conn.): Delilah, ATV.

Barron, Lee and Ian Inglis. 2005. 'We're not in Kansas any more', in Russell Reising (ed.), *Speak to Me: The Legacy of Pink Floyd's* The Dark Side of the Moon, pp. 56–66. Aldershot: Ashgate.

Barrow, Tony (ed.). 1967. *Magical Mystery Tour.* London: NEMS.

Barthes, Roland. 1972 (orig. 1957). *Mythologies*. New York: Hill & Wang.

Beach Boys, The. 2006. *Pet Sounds* (DVD), chap. 1: 'The Making of *Pet Sounds*'. Capitol Records.

Beatles, The. 1983. *The Beatles Complete*. London: Wise Publications.

—— 1993. *The Beatles: Complete Scores*. Transcribed by Tetsuya Fujita, Yuji Hagino, Hajime Kubo and Goro Sato. Milwaukee: Hal Leonard Publications.

—— 2000. *The Beatles Anthology*. San Francisco: Chronicle Books.

—— 2003a. *The Beatles Anthology* (DVD), episode 5, chap. 4: 'New Musical Directions: *Rubber Soul* and *Revolver*'. Apple Corps Limited.

—— 2003b. *The Beatles Anthology* (DVD), episode 6, chap. 6: 'The Making of "Strawberry Fields Forever"'. Apple Corps Limited.

—— 2003c. *The Beatles Anthology* (DVD), episode 6, chap. 8: 'Sgt. Pepper's'. Apple Corps Limited.

—— 2003d. *The Beatles Anthology* (DVD), special features, chap. 3: 'Back at Abbey Road, May 1995'. Apple Corps Limited.

Belmo. 1999. *20th Century Rock and Roll: Psychedelia*. Burlington (Ont.): Collector's Guide Publishing.

Bennett, H. Stith. 1983. 'Notation and identity in popular music', *Popular Music* 3, 215–34.

Benson, Alan (director). 1992. 'The Making of *Sgt. Pepper*', *The South Bank Show*. Buena Vista International, Inc.

Bishop, Malden. 1963. *The Discovery of Love: A Psychedelic Experience with LSD-25*. New York: Dodd, Mead & Co.

Blake, Peter. 2006. *Interview, University of Northumbria, Newcastle upon Tyne*. 11 May (unpublished).

Blake, William. 1987 (orig. 1804–20). 'The poet's motto from Jerusalem', in Stanley Kunitz (ed.), *The Essential Blake*, p. 91. Hopewell (NJ): Ecco Press.

Booker, Christopher. 1969. *The Neophiliacs: The Revolution in English Life in the Fifties and Sixties.* London: Collins.

Brewster, Bill and Frank Broughton. 1999. *Last Night a DJ Saved My Life: The History of the Disc Jockey.* London: Headline.

Brodax, Al. 1968. *The Beatles in Yellow Submarine.* Manchester: World Distributors.

Bromell, Nick. 2000. *'Tomorrow Never Knows': Rock and Psychedelics in the 1960s.* Chicago: University of Chicago Press.

Brown, Peter and Steven Gaines. 1983. *The Love You Make: An Insider's Story of the Beatles.* London: Macmillan.

Burke, Ken and Dan Griffin. 2006. *The Blue Moon Boys: The Story of Elvis Presley's Band.* Chicago: Chicago Review Press.

Burns, Gary. 1987. 'The myth of the Beatles', *South Atlantic Quarterly* 86, 169–80.

Buskin, Richard. 1999. 'Bruce Swedien', in *Inside Tracks*, pp. 273–7. New York: Avon.

Campbell, Joseph. 1949. *The Hero with a Thousand Faces.* Princeton: Princeton University Press.

Chanan, Michael. 1995. *Repeated Takes: A Short History of Recording and Its Effects on Music.* London: Verso.

Christgau, Robert. 1975. 'The basement tapes: Bob Dylan goes public', *Robert Christgau: Dean of American Rock Critics.* <http://www.robertchristgau.com/xg/rock/dylan-75.php>. Accessed 5 January 2007.

—— 1981. 'Symbolic comrades', *Robert Christgau: Dean of American Rock Critics*, <http://www.robertchristgau.com/xg/rock/lennon-81.php>. Accessed 14 January 2007.

Clayson, Alan. 1990. *The Quiet One: A Life of George Harrison.* London: Sidgwick & Jackson.

—— 1991. *Ringo Starr.* London: Sidgwick & Jackson.

Cloud, Cam. 1999. *The Little Book of Acid.* Berkeley: Ronin.

Cohen, Sidney. 1966. *The Beyond Within: The LSD Story.* New York: Atheneum.

Coleman, Ray. 2000. *Lennon: The Definitive Biography*, 20th anniversary edn. London: Pan Books.

Connolly, Ray. 1983. 'An introduction by Ray Connolly', in *The Beatles Complete*, pp. 9–31. London: Wise Publications.

Covino, William A. and David A. Jolliffe. 1995. 'Style', in *Rhetoric: Concepts, Definitions, Boundaries*, pp. 87–8. Boston: Allyn and Bacon.

Cunningham, Mark. 1996. *Good Vibrations: A History of Record Production.* Chessington: Castle Communications.

Davies, Hunter. 1992. *The Beatles: The Only Authorized Biography*, 2nd edn. London: Arrow Books.

DeRogatis, Jim. 1996. *Kaleidoscope Eyes: Psychedelic Rock from the '60s to the '90s.* Secaucus (NJ): Carol Publishing Group.

—— 2004. 'Idle worship, or revisiting the classics', *Jim DeRogatis Home Page*, <http://www.jimdero.com/News2004/July4SgtPeppers.htm>. Accessed 26 August 2006.

—— and Carmél Carrillo (eds). 2004. *Kill Your Idols: A New Generation of Rock Writers Reconsiders the Classics.* Fort Lee (NJ): Barricade Books.

Dillon, George. 1994. 'Rhetoric', in Michael Groden and Martin Kreiswirth (eds), *The Johns Hopkins Guide to Literary Theory and Criticism*, pp. 615–18. Baltimore: Johns Hopkins.

Dowlding, William J. 1989. *Beatlesongs*. New York: Simon & Schuster.

Eagles, Bill (director). 1997. *Psychedelic Science*. BBC.

Ehrenreich, Barbara, Elizabeth Hess and Gloria Jacobs, 1997 (orig. 1992). 'Beatlemania: a sexually defiant consumer subculture?', in Ken Gelder and Sarah Thornton (eds), *The Subcultures Reader*, pp. 523–36. London: Routledge.

Ellen, Mark. 2002. '*Sgt Pepper's Lonely Hearts Club Band*: the complete picture', *MOJO*, The Psychedelic Beatles Special Edition, 102–5.

Emerick, Geoff and Howard Massey. 2006. *Here, There and Everywhere: My Life Recording the Music of the Beatles*. New York: Gotham Books.

English, Rich. 2004. 'The Dry Piper: the strange life and times of Bill Wilson, founder of AA', *Modern Drunkard Magazine*, <http://www.moderndrunkardmagazine.com/issues/01-05/0105-dry-piper.htm>. Accessed 22 January 2007.

Evans, Mike. 1984. *The Art of the Beatles*. New York: Beech Tree.

Everett, Walter. 1999. *The Beatles as Musicians:* Revolver *through the* Anthology. Oxford: Oxford University Press.

—— 2001. *The Beatles as Musicians: The Quarry Men through* Rubber Soul. Oxford: Oxford University Press.

—— 2006. 'Painting their room in a colorful way: the Beatles' exploration of timbre', in Kenneth Womack and Todd F. Davis (eds), *Reading the Beatles: Cultural Studies, Literary Criticism and the Fab Four*, pp. 71–94. Albany: State University of New York Press.

Fielding, Steven. 2002. *The Labour Governments, 1964–1970: Labour and Cultural Change*. Manchester: Manchester University Press.

Fish, Stanley. 1995. 'Rhetoric', in Frank Lentricchia and Thomas McLaughlin (eds), *Critical Terms for Literary Study*, pp. 203–22. Chicago: University of Chicago Press.

Fort, Joel. 1969. *The Pleasure Seekers: The Drug Crisis, Youth and Society*. New York: Grove Press.

Frith, Simon. 1981. '"The magic that can set you free": the ideology of folk and the myth of the rock community', *Popular Music* 1(1), 159–68.

—— and Howard Horne. 1987. *Art into Pop*. London: Methuen.

Gabree, John. 1991 (orig 1967). 'The Beatles in perspective', in Charles Nieses (ed.), *The Beatles Reader*, pp. 131–7. Ann Arbor (Mich.): Popular Culture Ink.

Garbarini, Vic, Brian Cullman and Barbara Graustark. 1980. *Strawberry Fields Forever: John Lennon Remembered*. New York: Bantam.

Gelatt, Roland. 1977. *The Fabulous Phonograph 1877–1977*, 3rd edn. London: Collier-Macmillan.

Gillett, Charlie. 1970. *The Sound of the City: The Rise of Rock and Roll*. London: Souvenir Press.

—— 1996. *The Sound of the City: The Rise of Rock and Roll*, 3rd edn. New York: Da Capo Press.

Gleed, Paul. 2006. "'The rest of you, if you'll just rattle your jewelry [*sic*]": the Beatles and questions of mass culture', in Kenneth Womack and Todd F. Davies (eds), *Reading the Beatles: Cultural Studies, Literary Criticism and the Fab Four*, pp. 161–8. Albany: State University of New York Press.

Goldman, Albert. 1988. *The Lives of John Lennon.* New York: Bantam.

Grof, Stanislav. 1980. *LSD Psychotherapy: Exploring the Frontiers of the Hidden Mind.* Alameda (Calif.): Hunter House.

Grout, Donald J. and Claude V. Palisca. 2006. *A History of Western Music.* New York: W.W. Norton & Company.

Harris, John. 2007. 'The day the world turned Day-Glo!', *MOJO, Sgt. Pepper* Anniversary Edition, 72–89.

Harrison, George. 1970. 'All Things Must Pass', *All Things Must Pass.* Parlophone (CD reissue: 1987).

——— 1980. *I, Me, Mine.* New York: Simon & Schuster.

Hertsgaard, Mark. 1995. *A Day in the Life: The Music and Artistry of the Beatles.* New York: Delacorte Press.

Heylin, Clinton (ed.). 1992. *The Penguin Book of Rock & Roll Writing.* New York: Penguin Books.

Hobsbawm, Eric. 1994. *Age of Extremes: The Short Twentieth Century, 1914–1991.* London: Michael Joseph.

Hofmann, Albert. 1983. *LSD, My Problem Child: Reflections on Sacred Drugs, Mysticism, and Science.* New York: Putnam.

Horowitz, Michael and Cynthia Palmer. 1977. *Moksha: Aldous Huxley's Classic Writings on Psychedelics and the Visionary Experience.* New York: Stonehill.

Huckvale, David. 1990. '*Twins of Evil*: an investigation into the aesthetics of film music', *Popular Music* 9(1), 1–35.

Inglis, Ian. 2001. 'Nothing you can see that isn't shown: the album covers of the Beatles', *Popular Music* 20(1), 83–97.

Jarrett, Michael. 'Concerning the progress of rock and roll', *Michael Jarrett Home Page*, <http://www2.yk.psu.edu/~jmj3/saq.htm>. Accessed 5 January 2007.

Jones, Steve. 1992. *Rock Formation: Music, Technology and Mass Communication.* London: SAGE Publications.

——— and Martin Sorger. 2000. 'Covering music: a brief history and analysis of album cover design', *Journal of Popular Music Studies* 11 & 12, 68–102.

Julien, Olivier. 1998. *Le Son Beatles* ['The Beatles' Sound']. PhD dissertation in Musicology, University of Paris-Sorbonne (Paris IV).

——— 1999. 'The diverting of musical technology by rock musicians: the example of double-tracking', *Popular Music* 28(3), 357–65.

——— 2006. '"Purple Haze", Jimi Hendrix et le Kronos Quartet: du populaire au savant?' ['"Purple Haze", Jimi Hendrix and the Kronos Quartet: from popular music to art music?'], *Analyse Musicale* 53, 67–74.

Kehew, Brian and Kevin Ryan. 2006. *Recording the Beatles.* Houston (Tex.): Curvebender.

Keightley, Keir. 2001. 'Reconsidering rock', in Simon Frith, Will Straw and John Street (eds), *The Cambridge Companion to Pop and Rock*, pp. 109–42. Cambridge: Cambridge University Press.

Kimsey, John. 2002. 'What up, dogma?: contemporary rock and primitive correctness', *Habits of Waste: A Quarterly Review of Popular Culture* 1(3), <http://www.habitsofwaste.wwu.edu/issues/3/iss3art1a.shtml>. Accessed 22 August 2006.

Kinsey, Alfred C. 1948. *Sexual Behavior in the Human Male*. Philadelphia: W.B. Saunders.

—— 1953. *Sexual Behavior in the Human Female*. Bloomington (Ind.): Indiana University Press.

Kleps, Art. 1975. *Millbrook: The True Story of the Early Years of the Psychedelic Revolution*. Oakland: Bench Press.

Kozinn, Allan. 1995. *The Beatles*. London: Phaidon.

LaVere, Stephen C. 1990. Liner notes of *Robert Johnson: The Complete Recordings*. Sony.

Leaf, David. 1996. Liner notes of the Beach Boys' *The Pet Sounds Sessions*. Capitol Records.

Leary, Timothy. 1995. *High Priest*. Berkeley: Ronin.

——, Ralph Metzner and Richard Alpert. 1964. *The Psychedelic Experience: A Manual Based on the Tibetan Book of the Dead*. New Hyde Park (NY): University Books.

Lee, Martin and Bruce Shlain. 1985. *Acid Dreams: The Complete Social History of LSD – The CIA, the Sixties, and Beyond*. New York: Grove Press.

Lennon, John. 1964. *In His Own Write*. London: Jonathan Cape.

—— 1965. *A Spaniard in the Works*. London: Jonathan Cape.

Lewisohn, Mark. 1987. Liner notes of the Beatles' *Sgt. Pepper's Lonely Hearts Club Band*. Parlophone (CD reissue).

—— 1988a. 'The Paul McCartney interview', in *The Beatles Recording Sessions: The Official Abbey Road Studio Session Notes, 1962–1970*, pp. 6–15. New York: Harmony Books.

—— 1988b. *The Beatles Recording Sessions: The Official Abbey Road Studio Session Notes, 1962–1970*. New York: Harmony Books.

—— 1992. *The Complete Beatles Chronicle*. London: Hamlyn.

Lilly, John C. 1972. *The Center of the Cyclone: An Autobiography of Inner Space*. New York: Julian Press.

McCabe, Peter and Robert D. Schonfield. 1972. *Apple to the Core: The Unmaking of the Beatles*. London: Martin Brian & O'Keefe.

MacDonald, Hugh. 2001. 'Cyclic form', in Stanley Sadie (ed.), *The New Grove Dictionary of Music and Musicians*, vol. 6, 2nd edn, pp. 797–8. London: Macmillan.

MacDonald, Ian. 1994. *Revolution in the Head: The Beatles' Records and the Sixties*. New York: Henry Holt.

—— 1998. *Revolution in the Head: The Beatles' Records and the Sixties*, 2nd edn. London: Pimlico.

—— 2003. 'Pulse of the machine', in *The People's Music*, pp. 148–52. London: Pimlico.

MacDonald, Kari and Sarah Hudson Kaufman. 2002. '"Tomorrow Never Knows": the contribution of George Martin and his production team to the Beatles' new sound', in Russell Reising (ed.), *'Every Sound There Is': The Beatles' Revolver and the Transformation of Rock and Roll*, pp. 139–57. Aldershot: Ashgate.

MacFarlane, Thomas. 2005. *The Abbey Road Medley: Extended Forms in Popular Music*. PhD dissertation in Music Composition, New York University.

McKenna, Terence. 1992. *Food of the Gods: The Search for the Original Tree of Knowledge*. New York: Bantam.

Madow, Stuart and Jeff Sobul. 1992. *The Color of Your Dreams: The Beatles' Psychedelic Music*. Pittsburgh: Dorrance.

Marcus, Greil. 1980. 'The Beatles', in Jim Miller (ed.), *The Rolling Stone Illustrated History of Rock & Roll*, 2nd edn, pp. 177–89. New York: Random House.

Martin, George with Jeremy Hornsby. 1979. *All You Need Is Ears*. New York: St Martin's Press.

—— with William Pearson. 1994. *Summer of Love: The Making of Sgt. Pepper*. London: Macmillan.

—— 2004. *Conference at the University of Paris-Sorbonne (Paris IV)*. 17 June (unpublished).

Martin, Marvin. 1996. *The Beatles*. New York: Watts.

Mellers, Wilfrid. 1973. *Twilight of the Gods: The Beatles in Retrospect*. London: Faber and Faber.

Melly, George. 1970. *Revolt into Style*. London: Allen Lane.

Middleton, Richard. 1990. *Studying Popular Music*. Buckingham: Open University Press.

Miles, Barry. 1997. *Paul McCartney: Many Years from Now*. New York: Henry Holt.

Millard, Andre. 1995. *America on Record: A History of Recorded Sound*. Cambridge: Cambridge University Press.

Moore, Allan F. 1997. *The Beatles: Sgt. Pepper's Lonely Hearts Club Band*. Cambridge: Cambridge University Press.

—— 2000. 'Sgt. Pepper's Lonely Hearts Club Band', in Anthony Aldgate, James Chapman and Arthur Warwick (eds), *Windows on the Sixties*, pp. 138–53. London: I.B. Tauris.

—— 2002. *Rock: The Primary Text*, 2nd edn. Aldershot: Ashgate.

—— 2008. 'The track', in Amanda Bayley (ed.), *Recorded Music: Society, Technology and Performance*. Cambridge: Cambridge University Press (forthcoming).

Moorefield, Virgil E. 2001. *From the Illusion of Reality to the Reality of Illusion: The Changing Role of the Producer in the Pop Recording Studio*. PhD dissertation in Composition, Princeton University.

—— 2005. *The Producer as Composer*. Cambridge (Mass.): The MIT Press.

Nattiez, Jean-Jacques. 1987. *Musicologie Générale et Sémiologie* ['General Musicology and Semiology']. Paris: Christian Bourgois Editeur.

Neumeyer, David. 1987. 'The ascending *Urlinie*', *Journal of Music Theory* 31(2), 275–303.

Neville, Richard. 1970. *Play Power*. London: Jonathan Cape.

Noebel, David A. 1982. *The Legacy of John Lennon*. Nashville: Nelson.

Norman, Philip. 1981. *Shout! The True Story of the Beatles*. New York: Penguin Books.

Northcutt, William M. 2006. 'The spectacle of alienation: death, loss and the crowd in *Sgt. Pepper's Lonely Hearts Club Band*', in Kenneth Womack and Todd F. Davies (eds), *Reading the Beatles: Cultural Studies, Literary Criticism and the Fab Four*, pp. 129–46. Albany: State University of New York Press.

Nuttall, Jeff. 1970. *Bomb Culture*. London: Paladin.

O'Dell, Denis. 2002. *At the Apple's Core: The Beatles from the Inside*. London: Peter Owen Ltd.

O'Grady, Terence J. 1983. *The Beatles: A Musical Evolution*. Boston: Twayne.

Palmer, Robert. 1992. 'Rock begins', in Anthony DeCurtis and James Henke with Holly George-Warren (eds), *The Rolling Stone Illustrated History of Rock & Roll*, 3rd edn, pp. 3–16. New York: Random House.

Park, James. 2004. 'Becoming more authentic: the positive side of Existentialism', *An Existential Philosopher's Museum*, <http://www.tc.umn.edu/~parkx032/HMS-PG1.html>. Accessed 1 July 2005.

Patterson, R. Gary. 1996. *The Walrus Was Paul*. Nashville: Dowling Press.

Pattison, Robert. 1987. *The Triumph of Vulgarity: Rock Music in the Mirror of Romanticism*. Oxford: Oxford University Press.

Peel, Ian. 2002. *The Unknown Paul McCartney: McCartney and the Avant-Garde*. London: Reynolds & Hearn.

Peyser, Joan. 1969. 'The music of sound, or, the Beatles and the Beatles', in Jonathan Eisen (ed.), *The Age of Rock: Sounds of the American Cultural Revolution*, pp. 126–37. New York: Vintage Books.

Poirier, Richard. 1969. 'Learning from the Beatles', in Jonathan Eisen (ed.), *The Age of Rock: Sounds of the American Cultural Revolution*, pp. 160–79. New York: Random House.

Porter, Steven Clark. 1979. *Rhythm and Harmony in the Music of the Beatles*. PhD dissertation, City University of New York.

Porterfield, Christopher. 2006. 'Pop music: the messengers', in June Skinner Sawyers (ed.), *Read the Beatles: Classic and New Writings on the Beatles, Their Legacy and Why They Still Matter*, pp. 101–14. New York: Penguin Books.

'Psychedelic rock', *Wikipedia*, <http://en.wikipedia.org/wiki/Psychedelic_rock>. Accessed 9 January 2007.

Reck, David B. 1985. 'Beatles orientalis: influences from Asia in a popular song tradition', *Asian Music* XVI(1), 83–149.

Reeve, Andru J. 1994. *Turn Me on Dead Man*. Ann Arbor (Mich.): Popular Culture Ink.

Reising, Russell (ed.). 2002. *'Every Sound There Is': The Beatles' Revolver and the Transformation of Rock and Roll*. Aldershot: Ashgate.

Reising, Russell. 2006. 'Vacio luminoso: "Tomorrow Never Knows" and the coherence of the impossible', in Kenneth Womack and Todd F. Davies (eds), *Reading the Beatles: Cultural Studies, Literary Criticism and the Fab Four*, pp. 111–28. Albany: State University of New York Press.

Riley, Tim. 1989. *Tell Me Why: A Beatles Commentary*. New York: Vintage Books.

Risset, Jean-Claude. 1998. 'La musique et les sons ont-ils une forme?: des illusions auditives conçues sur le modèle des illusions visuelles' ['Do music and sounds have a shape?: of auditory illusions conceived on the patterns of visual illusions'], *La Recherche* 305, 98–102.

Rothenbuhler, Eric W. 2007. 'For-the-record aesthetics and Robert Johnson's blues style as a product of recorded culture', *Popular Music* 26(1), 65–81.

Roxon, Lillian. 1969. *Rock Encyclopedia*. New York: Grosset & Dunlap.

Said, Edward W. 1978. *Orientalism*. New York: Random House.

Sandford, Christopher. 2005. *McCartney*. London: Arrow Books.

Savage, Jon. 1997. '100 greatest psychedelic classics', *MOJO* 43, 56–67.

Schaffner, Nicholas. 1978. *The Beatles Forever*. New York: McGraw-Hill.

Schofield, Carey. 1983. *Jagger*. London: Methuen.

'Sgt. Pepper's Lonely Hearts Club Band', *Icons: A Portrait of England*, <http://www.icons.org.uk/theicons/collection/sgt-pepper>. Accessed 18 December 2006.

Shaw, Arnold. 1969. *The Rock Revolution*. London: Collier-Macmillan.

Sheff, David. 2000. *All We Are Saying: The Last Major Interview with John Lennon and Yoko Ono*, 2nd edn. New York: St Martin's Griffin.

Sheppard, John (director). 1987. *It Was Twenty Years Ago Today*. Granada Television, UK.

Shoales, Ian. 1985. 'Rock music today', in *I Gotta Go: The Commentary of Ian Shoales*, pp. 125–7. New York: Perigee.

Skinner Sawyers, June (ed.). 2006. *Read the Beatles: Classic and New Writings on the Beatles, Their Legacy and Why They Still Matter*. New York: Penguin Books.

Sless, David. 1986. *In Search of Semiotics*. London: Croom Helm.

Somach, Denny, Kathleen Somach and Kevin Gunn. 1991. *Ticket to Ride: A Celebration of the Beatles Based on the Hit Radio Show*. New York: Quill.

Sonnenschein, David. 2001. *Sound Design: The Expressive Power of Music, Voice, and Sound Effects in Cinema*. Studio City (Calif.): Michael Wiese Productions.

Soto-Morettini, Donna. 2006. *Popular Singing*. London: A. & C. Black.

'Sound Design', *Wikipedia*, <http://en.wikipedia.org/wiki/Sound_Design>. Accessed 12 November 2006.

Southall, Brian, Peter Vince and Allan Rouse. 1997. *Abbey Road: The Story of the World's Most Famous Recording Studios*, 2nd edn. London: Omnibus Press.

Spector, Phil. 1963a. Liner notes of *A Christmas Gift for You from Phil Spector*. Phil Spector Records (CD reissue: 1989).

—— 1963b. 'Silent Night', *A Christmas Gift for You from Phil Spector*. Phil Spector Records (CD reissue: 1989).

Stevens, Jay. 1987. *Storming Heaven: LSD and the American Dream*. New York: Harper.

Suczek, Barbara. 1972. 'The curious case of the "death" of Paul McCartney', *Urban Life and Culture* 1(1), 61–76.

Sullivan, Henry W. 1995. *The Beatles with Lacan: Rock 'n' roll as Requiem for the Modern Age*. New York: P. Lang.

Taylor, Alistair. 2001. *A Secret History*. London: John Blake.

Taylor, Derek. 1987. *It Was Twenty Years Ago Today*. New York: Bantam.

Thomson, Elizabeth and David Gutman (eds). 1988. *The Lennon Companion: Twenty-Five Years of Comment*. London: Papermack.

Thoreau, Henry David. 1983. *Walden.* New York: Penguin Books.

Thorgerson, Storm.1989. *Classic Album Covers of the 60s.* Limpsfield: Paper Tiger.

Townshend, Pete. 2000. 'I know that it's a dream', *MOJO*, Special Edition: John Lennon – His Life, His Music, His People, His Legacy, 146.

Turner, Steve. 1994. *A Hard Day's Write.* London: Carlton.

Wagner, Naphtali. 2001. 'Tonal oscillation in the Beatles' music', in Yrjö Heinonen, Marcus Heuger, Sheila Whiteley, Terhi Nurmesjärvi and Jouni Koskimäki (eds), *Beatles Studies 3: Proceedings of the Beatles 2000 Conference*, pp. 87–96. Jyväskylä: University of Jyväskylä.

—— 2003. 'Domestication of blue notes in the Beatles' songs', *Music Theory Spectrum* 25(2), 353–66.

—— 2006. 'Starting in the Middle: Auxiliary Cadences in the Beatles' Songs', *Music Analysis* 25(1), 155–70.

Weber, Max. 1947. *The Theory of Social and Economic Organization.* New York: Free Press.

Wenner, Jann S. 2000. *Lennon Remembers*, 2nd edn. New York: Verso.

Whitcomb, Ian. 1994. *After the Ball: Pop Music from Rag to Rock*, 2nd edn. New York: Limelight Editions.

White, Hayden. 1978. 'The Noble Savage theme as fetish', in *Tropics of Discourse: Essays in Cultural Criticism*, pp. 183–96. Baltimore: Johns Hopkins.

Whiteclay, John (ed.). 1999. *The Oxford Companion to American Military History.* Oxford: Oxford University Press.

Whiteley, Sheila. 1992. *The Space Between the Notes: Rock and the Counter-Culture.* London: Routledge.

Whitley, Ed. 2000. 'The postmodern White Album', in Ian Inglis (ed.), *The Beatles, Popular Music, and Society: A Thousand Voices*, pp. 105–25. New York: St Martin's Press.

Wilde, Oscar. 1965 (orig. 1895). *The Importance of Being Earnest.* New York: Avon.

Williams, Richard. 2003. *Phil Spector: Out of His Head*, 2nd edn. London: Omnibus Press.

Womack, Kenneth and Todd F. Davis. 2006. 'Mythology, demythology, remythology: the Beatles on film', in Kenneth Womack and Todd Davis (eds), *Reading the Beatles: Cultural Studies, Literary Criticism and the Fab Four,* pp. 97–110. Albany: State University of New York Press.

Wordsworth, William. 1973 (orig. 1802). 'Preface to *Lyrical Ballads*', in Harold Bloom and Lionel Trilling (eds), *Romantic Poetry and Prose*, pp. 594–611. Oxford: Oxford University Press.

Yogananda, Paramahansa. 1956. *The Autobiography of a Yogi.* Los Angeles: Self-Realization Fellowship.

Young, Warren and Joseph Hixson. 1966. *LSD on Campus.* New York: Dell.

Zak, Albin J. 2001. *The Poetics of Rock: Cutting Tracks, Making Records.* Berkeley: University of California Press.

Zappa, Frank. 1966. Liner notes of the Mothers of Invention's *Freak Out!* Rykodisc (CD reissue: 1987).

Index of names

Index of songs, albums, films and musical works